ERRATUM

Page xi, line 3. After 'Greater' insert:
'London Archive) and partly in the archive
of St George's'

A History of
The Royal Dental Hospital
of London
and School of Dental Surgery
1858–1985

A History of
The Royal Dental
Hospital of London
and
School of Dental Surgery
1858–1985

ERNEST G. SMITH & BERYL D. COTTELL

THE ATHLONE PRESS
London & Atlantic Highlands, NJ

First published 1997 by
THE ATHLONE PRESS
1 Park Drive, London NW11 7SG
and 165 First Avenue,
Atlantic Highlands, NJ 07716

British Library Cataloguing in Publication Data
*A Catalogue record for this book is available
from the British Library*

ISBN 0 485 11517 4

Library of Congress Cataloging-in-Publication Data

Smith, Ernest G., 1924–
    The Royal Dental Hospital of London and School of Dental Surgery,
1858–1985 / Ernest G. Smith and Beryl D. Cottell
        p.   cm.
    Includes index.
    ISBN 0-485-11517-4
    1. Royal Dental Hospital—History. 2. Royal Dental Hospital.
School of Dental Surgery—History. 3. Dental schools—England–
–London—History.   I. Cottell, Beryl D., 1921–   . II. Title.
    [DNLM: 1. Royal Dental Hospital. 2. Royal Dental Hospital.
School of Dental Surgery. 3. Education, Dental—history—London.
4. Dentistry. Operative—education—London.   WU 19 S646r 1997]
RK119.R69S64 1997
362. 1'976'009421—DC21
DNLM/DLC
for Library of Congress   97–11096
                                                              CIP

Typeset by Ensystems, Saffron Walden

Printed and bound in Great Britain by
Cambridge Univesity Press

Contents

List of Illustrations

Introduction

This History of the Royal Dental Hospital of London has been thirty-five years in the writing. The work started in 1958, the year of the institution's Centenary, when the late Mr C Bowdler Henry, then Senior Surgeon and Chairman of the Medical Committee, undertook the task, with the intention of publishing the work in connection with the centenary celebrations. He gathered a mass of detailed information about events up to the inauguration of the National Health Service in 1948 but never got around to completing the task.

There the matter rested for nearly thirty years while the momentous events in the history of the institution related in these pages were unfolding, and the co-authors of the present work were actively, not to say strenuously, engaged in them. Came the climax, in 1985, when the Royal's history came to an end and its Dental School was formally merged with the Dental School at Guy's Hospital. There the survivors of the wreck, including the late Professor WJB Houston, the last Dean of the Royal Dental Hospital of London School of Dental Surgery, decided that the account of the life and work of the institution which they had served should be completed, in order that the record should not perish. The Dental Funds Committee of the United Medical and Dental Schools of Guy's and St Thomas's Hospitals agreed to sponsor the work and Professor Houston asked us to undertake it.

Agreeing that a history of what was a unique institution needed to be recorded we undertook the task, conscious that our only qualification for it was our knowledge of and respect for the Royal. Because we both had a number of other commitments it took far longer than anyone thought it would, and the result is now presented for judgement. We know that what we have produced has deficiencies; in particular we have been unable to deal adequately with the technical and scientific contributions made by the staff of the Royal to the advancement of the science and art of dentistry.

The Royal Dental Hospital was not only a place where people learned to be dentists and other people came to receive dental treatment; its growth and life were part of the social activity of the community and the way it developed and the changes it experienced were related to the needs of the community. We have tried to tell the story of the Royal in the context of the changes in social and economic conditions which have taken place during its lifetime. The changes have been great; it seems remarkable now that in Victorian London, in a society based upon laissez-faire capitalism and controlled by market forces, a group of men was unselfishly concerned to raise the standards of the dental profession by providing proper training and qualification for those who engaged in it. It is equally remarkable that they were able to do this because another group of people were prepared to give money to provide dental treatment for the very poor. It was, of course, nothing new – the great Teaching Hospitals had operated in this way for centuries; and for the people who did it – the group of dental surgeons who founded the Dental Hospital – it was not remarkable at all, it was the natural way to go about it.

The foundation of the Hospital was brought about in the midst of controversy. Those who founded it believed that their objective of establishing a recognised qualification in dentistry could best be achieved under the *aegis* of the Royal College of Surgeons. The majority of practising dentists, who had not been consulted in the matter, were inclined to the view – and many held it very strongly – that the way forward was to set up a separate and independent body to supervise the professional education and examination of dentists. As the historian of the movement for the reform of the dental profession, Alfred Hill, recounts, the animosity between the two groups was both bitter and undisguised. Victorian gentlemen were capable of quarrelling over what they saw as matters of principle in the most uninhibited fashion and the vituperation which members of the two sides directed at each other has to be read to be believed.

In the event, as we relate, the greater influence and political ability of the former group prevailed at the time. But only when we had finished the book did we realise that their opponents, James Robinson and his fellow Independents, had the victory in the end. After degrees in dental surgery were introduced more and more entrants to the profession chose a degree rather than the diploma as their qualification. At the Royal adherence to the Royal College probably survived more strongly than elsewhere – even in the 1960s there were those there who looked upon what they called the double qualification – LRCP, MRCS, LDS – as the ideal. But this traditional attitude was severely jolted by the attack upon the Royal's aims and methods by the University Grants Committee in 1956 and at the Royal as elsewhere the profession began to separate itself from the Royal College. Now the Independents of the 1850s can be seen to have been vindicated and for practical purposes dentistry is an independent profession.

We thought it right to append the list of names from the War Memorial which was near the entrance to the Hospital but which disappeared during the conversion work after the building was sold. It seemed to us wrong that the record which our predecessors were careful to make should be lost.

Our principal sources for this book were the Minute Books, Annual

Reports and other records of the Hospital and School. After the Royal closed in 1985 these were held partly in the Library of Guy's Hospital Medical and Dental Schools (but have now been transferred to the Greater Hospital at Tooting. We have to thank Mr Andrew Batser and his colleagues in the Library at Guy's for their ready and patient assistance, and Dr TR Gould, Honorary Archivist at St George's Hospital for allowing access to his collection and helping us to find the information we sought. Reference was also made to material in the Guildhall Library, Westminster Public Library, the Library of Charing Cross Hospital Medical School and the Newspaper Archive at the British Library.

Much information came from articles and reports in the dental journals and newspapers of the period. Other sources have been mentioned in the text and are listed in the Bibliography.

As has been mentioned, Mr C Bowdler Henry carried out extensive research into the history of the institution from its beginning up to the inception of the National Health Service. We have benefited from access to his unpublished material and his collection of papers, now in the Library of the British Dental Association.

We are indebted to a number of individuals for help, guidance and labour. The late Professor WJB Houston inspired us to undertake the project and provided facilities for the work. The Dental Funds Committee at Guys agreed to finance it and Professor B. G. N. Smith, Mrs Susan Smith and Miss G. Bussey gave invaluable assistance in getting our typescript into publishable form.

EG Smith London Bridge
BD Cottell

1

Memorialists and Independents

The history of the Royal Dental Hospital of London is an important component of the history of the development of dentistry and the dental profession in this country. It was the creation of the Hospital by the Odontological Society of London which made possible the establishment of the first dental school and it was the members of the Society who brought about the inauguration of the qualification 'Licentiate in Dental Surgery', which was the foundation of the profession as it stands today. Conversely, the history of the movement for the reform of dentistry in the first half of the nineteenth century forms part of the history of the institution, and it is necessary to look at this briefly.

At the beginning of the nineteenth century dentistry in England was carried on by three classes of practitioners. There were what have been referred to as the 'irregulars', surgeons, apothecaries, druggists, barbers and blacksmiths – in fact anyone who considered himself capable – could and did pull out teeth, as a sideline to their regular business, and collected money for doing it. An example of the state of affairs is the much-quoted signboard from Ottery St Mary, Devon, once in the possession of the Royal Dental Hospital:

> The Smith-Glazier; Let Blood and Drawe Teeth, Tea Kittels
> & Potts, Buckitts, Lantern Cups to be Handled Heare.

There were those who made dentistry their trade more or less exclusively and who, like many another tradesman, had served an apprenticeship in order to learn it. Finally, there were the medically qualified men who considered dentistry an important speciality and practised it exclusively, bringing to it their training and experience and making it the subject of scientific study. The first class had existed since mankind had discovered that one way of obtaining relief from the torment of toothache was to have the offending tooth taken out; the others had only come into existence during the eighteenth century. Unless they practised within the City of London or a seven-mile radius of its boundaries, none of these practitioners were subject to any controls other than those imposed by their consciences and the law of torts. Those with London practices were subject to the requirements and regulations of the College of Surgeons, the College of Physicians or the Society of Apothecaries, if they were members of those bodies; but those practitioners who were not members of the professional bodies and, indeed, those who had no formal qualifications of any kind, were subject to no more control than their provincial colleagues.

In comparison, at the same time medical practice was beginning to evolve into a disciplined and regulated profession. Although there was no statutory system of control over qualification and practice until 1858, the medical corporations kept a watchful eye on the activities of their members and on those of the unqualified practitioners and used their powers over the former and those of the common law against the others in an attempt to establish standards of competence and an ethical code. The Society of Apothecaries, which was established in 1607, had from the beginning required candidates for membership to pass an entrance examination to prove that their general education was of an appropriate standard, to serve a seven year apprentice-ship, and to pass a searching examination before admission. Originally sellers and dispensers of medicines, apothecaries had become, by the middle of the eighteenth century, practitioners of medicine and the Society, for practical purposes, had become a College of general medical practitioners. So much so, that when in 1815 Parliament first legislated to control the practice of medicine and the training of medical practitioners it was the Society which was appointed to give effect to the new laws. Under these powers, it appointed examiners, decided the curriculum of training and supervised teaching until 1858, when the Medical Act created the General Medical Council and transferred these functions to it. Despite these efforts at control, however, as Dr Cameron has noted in his history of Guy's Hospital, (*Mr. Guy's Hospital*, HC Cameron) when all those who were engaged in medical practice were required to register in 1858, only one third possessed a formal qualification of any sort.

Pressure from dental practitioners for the training, qualification, registra-tion and regulation of members of their profession existed from the early part of the eighteenth century. However, the campaign for the reform of dentistry in England is generally considered to have started with the publication in 1841 by George Waite, FRCS of the pamphlet *An Appeal to Parliament, the Medical Profession and the Public on the present State of Dental Surgery*, of which Bowdler Henry says:

> After painting a dismal, but perfectly true, picture of the state of dental practice, Waite urged that the interests of the public and of the profession itself demanded legislative action. The legislature and the medical profes-sion must recognise dentistry as a legitimate branch of medicine; no person should be allowed to practise without having undergone examin-ation by the Royal College of Surgeons. He demanded that 'dentistry,

which is a de facto branch of surgery', be placed on a legitimate footing. He made valuable suggestions regarding the course of study which he thought dentists should pursue. This course was to last three years at least and it was to include instruction in chemistry, anatomy, physiology and surgery and attendance on hospital practice. The proposed measures could be incorporated in the Medical Reform Bill of Mr Benjamin Hawes, MP, which was at this time agitating the medical world. Waite's proposals strike us as being extraordinarily well considered; he saw clearly all the deficiencies in the existing system or lack of system, and he indicated the appropriate remedies – a proper curriculum, organised instruction, a licence or qualifying diploma to be issued by the College of Surgeons. It may in fact be said that the whole subsequent history of the dental reform movement is the story of the struggle to achieve the objects so clearly laid down by this far-sighted dental practitioner in 1841.

Waite's ideas seem to have failed to attract the support of many of his colleagues, although in 1843 a group of eminent dental practitioners wrote to the Home Secretary asking for the Medical Reform Bill to be extended so as to require 'parties purposing to practise as dentists to pursue a course of education similar to that followed by those intending to practise surgery and to gain for themselves a similar diploma'. In the event Mr Hawes' Bill (which was primarily concerned with the qualification and registration of medical and surgical practitioners) failed to reach the statute book. The Royal College of Surgeons had recently gained that title by Royal Charter, together with the power to confer upon members considered meritorious the distinction of Fellow. At the same time as their approach to the Home Secretary the group of dental practitioners addressed a 'Memorial' to the College asking for members practising dentistry to be eligible for the Fellowship (Appendix I). From the response the Memorialists received the impression that for a Member of the Royal College of Surgeons to practice dentistry solely was somewhat derogatory.

For more than a decade after this there is no record of any specific action for reform. Indeed, the indications are that the majority of dentists of Great Britain were not greatly concerned to advance their profession. In evidence of this are the facts that no dental societies existed or were formed and that attempts to start two dental journals, *The British Quarterly Journal of Dental Science* (1843) and *The Forceps* (1844) failed, the first after two issues and the second after two years. Some scientific progress was made, however; John Tomes, then dental surgeon at the Middlesex Hospital, produced in 1848 his book, *A Course of Lectures on Dental Physiology and Surgery*, based upon his histological research and wide clinical experience, which became a standard work of reference.

Nevertheless, there were some advocates of change, and by 1855 these had resolved themselves into two contending parties, which have come to be referred to as The Memorialists, and included those who had 'memorialised' the Royal College of Surgeons in 1843, and The Independents respectively. Briefly summarised, the difference between them was that the former wanted the education and training of dentists and the regulation of the profession to be placed under the control of the Royal College of Surgeons; whereas the Independents, on the other hand, proposed to set up a College of Dentists to assume these functions. The contest between the two was closely fought. The Memorialists formed the Odontological Society of London on 10th November 1856; the Independents formed their College of Dentists on 11th November 1856. But well before then, in December 1855, the Memorialists had, without publicity, submitted to the Royal College of Surgeons their request that dentistry be recognised as a special branch of surgery and that the Royal College institute an examination in dental surgery.

There were two main obstacles to progress – the absence of a definitive curriculum and properly supervised training and the fact that its charter did not empower the Royal College of Surgeons to introduce a dental qualification. The Independents proposed to meet these deficiencies by making these functions the responsibility of the College of Dentists – in fact, the root of their opposition to the proposals of the Memorialists was their conviction that surgeons were not competent to supervise the training of dentists or to examine them. On the other hand, the Memorialists, many of whom were members of the Royal College of Surgeons, were convinced that the authority and status of the College were essential to the achievement of the required improvement of the dental profession.

At this stage the two contending bodies were proceeding along divergent roads. The Independents set about collecting together their membership and establishing a means of training, with considerable dissension among themselves as they tried to design standards for both, whilst maximising the appeal of membership to practising and prospective dentists. Their proposals envisaged the provision of instruction in anatomy and physiology, the elements of chemistry and natural philosophy, dental surgery, pathology and dental practice. There was to be 'a sound and practical examination' but the trainee dentist was not bound by any curriculum and was free to acquire the necessary knowledge 'according as his own taste and opportunities may lead him on his way.' On 5th October 1859 the College opened the Metropolitan School of Dental Science at its headquarters in Cavendish Street, where there were formal lectures by medical men and demonstrations of anatomical specimens and instruments, but no facilities for clinical work. To provide these, special arrangements were proposed for students to attend the dental practice at the Westminster Dispensary, but these seem never to have been satisfactorily implemented. In 1861, having failed in this attempt to provide clinical practice for its students, the College decided to establish a dental hospital and the National Dental Hospital was opened in Great Portland Street in November 1861.

Very soon the College combined this institution with the Metropolitan School of Dental Science to form a complete dental teaching hospital, which amalgamated with University College Hospital and Medical School in 1914.

Meanwhile, the Odontological Society had pursued its campaign to engage the Royal College of Surgeons in the movement for dental reform. In February 1857 the Society tried to persuade the Royal College to take advantage of the Bill for the regulation of the medical profession then before Parliament to obtain power to establish 'a department of dental surgery'. The response of the Royal College, having, it seems, agreed with the other medical corporations on the contents of the Medical Bill and being reluctant to re-open what was most probably a delicate negotiation, was a counter-suggestion that the Society itself might petition Parliament for an addition to the Bill giving themselves or the Royal College appropriate powers. The Bill then under discussion was, in fact, withdrawn, but in May 1857 another similar Bill was introduced and a deputation from the Society consisting of Messrs. JH Parkinson, WA Harrison and John Tomes was successful in persuading its Parliamentary sponsors to insert the following addtional clause:

It shall, notwithstanding anything herein contained be lawful for Her Majesty, by charter, to grant to the Royal College of Surgeons of England power to institute and hold examinations for the purpose of testing the fitness of persons to practise as dentists, who may be desirous of being so examined, and to grant certificates of such fitness.

After a number of Parliamentary vicissitudes a Bill incorporating this provision received the Royal Assent as the Medical Act 1858 on 2nd August of that year. But by that date the Odontological Society had decided to proceed with plans for a dental school, regardless of the outcome of the negotiations with the Royal College and the Parliamentary process. The formal decision was made by the Society at a meeting on 11th June 1858, when the report of the committee it had appointed 'to draw out a plan of a Dental School' was approved. This report included a complete curriculum for the education of dental students, which, since the Bill was still in the balance, it was agreed should be 'such as would be received by the College of Surgeons should that College form a dental department, and . . . such as would be received by an independent Dental Institution, should it ultimately be found necessary to found such an institution' and recommended the establishment of a dental hospital supported by voluntary contributions in order to provide facilities for practical training and clinical experience. In consequence of this decision, the Dental Hospital of London was opened at 32, Soho Square on 1st December 1858, and the London School of Dental Surgery at the same address on 1st October 1859.

The dates of some of the main events in this period in the history of dental reform are indicative of the intense rivalry between the Memorialists and the Independents. The former brought their Odontological Society of London into being on 10th November 1856, and the Independents established the College of Dentists on the following day. It will have been noted that the opening of the London School of Dental Surgery was followed within four days by that of the Metropolitan School of Dental Science (no doubt considerable thought was expended in arriving at a title which distinguished the latter from its rival without diminishing its status). But the Independents had already missed the boat. In the first place, they had failed to make adequate arrangements for clinical experience for the pupils at their School – their dental hospital did not open until 1861. More importantly, they were out-manoeuvred by the Memorialists and the Royal College of Surgeons, who seem to have included some adept politicians, by the introduction of the Dental Qualification Clause into the Medical Bill. The College of Dentists, starting from scratch to provide dental training and a dental qualification, could not compete with the prestigious Royal College once it was empowered to do the same.

The episode is, perhaps, a neat epitome of the theory of progress through conflict – thesis; antithesis; synthesis. The controversy continued for a while, with much heated correspondence in the dental journals and some unmannerly name-calling, and a steady drift of members from the College to the Society. In 1863 the College of Dentists threw in the towel. Its members were accepted as members of the Odontological Society (henceforward 'of Great Britain'), its assets were transferred to the Society, and it ceased to exist.

Following their decision of 11th June 1858, the first practical task which faced the Odontological Society was that of setting up the proposed hospital. They established a Dental Hospital Organisation Committee, which proposed that the School should implement the curriculum adopted by the Society. Because of its historical importance this, the first curriculum for a dental school in this country, is reproduced in full:

Lectures and Hospital Practice to be attended at the existing School and Hospital.

Courses of Lectures.

2 Anatomy with Dissections (one being Special)
2 Physiology and Pathology
1 Practice of Physics
1 Practice of Surgery
1 Materia Medica
1 Chemistry 1 Practical Chemistry
1 Metallurgy
2 Dental Anatomy and Physiology (Human and Comparative)
2 Dental Surgery
2 Mechanical Dentistry

Hospital Attendance

6 months Medical practice and attendance on Clinical Lectures
2 year's attendance at a recognised Dental Hospital, or at the Dental Department of a recognised General Hospital.

Candidates for examination will be required to bring proof of being 21 years of age, and having been engaged at least 4 years in the acquirement of professional knowledge, and that a period of not less than 3 years has been employed in acquiring a practical familiarity with the details of Mechanical Dentistry under the instruction of a recognised Practioner.'

What sort of society was it in which these events occurred and what motivated the Memorialists and the Independents? Professor Best (*Mid-Victorian Britain, 1851–75*) concurs with many other historians that the mid-Victorian period was one of relative calm between times of unrest, during which there was a high degree of consensus about fundamental moral values. There was a common acceptance of a hierarchical social order and a common cult of 'respectability' and 'independence' which, with the practice of deference – 'knowing one's place' – and the belief that by hard work and application – 'self-help' – an individual could improve himself and his position in society, made the manifest social inequalities acceptable. Ambitions for respectability and independence and the desire for improvement are apparent in the Dental Reform Movement of the nineteenth century. But these are largely self-centred motives and there was clearly something more; the words of the reformers show that they were concerned that members of the profession should be enabled and required to provide a better service.

Dentists were not unique, in the mid-nineteenth century, in their zeal for professional discipline and qualification. The professionalisation of occupations, from accountants to sanitary engineers, and the formation of organisations responsible for regulating the qualification and practice of their members was an important element in the development of nineteenth century British society – of all such organisations in existence during the last decade of the century, three-quarters had come into being since its beginning. Furthermore, as Anthony King points out in his introduction to *Town Swamps and Social Bridges* (Godwin, G., Leicester, 1972 ed.)

the creation of professional associations with established criteria for recruitment, shared norms of professional behaviour, and a distinctive ethic governing members' conduct was a major factor in the development of Victorian technology. Purpose-built premises, specialist libraries and the institution of regular meetings made possible a more adequate exchange of ideas and information, an indispensable part of scientific activity.... It is clear that these organisational changes, dependent as they were on technical improvements in the communication and distribution system, immensely increased the rate at which the corpus of any particular knowledge grew, whether in medicine, science, politics or the arts. The exponential growth of science, a phenomenon so well recognised in the twentieth century, owes much to the organisational and institutional infrastructure laid in the nineteenth century.

In addition to these considerations of personal standing and professional standards there was concern for the less fortunate. In the late 1850s, particularly for the large number of people who were not blessed with or successful in achieving wealth or station, there was little to relieve the harsh and sordid conditions of life in the towns and cities – not that things were much better in the country villages, despite the romantic folk memory of idyllic rural bliss – governed as they were by the gospel of work and the doctrines of individualism and economic laissez-faire. Although efforts to improve conditions had commenced, their successes were largely in the future. The Public Health Act of 1848 had empowered local authorities to facilitate sanitary improvement, and although the duty was optional, many had accepted it. Nevertheless, many of the London slums were unspeakably vile, as Charles Dickens described (*Great Expectations* was published in 1861) and some of the measures adopted to do away with them made matters worse. New roads – Charing Cross Road, Shaftesbury Avenue, Victoria Street, Northumberland Avenue – were built through some of the worst slum areas, but the accommodation thus destroyed was not replaced. In consequence, the people so displaced added to the overcrowding and squalor in the remaining slums. The Thames in London was an open sewer and 1858 was the year of its 'great stink', which motivated Parliament to face the problem of urban sanitation. There was a cholera outbreak in London, albeit the last, in 1866–67. Florence Nightingale's reform of hospital nursing had only just started (the Crimean War ended in 1856) and public executions and the transportation of convicts to Australia continued until 1868. Sending small boys up chimneys to sweep them was not made illegal until 1875.

The society in which the dental reformers worked was, therefore, one which differed markedly from modern British society, although the transition from that society to the society of the present day was already under way. But it was not much different from some other modern societies; many of the citizens of Rio de Janeiro, Calcutta and Soweto would have found London of the mid-nineteenth century very much like their home towns. It was a society based upon class distinction, in which culture and beauty, luxury and splendour existed for those in high positions, and wealth and esteem for those with professional skills and successful businesses. Members of 'the industrious working class' if they worked hard and subject to periods of depression and unemployment, were able to live comfortably by their standards; but there remained a large group of people, variously described as 'the labouring poor', 'the indigenous poor' or 'the dangerous classes', who lived in poverty. These were the people who inhabited the slums of London and elsewhere, whose lives were described by Mayhew (*London Labour and the London Poor*). They lived from hand to mouth, the men by labouring when there was work, by petty trading and thieving at other times, the women by domestic service, cleaning and laundering and, often, by prostitution when other means failed.

The plight of the poor was of great concern to many of the educated and wealthy, for a variety of reasons. Some of the reasons were altruistic – Christian charity was a real force – and others were practical; if the insanitary conditions of the poor bred cholera, the disease could not be confined to their quarters. When the dentists came to set up their dental hospital they were able to draw upon this fund of charitable goodwill. The prospectus which they issued in August 1858 set out as follows:

The Dental Hospital of London is founded for the purpose of affording to the poor generally the means of obtaining gratuitous relief and advice, in such cases as are included in the special practice of Dental Surgery; and also for affording an opportunity of instruction to those who enter the Dental profession. In existing general hospitals, the Dental forms but a subordinate department, the duties of the Dental Surgeon are mainly confined to the extraction of teeth, and the treatment of affections of the gums; and his services are generally only available on one or two days in the week. On other days the patients are necessarily left to the care of students, whose attention has not been specially directed to the practice of Dental Surgery. (The last sentence seems to have ruffled feathers, because at a meeting of the Publication Committee on 14th October 1858 it was decided to delete it from future editions).

Statistical records show that the teeth of the lower orders are very defective, the average of decayed permanent teeth in young persons, between the age of six and fifteen, ranging as high as 24 or 25 per cent., while in adults the percentage is very much greater; and it is not too much to affirm that, in the majority of instances, such teeth are lost to the poor, after much suffering, for want of timely remedial treatment. Independently, however, of the immediate suffering produced by diseased teeth, their loss is often the cause, the sole cause, of visceral derange-ments, exhibiting themselves under more or less aggravated forms of dyspepsia, etc., the debilitating and depressing effects of which are too well known to make it necessary to dilate upon them here; but the results warrant the directing special attention to a point of no small importance in its consequences, namely, the effects such evils have upon the physical efficiency of the working portion of the community; and yet, with this serious amount of mischief arising from the loss of such important organs, no opportunity has hitherto been afforded to the poor of preserving them by remedial treatment, except at one or two special institutions, which, from various circumstances are altogether unequal to meet the demands made upon them.

To those who interest themselves in the subject, it will be apparent from statements that, in common charity towards our poorer brethren, an institution on an extended scale for the proper treatment of teeth is called for; but there are other and strong reasons which render the formation of such an Hospital necessary.

Besides the substantial benefits which this Hospital will confer upon the poorest classes, upon domestic servants, and upon those whose earnings are too small to enable them to defray the expense of the professional assistance required in such cases, it will be a means of affording practical instruction to those students who may wish to make themselves acquainted with the principles of Dental Surgery, either to meet the requirements of general practice, or to gain the necessary facility for practising that special branch as army or navy surgeons.

This latter point the Committee who have undertaken the formation of this hospital consider of no small importance as, at the present time, little opportunity exists for the dental pupil to obtain the requisite knowledge for performing the various operations on the teeth, such as regulating, filling, etc.; and, consequently in the majority of cases, experience in these most difficult and delicate operations has to be acquired after the commencement of his professional career, as a practitioner.

Not doubting that the importance of these facts will be acknowledged, the Committee feel that they have the strongest grounds for urging their richer brethren to support the Hospital they now bring under the notice of the public; and they believe that their appeal will meet with favour, and command the sympathy of the charitable; and likewise claim the aid of those who employ large numbers of workpeople and artisans.

Donations and subscriptions will be thankfully received by the Treasurer, at his residence, 36, Sackville Street, Piccadilly; or at the Union Bank of London, Argyll Place, Regent Street.

This Prospectus was issued by the Dental Hospital Organisation Committee, set up by the Odontological Society on 11th June 1858, under the chairmanship of Mr WA Harrison, with Alfred Hill (author of *History of the Reform Movement in the Dental Profession*) as its Honorary Secretary. In setting about its task the Committee would have been able to draw on the experience of those who during the previous 150 years had set up a number of voluntary hospitals and dispensaries up and down the country. The procedure followed more or less the same general plan, initiated by a group of enthusiasts who set out to raise funds for the project, by public appeal, by direct approach to individuals and by organising fund-raising functions, such as dinners and concerts. They appointed a Board or Committee of Management comprising influential people capable of attracting subscribers and benefactors and of controlling the finances and managing the institution. The Managing Committee usually tried to secure a prominent personage – a member of the Royal Family if possible – to act as patron and president, invited senior physicians and surgeons to act as consulting officers and appointed the honorary professional staff, who would direct the treatment and training carried out in the institution. The Managing Committee usually appointed a House Committee, which met weekly to manage the day-to-day affairs of the hospital, with a paid secretary who worked to their instructions. A Collector was appointed for the collection of money, paid on a commission basis. Subscribers of a certain amount became the Governors of the charity; there was an Annual Meeting of Governors, to which the Committee of Management submitted a report and which elected the Committee for the subsequent year, and was responsible for the bye-laws of the charity.

Governors were given tickets, or 'letters', as they were called, to give to deserving persons to enable them to obtain treatment at the hospital. At some voluntary hospitals only those who had letters were seen, except in emergency, at others the letters entitled the bearers to special or extra treatment.

In this connection, the Dental Hospital's Prospectus included the following 'Abstract of Laws':

Donors of ten guineas, in one payment, shall be considered Life Governors, and be entitled to recommend annually an unlimited number of patients requiring ordinary relief, and three patients for special operations; and also to vote at all elections. Annual subscribers of one guinea shall be entitled to the same privileges.

It is interesting to note that although the authors of the Prospectus refer to their object of affording free treatment 'to the poor generally' – a point which they had to establish if their institution was to have legal charitable status – the document is designed to appeal to members of the middle and upper classes from whom, of course, the money was to come. Reference is made to the benefits likely to accrue to employers in the maintenance of the efficiency of their workpeople and domestic servants. This leads to the question frequently raised, who benefited from the letters for treatment issued by governors of charitable institutions? Clearly there was a temptation for the letters to be used by the donors to help their employees, with a tacit assumption that a subscription to the local voluntary hospital provided access to a kind of 'health service' for them. As early as 1844, an article in the dental journal *Forceps*, complained that those who could afford to pay were admitted to hospitals, to the disadvantage of the poor:

As if the poor were not at sufficient disadvantage every difficulty is thrown in the way of their obtaining admission to one of these charities. A letter has to be obtained and the friends of the patient are frequently bandied from house to house and made to waste day after day before they are successful; then they may not have the necessary quantity of linen and this has to be bought or perchance begged; and lastly, security in case of death.

In the report on the opening of the Dental Hospital of London in the *British Journal of Dental Science* (November 1858), the writer remarked:

With regard to the working of the Dental Hospital, we think the Committee will have to exercise great caution with regard to the patients admitted. In every hospital great abuses exist, and it is a well-known fact that persons often seek the advice afforded at charitable institutions whose means well enable them to pay for medical aid. An institution established for a special purpose, like the Dental Hospital is peculiarly open to such abuse, and therefore the laws which regulate the admission of patients should be very stringent and vigorously enforced, and the class relieved should be those who cannot afford to pay, and those alone.

The problem of who was to benefit from the treatment provided was a recurring one, as will be seen. To some extent it was caused by watchful members of the dental profession anxious that those able to pay them for their services should not get free treatment from the Hospital, but this was by no means the whole story. Much later, in the 1890s, when the question of providing free dentures was debated, the view was expressed by the Management Committee that handing out false teeth free of charge would lead to the 'pauperisation' of the recipient. This view was very typical of the times, and part of the very serious concern over what to do about poverty. The self-evident fact that large numbers of what were called the labouring classes suffered from it led to the introduction in 1834 of the system of poor relief based upon the Workhouse. The difficulty was to distinguish between the indigent poor – those who, because of age or infirmity, lacked the ability to earn a living – and those who were capable of work. It was felt that public relief corrupted the low-paid and unemployed able-bodied poor, undermining the character and independence of individuals and their families – pauperising them, in fact.

The result of the continued relief of pauperism is seen to be the creation of a definite pauper class which not only won't work, but really can't work, which is physically too weak and mentally too shiftless and dependant to undertake severe physical toil. (Bryce, J., *The American Experience in the Relief of the Poor*, 1871).

The Workhouse system was adopted to provide for the needs of the first category without tempting those of the second category to take advantage of it. Those admitted to the Workhouse were subjected to a disciplined regime of orderly behaviour, plain diet and hard work; it was, in the words of a contemporary commentator, 'a machine for grinding men good'. As such, people in need had recourse to it only as a last resort. This apparently harsh attitude was based upon what was seen as a law of nature designed to maintain the human population at the level which could be maintained by the current production of the means of subsistence. If the population rose above that level a natural process of starvation would reduce it appropriately. Unemployment and poverty were signs that the level had been exceeded and attempts to relieve those suffering from them (and especially the relief of those receiving low wages) would be either ineffective or, if successful, could lead to the growth of a huge class of 'hereditary paupers' and to the eventual destruction of society. Hence the concern of those running the Dental Hospital that only the indigent poor should benefit from its services was not just stinginess; as a general principle, they believed, giving people things for nothing was personally harmful and potentially socially disruptive.

The need to make sure that the recipients of charity were 'deserving' led in the 1860s to the formation of the Charity Organisation Society, the services of which were, at a later stage, considered by the Hospital authorities during the debate about free dentures. One of the stated objects of that body was the stamping out of mendacity; its members seem to have started from the assumptions that most charities were gullible and foolishly soft-hearted, and that many applicants for relief were liars and frauds. They undertook, by a system of visiting and enquiry, to check need, investigate fraud, eliminate waste and avoid duplication and sought to monitor the activities of charities.

The Dental Hospital and School inaugurated by the Odontological Society claimed to be the first such institution in Great Britain – indeed, it was preceded in the English-speaking world only by the one in Baltimore, USA, which was founded in 1839. But it was not quite the first venture into this field in this country. In 1840 there was established in Windmill Street, Tottenham Court Road, The London Institution for Diseases of the Teeth, to provide dental treatment for the poor, among the founders of which were WA Harrison and Edwin Saunders, both of whom were later prominent in the affairs of the Odontological Society and the founding of the Dental Hospital of London. A report issued in 1844 indicates that although it was open only on Tuesday and Friday mornings nearly 6000 patients attended the Institute during the first four years of its existence. From the point of view of this History, however, the importance of the Institute is that its founders clearly envisaged it as a place at which clinical instruction in dentistry would be available to students. In 1844, in a letter in *The Forceps* referring to an earlier statement in the journal with reference to dental training, that 'there is neither hospital or dispensary expressly for diseases of the teeth', Harrison and Saunders said that pupils were received at the Institution where they were able to see treatment and operations carried out, and to carry them out themselves under supervision. The Institution seems to have lasted for about twelve years and the reasons for its closure are not known; perhaps its scale of operation was too limited for it to gain the necesssary support and influence. But it is clear from their letter that Harrison and Saunders conceived the idea of a teaching dental hospital as early as 1840. Their pioneering work, however, does not invalidate the claim of the Dental Hospital of London to be the first because although it provided clinical teaching and experience the London Institution made no provision for teaching the non-clinical subjects.

The oldest existing dental hospital in the British Isles at the time of writing is the Birmingham and Midland Counties Dental Dispensary (later the Birmingham Dental Hospital), which opened in January 1858. This, however, had no teaching function in its early days and it was not until 1880 that it was recognised as a dental school by the Royal College of Surgeons. However, as the first dental hospital the institution at Birmingham preceded the Dental Hospital of London, albeit only by a few months.

2

Saunders and the move to Leicester Square

The new institution formally came into being at a meeting of the Odontological Society at 32 Soho Square on 6th October 1858, at which the Chairman of the Organising Committee reported that a Committee of Management, Trustees, Honorary Officers and a medical staff had been appointed and regulations ('Laws') governing the administration of the charity had been drawn up. A lease at a rent of £170 per year had been taken of the house in which the meeting was held, to provide a home for the new Hospital and School – it was hoped to raise a proportion of the rent by letting off parts of the building not required for immediate use. The sum of £192.5.8d had been raised, and a further £63 had been promised, towards the cost of opening. At the conclusion of his report, the Chairman of the Organising Committee formally handed over the Hospital and the funds to the Committee of Management, which proceeded to establish committees to arrange the furnishing of the premises, the provision of instruments and the publication of prospectuses and advertisements. Alfred Hill was appointed Honorary Secretary to the Hospital.

32 Soho Square was built in 1776 or thereabouts, and stood on the south-west corner of the Square, its rear portion extending into Dean Street. David Hepburn, who was House Surgeon in 1875, by which time the institution had moved to Leicester Square, in an address to the Students' Society in 1905, recalled the earlier days at Soho Square, where he must have been a student, giving the following account of what he referred to as 'the small and unostentatious hospital in that quiet corner of Soho Square, which was our original home':-

I well remember the old house, with its large and elegantly proportioned rooms. It was of historic interest, too, having once been the residence of Sir Joseph Banks, the distinguished naturalist, and President of the Royal Society. It had also been the home of the Linnaean Society, and in all respects it was a dignified abode for a scientific school, and a much needed charity.

An entrance hall of considerable dimensions served as a waiting room for patients. Off this the operating rooms opened, that reserved for conservative operations and consultations being the original dining room of the house. It contained three or four operating chairs, book cases, writing table and other necessary furniture. Upstairs, in a lofty well-proportioned apartment, with a large alcove curtained off for use as a library and committee room, the Odontological Society held its meetings. Various rooms were let as offices to 'The Council of Medical Education', and in the upper storey of the house one room was set apart for the Museum of the Odontological Society. Another was used as a lecture room, and this was adapted by joining two rooms with an open arch. In one of these were four raised forms and narrow desks facing the lecturer's table, and the other was elaborately fitted up with benches, furnaces for melting and porcelain work, lathes, plaster and sand boards, all the instruments and tools necessary for bone, vulcanite and metal working; in fact, every appliance required in the province of dental mechanics.

Hepburn's illustration, taken after the Dental Hospital had moved to Leicester Square and the premises were occupied by the Hospital for Diseases of the Heart, shows the nicely proportioned facade squeezed between rather drab neighbours. Hepburn refers only to chairs used for conservation – according to the Annual Reports the total chair number had reached eleven by 1865, which must have been a little before his time. The premises were considerably larger than the illustration suggests, because they extended behind the neighbouring house, which was on the corner of Soho Square and Frith Street.

The letting of accommodation to other organisations to which he refers was to make use of surplus accommodation and provide revenue. Arrangements were made in January 1859 to allow the use of the large Meeting Room and the Board Room by the Odontological Society for their meetings for a sum of £30 per annum and, with the agreement of the Odontological Society, that the General Council of Medical Education and Registration should use the Board Room, large Meeting Room and a back room on the first floor for a sum of £160 per annum. When courses of lectures and demonstrations commenced later in the year a room in the basement was used for demonstrations 'in the various proceedings incidental to mechanical dentistry'.

It is not easy to reconstruct the Hospital and School of those early days. The only source of information is the Minute Book, the first volume of which covers the period 1858 to 1882. On the face of it this is an impressive volume, commencing with the record of the initial meeting on 6th October 1858. It is in a neat copperplate hand and has illuminated headings of splendid appearance. But it is not, it seems, the original record as far as the period from October 1858 to April 1859 is concerned for, although at each meeting it is recorded that the minutes of the preceding meeting were read and confirmed none have been signed by the Chairman. This suggests that there was another minute book for this period and that someone decided that it was not sufficiently dignified and set in motion the process of transcribing it into the present grandiose format. It is tempting to think that this someone was Alfred Hill – he was, after all, Honorary Secretary and a historian and must have been conscious of the importance to dental history of the records for which he was responsible.

The transcription process apparently did not catch up with events until April 1859 because the record of the meeting on the 20th of that month is the first to be signed. As well, alas, this marks the end of the illuminated manuscript; for a time the minutes are set out in such form that someone could go back later and fill in the coloured headings and initial letters, but they remain still as pencilled drafts. By the end of 1866 even this attempt has been abandoned and the record continues in ordinary manuscript.

The Minutes of the early meetings reveal that the Committee of Management had to learn the business of adminstration as it went along. When the Organising Committee handed over, although the dental surgeons who would be responsible for the care of the patients of the hospital had been appointed (S Cartwight, Jnr., WA Harrison, R Hepburn, C Rogers, J Tomes and T Underwood), there was no administrative staff other than the committee members themselves – Arnold Rogers was Honorary Treasurer, Alfred Hill, as has been mentioned, Honorary Secretary, and Rogers, Edwin Saunders and James Robinson were Trustees. The Chairman of the Committee, Campbell Greig De Morgan, is not previously recorded among those concerned with dental reform and dental education. He was a distinguished surgeon and anatomist who had collaborated with John Tomes, and it was no doubt through this connection that he became involved in the affairs of the Dental Hospital. The first administrative appointment made was that of Mr T Champion as Porter, from 14th October 1858, at a wage of one guinea per week, plus accommodation for himself and his wife. At about the same time Mr J Hall was appointed as temporary assistant to the Honorary Secretary at a similar rate of pay. His job, however, was probably part-time only; one of his successors who resigned in 1870 gave as his reason for doing so the fact that his other professional commitments had increased. The appointment was not, as things turned out, temporary – although individuals came and went the post was always filled except for a short period in 1870 when the unsuccessful experiment was made of combining the post with that of House Surgeon. For the record, the first student to be enrolled is said to have been William Frederick Forsyth, aged 22. He gained his LDS within a year, so he must have been experienced in the profession before he entered the School. He died in 1922, aged 85.

The duties of the Assistant to the Honorary Secretary were laid down by the Management Committee and consisted of 'the arrangement of book-keeping, keeping the lists of subscribers, receiving any information at the Office, which he will convey to the Honorary Secretary for his advice' while the Honorary Secretary 'will undertake the arrangements for all Board meetings, keeping the minutes of all meetings entered, the agenda, petty cash and standing order book'.

A third appointment at this time was that of Mr HC Large, as Collector, from 21st October, whose job it was to 'get in', in the phrase used in the Minutes, the subscriptions and donations upon which the institution depended. His remuneration was to be a percentage of the amount got in, although the Minutes coyly refrain from specifying what the percentage would be, referring only to 'the customary rates'.

All three appointments seem to have been unfortunate. By the beginning of December Mr Champion became seriously ill and had to be replaced. Early in 1861 the auditors reported a small discrepancy in the Hospital's books for which they were unable to account. The Committee of Management instructed them to examine the accounts more thoroughly in order to establish the reason for the discrepancy, whereupon Mr Hall resigned. Later it was reported that the examination of the accounts had disclosed that he owed the Hospital £12.9.6d. Almost simultaneously Mr Large, the Collector, seems to have been invited to attend a meeting of the Management Committee in the course of which he found it appropriate to offer his resignation. The formal prose of the minute-writer fails to conceal the alacrity with which the Committee accepted this offer. Subsequently the minutes report that the Honorary Secretary was instructed to write to him about three subscriptions of one guinea for which receipts had been issued but which did not appear to have found their way into the Hospital's bank account. All this suggests that the two had been collaborating in an exercise of embezzlement and fraudulent book-keeping.

If this was the case – and although the Minutes on the subject are exceedingly reticent it seems reasonable to believe that it was – the Committee is to be congratulated on discovering the fraud without professional assistance – the auditors were subscribers to the charity acting in an honorary capacity – and on dealing with it so promptly. These Victorian surgeons and dentists knew how to look after themselves and their brainchild in the hard world and were capable of being quite ruthless in doing so. In fact, the Committee of Management exercised a very close control over financial matters. They received regular reports of bank balances, approved every payment before it was made and audited the petty cash expenditure each time it was reimbursed. The weak link at first, as no doubt Hall and Large appreciated, was on the income side, where the Collector seems to have had a free hand. But this was soon remedied, and we find at each meeting of the Committee detailed reports of subscriptions and donations. In 1958, one hundred years later, the accounting and reporting system which they originated was still in use in the School, basically unchanged in principle.

The institution occupied the premises in Soho Square from its birth in 1858 until 1874, during which period the workload increased rapidly. The Annual Reports record that 2,116 patients attended in 1859, the first full year of operation, and that the numbers of operations carried out reached a peak of 22,627 in 1872, falling slightly to 21,904 in 1873, evidence that the resources were strained to their limit and the justification for the move to Leicester Square in March 1874. The benefits in the way of dental treatment which the charity provided for poor people are frequently referred to in the Annual Reports. In 1859, the point is made that, in contrast with the situation at the majority of general hospitals, where the work of dental officers was largely restricted to extraction, 'the greater number of cases treated at this Hospital consists of operations other than mere extraction, which, but for this Institution, would have been entirely out the reach of the poor.' The ways in which patients qualified for treatment were set out in the Laws of the Charity, which provided as follows:

> That every poor applicant suffering pain shall have gratutitous advice, and any operative assistance that may be immediately necessary, without a letter of introduction; but that persons requiring special operations shall be admitted only by the recommendation of a Governor.

At first the work was carried out by the six Dental Surgeons, one of whom attended each morning, Sundays excepted, from 8.30 to 9.30, but the build-up of work soon made this an impracticable arrangement; by 1862 operations were averaging about 35 a day. To deal with the overload, six Assistant Dental Surgeons were appointed in 1863. One the these was to attend from 9.00 a.m. to 12 noon daily, and, it was decided,

> in the absence of the Dental Surgeon of the day the Assistant shall be responsible for the treatment of the patients and the general management of the Surgery. He shall exercise supervision over the students in respect to patients committed to their charge. No person shall be eligible for the office of Assistant Dental Surgeon unless he holds the Dental Diploma of the Royal College of Surgeons.

Thus was set the pattern for the clinical control of the establishment – the Consultant of the Day – which subsisted in principle, although latterly in attenuated form, until the closure of the Hospital in 1985. The Consultant of the Day was responsible for the clinical work of the institution on his day, whether or not he was physically present in the building. The Assistant Dental Surgeons were practitioners of experience and reputation and their status within the Hospital does not seem to have been very much inferior to that of their senior colleagues, except that they were not in the early years entitled to a share of students' fees. They were members of the Medical Committee and, as the records show, those who remained in post were in due course promoted to the senior rank as vacancies permitted.

One of the duties of the Dental Surgeons (presumably often carried out on their behalf by their juniors) was that of making sure that those presenting for treatment were qualified to have it – that is to say, that they were poor and in possession of a 'letter' from a Governor if they were to have more than emergency relief. This must have been a rather invidious task, apart from being time-consuming, but a necesary one. To provide free treatment for people who could afford to pay for it would be a breach of faith with those who had contributed to the charity and would attract criticism from the dental profession, the members of which were alert for any such threat to their livelihoods. The staff clearly felt that they failed to receive proper co-operation from individual Governors in carrying out this task. The annual reports of the Medical Committee, in the early years, frequently draw attention to the need for Governors to ensure that those to whom they give their recommendations are necessitous; the following, from the Report of January 1873 is a typical example:

They (i.e., the Medical Committee) would again call the attention of the Committee of Management to the large number of persons applying at the Hospital for relief, who, upon interrogation, are found to be able to pay for medical advice and attendance, and are not proper objects of charity. Their common observation that they can get better aid at the Hospital than elsewhere is, whilst flattering to the Staff, no ground, in the opinion of this Committee, for diverting the resources of the Institution from its legitimate object.

There were, however, at least two apparent departures from the principle that patients should be 'proper objects of charity'. In 1870 the Chief Commissioner of Metropolitan Police wrote to say that he had been authorised to pay an annual subscription of five guineas in return for the services which the Hospital was regularly giving to members of the Force; and in 1871 the Committee of Management agreed, in return for an annual subscription of ten guineas 'to admit on the same terms as other patients but as a matter of right and not of charity all servants of the General Post Office requiring dental treatment.' The anomaly was subsequently rectified, following a complaint that Post Office employees who were not entitled to the benefits of a charitable institution were receiving treatment and that some were passing their entitlement cards to strangers, by an agreement by the GPO that cards entitling their bearers to treatment would be issued only to those who were proper recipients of relief. So there was, perhaps, no departure from principle and the two arrangements are evidence only of the fact that the pay received by some policemen and postal workers was not sufficient to disqualify them as 'suitable recipients of charity'.

The appointments of Dental Surgeon and Assistant Dental Surgeon were honorary and carried no salary, although the senior Surgeons shared with the lecturers the surplus of students' fees over the School's expenses. Nevertheless, appointments to the staff of London medical charities were exceedingly valuable and much sought after because of the advantages they gave to the holders in their private practices, enabling them to attract richer and more remunerative patients. An incident at Charing Cross Hospital indicates the value placed upon such appointments. There, in 1836, a scandal arose because the Senior Surgeon had demanded – and got – a payment of £500 for securing the appointment of an Assistant House Surgeon (*The Two Pillars of Charing Cross*, Minney, RJ, London, 1967). There is every reason to believe that similar appointments at the Dental Hospital would have been equally sought after – but no evidence at all to suggest that there was any impropriety in the making of them there. That those who held such appointments were not slow to make the fact known was noticed in the report in *The Quarterly Journal of Dental Science* of the opening of the Dental Hospital in 1858, which included the barbed comment: 'Great publicity is given to the institution, and the names of the dentists in connection with it are printed in large letters in the circular sent to the affluent soliciting contributions for the relief of the indigent.' (It has to be noted that this was at the height of the war between the Odontological Society and the College of Dentists and that the Quarterly Journal was a committed supporter of the latter and, as such, eager to belittle the Society's achievement).

In 1868, the numbers of patients attending the Hospital having increased to some 55–60 per day, the Medical Committee suggested the appointment of a House Surgeon, to hold office for not less than three months, and to be granted a certificate at the successful completion of his term of office - the inference being that the post was to be, as such posts are still, a training one. In May 1869 detailed consideration was given to the appointment. The Committee of Management concluded that 'they felt the need of having some reliable Officer who could attend the Hospital during the greater part of the day to treat certain cases of emergency, such as Patients suffering acute pain, haemorrhage after operation, etc.' The hours of attendance were to be from 9.0 a.m. to 5.0 p.m., and it was thought that a salary of at least £100 per annum would be necessary to obtain a responsible and efficient person for the post. The efforts of the Management Committee were doubtless encouraged by an editorial article in the *British Journal of Dental Science* in August 1868. 'Why,' the article asked, 'should the poor policeman on his beat, the shop-girl obliged to keep up a cheerful appearance before customers, the fruit-seller at the windy corner, and other similar cases be expected to bear their pain after 12 o'clock in the day, until next morning, by the authorities of the Dental Hospital, any more than by the authorities of the General Hospital, to which, of course, they go to be treated by the resident dresser of the day?'

The difficulty was to find the money for the salary, and to this a most curious solution was devised, that of combining the duties of the post with those of Assistant Secretary. Mr MP Harding, formerly a prizeman at the Hospital and an honours graduate of University College, was appointed in

June 1869, and Mr B Soady, the Assistant Secretary, having agreed to resign his post in the interest of the Institution, undertook 'to instruct and fairly launch his successor in the duties of his office, and to leave in his hands the most minute instructions, to enable him to carry out the simple and systematic arrangements he, Mr Soady, had introduced' (Annual Report, 1869). In addition to the simple duties explained to him by Mr Soady, Mr Harding was required to provide the emergency clinic already referred to after 12 noon, and to deal with cases referred to him by his clinical superiors. As well, he was responsible for the custody and care of all instruments belonging to the hospital, and for the maintenance and control of medical supplies. If this was not enough, he was to maintain the casebooks and records of students' attendances and to manufacture the Hospital's supply of nitrous oxide, in which process he had been instructed in the laboratories of Messrs. J Bell and Company. In no circumstances was he to engage in private practice. It does not seem surprising that Mr Harding resigned in October 1870.

What he said in his letter of resignation is not recorded, but it was thereupon decided not to continue with the combined appointment. A new Assistant Secretary, Mr FT Procter, was appointed, and Mr M Stevens became House Surgeon, working from 9.0 a.m. to 2.0 p.m. for a salary of £40 p.a. (which was what was left of Mr Harding's £100 after deducting Mr Procter's salary). A year later we read that Mr Stevens applied for an increase in salary and for permission to 'practise on his own account' in the afternoons'. To this request the Medical Committee gave the following enigmatic reply:

> That in view of the purpose for which a House Surgeon was appointed the Medical Committee do not deem it desirable that the House Surgeon should be permitted to engage in private practice in any way during his term of office.

There seems to have been no comment upon the request for more money and Mr Stevens, following the example of his predecessor, shortly departed. His successor was Mr R Hepburn, Jnr., brother of David quoted above (p. 15) who started in March 1872. He left in November, having been asked to resign after enlarging a two-week leave of absence to one of five weeks.

Despite these experiences, the Hospital seems to have had little difficulty in the long term in obtaining House Surgeons, although there is no indication that the salary was increased for many years; £100 p.a. in 1862 equates with approximately £3,500 p.a. in today's terms. No doubt potential House Officers then, as now, considered themselves amply compensated for their low remuneration by the opportunity to gain experience and to work with the Senior Staff of the Hospital, who were among the leading members of the profession of their time.

The need for the appointment if the work of the institution was to be carried out economically is clear from the figures of patient attendances quoted in the Annual Reports; starting at 2,116 in 1859, the first full year of operation, these had increased eightfold by 1869; a considerable achievement in the first ten years of the institution's life – and at an average cost in that year of £0.033 per attendance (about £1.15 at current values). The money had been provided by a surprisingly small number of people – the 1869 Annual Report lists 143 Life Governors, most of whom would have provided no more than £10.50 during the decade, and 205 annual subscribers of £1.05, with a small number of miscellaneous donations. Many of these subscribers were members of the dental profession and their relatives, friends and patients and in the Annual Report for 1866 regret was expressed that although members of the profession had been generous and supportive the general public had not been especially forthcoming. Whatever their source, the contributions could not have been applied so effectively or made to go so far without the unremunerated efforts of the Dental Surgeons, Assistant Dental Surgeons and students attached to the Hospital. The scale of these efforts is indicated by the fact that the operations carried out during the year included about 14,000 extractions. These, it seems, would have been carried out by the Assistant Dental Surgeon of the day during his three hours of attendance, with such assistance from students as they were qualified to provide – a workrate of something approaching 15 per hour.

The method of working (which differs little, if at all, in principle from current practice) was described in September 1865 in an article in *The British Journal of Dental Science*, urging a visitor to the Hospital to

watch in turn the nine or ten chairs, attended to by careful earnest students, working to the benefit of the poor patients with as much zeal and care as if they were to receive a five guinea fee for each stopping, never attempting more than they feel themselves competent to accomplish, and at any moment of doubt or self-distrust honestly referring to the Dental Officer of the day, so that at no time is the poor patient the victim of inexperience or experiment.

It was during this period of the institution's life that the use of anaesthesia in dental practice began to be developed. The use of nitrous oxide in dental extraction had been demonstrated in America in 1844. In the 1840s ether and chloroform were beginning to be used in surgery, obstetrics and dentistry, and John Snow was using them in the out-patients' department of St George's Hospital for cases of tooth-drawing in the 1850s. A 'nitrous oxide clinic' had been set up in New York in 1863, exclusively for the painless extraction of teeth and preparing the mouth for dentures and SL Rymer, of the National Dental Hospital, tested the use of the gas on four subjects in December of that year. But it is not until 1865 that mention of anaesthesia at the Dental Hospital of London is recorded. In that year Mrs George Laurie, a prominent supporter of the Hospital and wife of a dental practitioner in the West End of London, wrote suggesting the introduction of chloroform to the practice of the Hospital and offering to contribute towards the cost of its provision. Asked to report upon this proposition, the Medical Committee (February 1866) gave their opinion as follows:

> That the administration of chloroform in very special cases is desirable on account of humanity and the benefits accruing to the students and pupils of the School. That the appointment of one or more Chloroformists to the Hospital would be advantageous and that upon the undertaking that Messrs. Potter and Clover had offered to attend one day in alternate weeks when necessary, this Committee recommend that the offer of these gentlemen be accepted.'

Mrs Laurie had probably done some lobbying among her friends, because in the next month are recorded a contribution from her of ten guineas and other contributions from several new subscribers who asked, like her, that their money be applied to the supply of chloroform. A Chloroform Fund was duly instituted. Mrs Laurie also urged that the use of chloroform at the Hospital be advertised, but the Committee of Management asked the Honorary Secretary to write to her to the effect that they thought such a step 'entirely inadvisable'. At the end of 1866 the Medical Committee said, in their Report to the Management Committee that they had 'much pleasure in recording the fact that operations have been conducted under the influence of chloroform, which, through the kind and liberal assistance of a Lady Governor, is now regularly administered whenever required.'

There were misgivings, however, about chloroform anaesthesia. Clover, who had said of Rymer's experiments with nitrous oxide in 1863 that 'they were not so successful as to induce anyone to adopt the practice of giving it', and who himself administered chloroform, said of it in a paper presented at a meeting of the Odontological Society in 1868:

> The experience of Dentists caused them to hail with gladness the introduction of anaesthetics, but they were soon found to be attended with inconvenience and danger. Those practitioners who gave the anaesthetic in strong doses not infrequently found their patients become so prostrate as to cause the greatest anxiety, and in a few cases death was produced'.

An event of considerable importance in the field of dental anaesthesia, therefore, was the demonstration in London of the use of nitrous oxide by Thomas Wiltberger Evans, an American dentist practising in Paris. On 31st March 1868 he anaesthetised eleven patients at the Dental Hospital in the morning, and in the evening gave a demonstration before a gathering of leading physicians, surgeons and dentists at the home of Robert Hepburn. On 2nd April he anaesthetised eight more patients at the Dental Hospital, and also assisted with five cases at the Central Ophthalmic Hospital; and on the following day he anaesthetised three cases at the Central Eye

Hospital, Moorfields. This done, Evans returned to Paris. On leaving London, however, he offered the sum of £100 to the Committee of Management of the Hospital for the purchase of apparatus and materials for the manufacture of nitrous oxide, or, if the Hospital decided to discontinue the use of the gas, for the provision of any other anaesthetic.

This offer was taken up and a joint committee was set up with the Odontological Society to investigate the use of nitrous oxide as an anaes-thetic in dentistry. The committee reported favourably in December 1868, after 1380 operations in which the gas had been administered and the use of nitrous oxide in dental surgery in this country was established. It is on this association with Evans and the committee of investigation that is based the Dental Hospital's claim to be the birthplace of nitrous oxide anaesthesia in Great Britain. It has to be said that nitrous oxide as then used was far from perfect – opinions differed whether it produced anaesthesia or asphyxia – and the best the committee of investigation could say was 'properly administered, it is as least as safe and efficient an anaesthetic for short operations as any other now in use'. It was not until the 1890s that Frederick Hewitt, whose work was also carried out at the Dental Hospital, perfected his method of delivering oxygen and nitrous oxide simultaneously.

By 1869, it became clear that the limit to what the institution could achieve had been reached – it seemed that the patient throughput of 17,926 in that year was the maximum possible in the accommodation available; the Medical Committee, in their report to the Committee of Management, gave their opinion that it could not be sustained and patient attendances did in fact fall during the following three years. This restriction was recognised in the Annual Report for 1869, in which the Committee of Management said that they could 'see a time fast approaching when they would be compelled to enlarge their accommodation, now barely sufficient for their necessities, and this enlargement can only be effected at a very considerable and permanent cost.' This wording is interesting in the evidence it provides of the attitude of the Committee – there is no suggestion that the institution should rest on its laurels and accept the limit of expansion imposed by its accommodation. On the contrary, the Report calls upon the Governors to accept that the time had come for a major step forward, involving 'a permanent increase in the scale of the enterprise and its cost.'

In their Report for 1871 the Managing Committee referred again to the lack of room for all those who sought relief at the Hospital, which prevented the number of operations in any year increasing above a certain level. To quote from the Report, the Committee called

the attention of the Governors and the general Public to the absolute necessity which exists for increased accommodation and, with this object in view, they invite the Public to subscribe to a fund to be specially devoted to the building of a Hospital of larger dimensions, or to giving increased accommodation in the present one; and they hope that they will not make this appeal in vain, as it is to the advantage of the Public that the powers of the Hospital for doing good should not in any way be abridged.

It is unlikely that today rebuilding on a new site or extending the existing premises – roofing over the back yard was discussed – would be the first remedies proposed for a lack of room in a building which, apart from the work of the House Surgeon, was in use for patient treatment only from nine o'clock to noon daily. Afternoon clinics, it seems reasonable to think, would at least be considered, but there is no record of any such suggestion. It is difficult to think of reasons for this. The clinical work was supervised by the Surgeons and Assistant Surgeons of the day, who received no remuneration for their services; perhaps it was considered unreasonable to ask them to give more than one morning per week, and difficult to recruit another five suitably experienced and public-spirited practitioners to cover the afternoons. Most probably the difficulty was that the students, who carried out much of the clinical work, had commitments elsewhere – their medical and surgical sessions for example – in the afternoons. It was in fact nearly twenty years before afternoon clinical sessions were implemented.

However, it is quite clear that 32 Soho Square, despite David Hepburn's sentimental memories of the place, was no longer a suitable building, and there were complaints of a lack of light as well as shortage of space. In the principal clinical room, for example, there were only two windows, with eight operating chairs in two ranks of four facing them, and this at a time when artificial lighting was rudimentary, if available at all. But there was for some of those in the Committee of Management another equally compelling reason for rebuilding. In the Annual Report, which was addressed to subscribing governors and the general public, the Committee referred to the need to extend in order to maintain and increase the work of the charity 'for the benefit of the Public'.

But when, in a letter published in March 1872 in the *British Journal of Dental Science*, Edwin Saunders, then one of the Hospital's Trustees , addressed an appeal for funds to members of the profession he made a different approach. He described the existing premises of the Hospital as 'in an obscure corner, known scarcely at all to its patrons, with imperfect light and scant room for the good work it undertakes' and asked 'Can we rest satisfied to introduce foreign visitors or our transatlantic friends to an institution on so inadequate a scale; and can we ever hope to raise our profession in social estimation while such a state of things continues to exist ?' He called upon the profession to subscribe so that the institution could be rebuilt in such a way 'as duly to reflect honour and credit upon the great body of Dental Surgeons'. In using these words Saunders was demonstrating and appealing to the Victorian proclivity for the creation of imposing buildings as evidence of respectability and standing, of which numerous examples exist, from railway termini to learned institutes.

His approach was justified by the results, because by the end of 1873 there seems to have been collected a Building Fund of £3,622 (some £96,000 in modern money); the list of subscriptions includes a number of sizeable donations from members of the dental profession, Saunders himself putting in £500 and his wife another £100. In fact, the evidence is that Edwin Saunders was the prime mover in the rebuilding scheme. He was, like several of his colleagues, a wealthy man and his home, Fairlawns, at Wimbledon, was a show-place with a garden large enough to allow tea-parties in connection with international medical and dental meetings. He had taken an interest in dental education in the early years of the movement for its reform, being associated with the establishment of the London Institution for Diseases of the Teeth in 1839, was one of the original Memorialists of 1843 and had been associated with the Dental Hospital and the Odontological Society from their beginnings. He was appointed Dental Surgeon to Queen Victoria and Prince Albert in 1847, a connection which doubtless brought him a number of distinguished patients.

His correspondence includes a letter of April 1867 from Florence Nightingale who wrote asking for an appointment and said 'I have broken four of my teeth lately (probably with gnashing my teeth at Ministers)'. Saunders was knighted in 1884 in recognition of his services to dental education, the first member of the profession to be so distinguished. He was, like many others among the dental reformers, a man of wide culture and many interests and was given to writing poetry, some of which was published in dental and other journals. The issue of the *British Journal of Dental Science* containing Saunders' appeal for the rebuilding fund for the Hospital also contains his verses entitled 'On the Illness and Recovery of HRH the Prince of Wales', (the Prince was ill with typhoid fever) beginning as follows:

> There was revelry and mirth,
> And cloudless was the sky,
> When a shadow crossed the earth,
> And a darkness passed by,
> A hundred hands would seize their brands,
> To shield him from the foe,
> But, oh, not one could save the son
> of England now laid low.

Saunders was not only enthusiastically in favour of a move to new premises; he had already decided where they were to be found. At the Annual Meeting of Governors in January 1872 he had called attention to Nos. 40 and 41 Leicester Square (the site now occupied by the Leicester Square Cinema) which he and others connected with the Hospital consulted by him thought would fully meet the needs of the institution. In April of that year the promoters of the Leicester Square scheme persuaded the Committee of Management to set up a small Building Committee to examine it, with Saunders as Chairman. The Committee's Report was swiftly prepared. It said that the premises would provide better facilities than those at Soho Square, would bring the institution more prominently to the notice of the public and that the alterations necessary could be carried out for a sum well within the Hospital's resources. In December the Committee of Management adopted the Report and recommended to the Annual Meeting of Governors on 30th January 1873 that the scheme be implemented.

Saunders, who seems to have been a competent political operator, arranged for details of the Report to be published in the *British Journal of Dental Science* so that the proposals received the maximum publicity immediately before the meeting. However, it seems that he may very nearly have overplayed his hand. Alfred Hill reports that when the Committee sought the opinion of the dental staff upon his proposals, which came to them 'hampered by what was felt to be restrictive and quietly coercive ideas':

> The manner in which the entire subject was presented to the medical comittee at first made it very difficult for that body to deal with it. It appeared that if an adverse vote were given by the medical officers the whole onus and responsibility of failure would rest upon them. Several of their number, not seeing the absolute necessity of a change of locality in the clear light in which Mr Saunders and his supporters had viewed it, resented this as an unjust conclusion. The consideration of the subject was fully entered into by them, and while all claimed an equal interest in and desire for the present and future prosperity of the institution to which they had been and still were devoting so much of their valuable time, they also maintained their undoubted right and privilege of freely expressing their individual opinions on so important a matter without the alleged imputation of opposition. (*Reform in The Dental Profession*, 1877, p. 236).

Hill adds that when the Medical Committee voted on the proposition there was a majority in favour of one only and that, if one of the members of the Committee had not had to retire during the debate because of illness, the votes would have been equal. (This is an early example of the insistence by the Medical Committee of the Hospital on its right to an make an independent assessment of propositions by higher authority and its refusal to be coerced).

From the same source (p. 237) comes the information, interesting in view of later developments, that there was another alternative proposition, for purpose-built premises rather than 'old ones converted to the nearest approach to convenience they would allow.' This was made by Mr Ash, a member of the Managing Committee and the founder of the dental supplies firm, who produced plans of proposed dental hospital buildings on sites available from the Metropolitan Board of Works which, he said, could be built for £4,000, undertaking to meet any extra cost himself. Hill says that Mr Ash's proposal was discussed but that eventually the decision was given in favour of the Saunders' plan. The minutes contain no reference to Ash's plan or any discussion of it – nor, in fact, do they record the report of the Building Committee or their discussion of it, merely the fact of the adoption of the Report.

The entire exercise was carried out with despatch, including the disposal of opposition and the alternative plan, all details of which were omitted from the official records, and the institution formally opened at 40 and 41 Leicester Square on Saunders's birthday, 12th March 1874. In due course, members of the profession subscribed to a testimonial to Mr Saunders in recognition of his efforts and generosity which, it was suggested at first, should take the form of a bust of him to be placed on the Hospital building. Saunders himself, however, thought the money should be used to found a scholarship at the Hospital and thus, in 1875, was inaugurated The Saunders Scholarship, henceforward to be acknowledged the blue riband among the undergraduate academic awards available at the Dental School. The list of Saunders Scholars from that date until 1985 contains the names of a number of people who went on to become renowned in their profession.

Saunders, in the traditions of the institution, is held to be something equivalent to the Founding Father; Bowdler Henry (to whose assiduous research the present authors are greatly indebted) included the following in a draft he prepared for a plaque for a portrait of Saunders:

> He was the virtual creator of the Royal Dental Hospital and School and was the leading spirit among those who made dentistry a profession in this country.

Perhaps this overstates the case; in considering the claim that he was a leading spirit in the reform movement it should be noted that in this connection Alfred Hill, a contemporary witness, writes 'Whatever influence Mr Saunders had was exerted, if at all, in a quiet manner during several years from the commencement of the new era in 1856.' It seems significant that although he petitioned with others for a dental qualification adminstered by the College of Surgeons, Saunders did not submit himself to the examination and gain the Licence when it was instituted, unlike many of his leading colleagues who did so in order give authority to the qualification and to encourage others to gain it. As to his being the 'virtual creator' of the Hospital, the same source points out that although Saunders accepted office as one of the Trustees on the foundation of the charity, he did not occupy a position as dental surgeon at the Hospital or a teacher at the School. The claim made on his behalf rests, it seems, on his effort in pushing through the move to Leicester Square – there can be no doubt that if a move had not been made the progess of the institution would have extremely hampered, or that Saunders brought about the move to Leicester Square with energy and resource; but his was not the only solution to the problem proposed, as has been seen, nor was it, in the long term, the best.

Records of the activities of the School in the early years are sparse. The original teaching curriculum has been referred to above (p. 6) but details of student numbers during the period from the opening of the School in October 1859 and the move to Leicester Square are not easy to come by. In distinction from the Hospital, which was a charity obliged by law and the need to maintain public confidence to keep proper accounts and publish annual reports, the School was conducted almost as a private business operated by an informal partnership of the Senior Surgeons (i.e., the Medical Committee) and as such it maintained only such records as they considered necessary and they certainly did not feel obliged to publish them. Strictly speaking, they were responsible to the Committee of Management. They had, of course, to satisfy the students and their parents that they gave value for money and the College of Surgeons that they maintained an appropriate academic standard if their students were to qualify for the Licentiate.

The Annual Report of the Hospital for 1860 said *en passant* that 'several' students had been admitted and in 1861 that the number of students 'had greatly increased'. Only in 1862 is the actual number given – 22. The Annual Report for 1868 said that students were attending the lectures and practice of the Hospital in increasing numbers, and that 'it is also found by the attendance of Foreign Students that the benefits of the Institution are appreciated on the Continent'. And in 1873 it was reported that 'the School exceeded in numbers some of the medical schools attached to general hospitals'.

Not all of these students would necessarily have been studying for the Diploma of the Royal College. A petition to the College in July 1874 for the amendment of the rules under which dentists in practice before 1859 could qualify for the Diploma contains the interesting information that between 1863 and 1873 only 69 candidates examined for it had complied with the regulations of the College by studying at a recognised school. This number gives an average of only 7 a year passing through the dental schools and highlights the fact that events so far constituted only a small step in the direction of the regulation of the profession. The number of dental students obtaining the Diploma was still very small in relation to the total number of dental practitioners and there was nothing whatever to prevent the unqualified man styling himself 'surgeon dentist' or 'dental surgeon.' In 1875 the following advertisement appeared in a Manchester paper: 'A dentist giving up business will sell his Instruments, Tools, etc; would teach a purchaser; price, including tuition, £20'.

Some of the Dental School's students may well have been such practitioners enrolled for specific courses to extend their knowledge with no intention of submitting to an examination. This was obviously of concern because in 1868 a rule was introduced that students entering the practice of the Hospital did so on the understanding that it was their intention to obtain the Diploma.

It was at about this time that C.J. Fox, *Editor of the British Journal of Dental Science* and a member of the staff of the Hospital, started a campaign for the registration and compulsory qualification of dentists.

No Minute Books now exist for the Medical Committee prior to 1875 and the Finance Committee before 1886, and no accounts for the School before 1905/06 (although this is not to say that they never existed) so it has not been possible to glean much information about the teaching work of the institution in the early days. In particular information about student numbers during this period is almost totally lacking. There seem to have been no formal rules for the conduct of students until 1868, when there was concern that some of them were using their attendance at the Hospital as a source of private gain, a practice of which the Medical Committee strongly disapproved and they asked for the co-operation of the Committee of Management in its prevention. It was this request which led to the introduction of the rules referred to earlier, the Management Committee itself intervening to have the provision inserted that all students should study for the Diploma of the College.

At the end of 1873 the first Dean of the Dental School was appointed by the Management Committee on the recommendation of the Medical Committee. He was Mr Thomas Arnold Rogers, who had been associated with the Odontological Society from its inception and had held office as its President.

3

Developments and Differences

The following notice was printed on the back of the Annual report of the Hospital for 1873, which was published early in January 1874:

NOTICE OF REMOVAL

This Hospital will be removed to the New Buildings, at No. 40 Leicester Square, on and after, Thursday, March 12th, 1874.

Leicester Square at this time was a particularly unprepossessing place, which accounted for some of the opposition to the move. Dickens, in Bleak House, had described the district as 'that curious region which is a centre of attraction to indifferent foreign hotels and indifferent foreigners, old china, gaming-houses, exhibitions and a large medley of shoddiness and drinking out of sight', and an historical account of the Square published in the very year in which the Hospital moved there, said that its condition had long been a disgrace to the metropolis:

Overgrown with rank and fetid vegetation, it was a public nuisance and an unwholesome fever-bed, in a sanitary point of view; covered with the debris of tin pots, kettles, cast-off shoes, old clothes and dead cats and dogs.

The picture of dirt and desolation which the Square seems to have presented must have been completed by the equestrian statue of George I which occupied the centre of the Square until 1872, when it was sold for scrap, from which the king's head, arms and legs had been cut off, and his mount mutilated and daubed with paint.

This state of affairs, however, was about to change. The disgraceful state of Leicester Square had not entirely escaped the attention of the authorities, and in 1869 it was proposed that the land be built over. However, it was ruled by the Master of the Rolls in 1873 that the centre of the Square had to be preserved as an open space and while this decision prevented the encroachments of speculative builders it did nothing to rescue the Square from its sorry state. At this stage, Mr Albert Grant, a company promoter who was anxious to appear in the role of a public benefactor, bought the Leicester Square area and converted the open space into a public garden which he handed over to the Metropolitan Board of Works in July 1874. 'It would be almost impossible to over-estimate the benefit conferred on the crowded inhabitants of one of the most popular parishes in London by the noble-spirited policy of Mr Albert Grant,' said a contemporary report. 'Stepping into the breach at almost the eleventh hour, he has touched the building-mad daemon of avarice with the wand of philanthropy, and rescued from the jaws of destruction one more breathing-place for the lungs of our half-stifled city.' Albert Grant seems in fact to have been a financial adventurer who had been accused of having enriched himself at the expense of 'those most susceptible and gullible of investors, the parson and the widow.' His real name was Gottheimer and the title by which he liked to be known, 'Baron Grant', was given to him by the King of Italy. However, whatever his motives, Albert Grant spent some £28,000 in laying out Leicester Square and rehabilitating it. His plans included the adornment of the Square with statues of eminent men formerly associated with the locality and at the suggestion of someone associated with the Hospital had agreed to substitute for the statue of Samuel Johnson, who had no particular association with the place, one of John Hunter ('whom', said the President of the Odontological Society, 'We have always regarded as the true Father of Dental Surgery in this country'), who had at one time lived in the Square.

The move of the Hospital itself contributed to this rehabilitation. No. 40 Leicester Square, which had been described as 'a dirty, dismal, dungeon-like place' had for a number of years housed the Leicester Square Soup Kitchen, which, under the aegis of the National Philanthropic Association, provided for the destitute a meal of soup and bread. These unpromising premises were selected by Saunders for conversion and adaptation to the needs of the Dental Hospital and School and, in addition to internal alterations and renovations, Saunders and his Building Committee proposed 'due architectural treatment' to the facade which, his Building Committee said in their Report, 'would present a noble and imposing elevation, and which in so conspicuous a position could not fail to lead to more exalted estimation both of the Institution and of the profession which it represents.'

The official opening of the new building on 12th March 1874 was preceded by a meeting held there by the Odontological Society on 2nd March, to which some 600 guests were invited. There was, it seems, a scramble to get the conversion work completed in time; the builders and decorators, personally supervised by Edwin Saunders, had worked throughout the preceding weekend and on the day itself it was impossible to hang some valuable paintings loaned for the occasion by members of the Society because the newly plastered walls had not sufficiently dried. In its report of the occasion the *British Journal of Dental Science*, stating its opinion that a new era was about to begin under brilliant auspices, reminded its readers, with a Victorian flourish, of the connection between the Society and the Hospital: 'So, as the Odontological Society was first originated and then gave birth to the Hospital, it will now gracefully lead the way to the new premises, and light them up to do honour to the entry of its offspring, grown so vigorous that, in fact, it has become the shelter of its parent' – a reference to the fact that the new premises, like those in Soho Square, provided accommodation for the Society.

The formal opening of the Hospital and School in their new home took place, as indicated earlier, on 12th March 1874, on which date the Dean, Rogers, had said that he would be happy to meet the students there at 9 o'clock. He welcomed them with an address which concluded: 'Let us resolve here and now that we will, with God's help, do our utmost to benefit our fellow men, to qualify ourselves to take the highest positions in our calling, and to make our School the first school in the world. And now let us begin.'

There seem to have been 60 students at this time – not all necessarily taking the full course for the Diploma – and since details of the syllabus were published (apparently for the first time) in the *British Journal of Dental Science* (XVII 1874, 408), it is appropriate to review the arrangements then in force.

The syllabus was, of course, designed to meet the requirements of the Royal College of Surgeons, which stipulated that the student should have been engaged over four years in the acquirement of professional knowledge. In the Calendar students were advised that

> an advantageous way of accomplishing all the objects of the Curriculum is by an apprenticeship (at as nearly 17 years of age as possible) to a competent Dental practitioner. The first two years may then be devoted to study, – including that of Mechanical Dentistry, – during which the pupil should also go through a systematic course of reading suitable to the requirements of the Curriculum, and then he should commence his attendance at the hospitals and schools, fulfilling his third year of Mechanical Dentistry in the interval between the Hospital Winter and Summer sessions.

The syllabus showed that the difficulty which afflicted the School up to its demise in 1985 – that of providing satisfactory facilites for students to cover the general medical and surgical requirements – existed from the very beginning. There were then, as there continued to be for the next hundred years, in addition to the basic scientific studies, three distinct parts in the training of the dental practitioner. These were the practical training in the materials and techniques involved in the production and fitting of dental appliances, training in general medicine and surgery to the extent required by the College, and the practical and theoretical training in clinical dentistry. The first part, until 1891, was obtained in a dental practice, supplemented by lectures and demonstrations at the School; the third part, in the clinics of the Dental Hospital; and the training in general anatomy and physiology and general medicine and surgery, in one of the general teaching hospitals.

The last was the part of the syllabus which created perennial difficulties, for the dental student found himself not always welcomed in the medical school. No specific accommodation was provided for him in the dissecting room, the lecture courses, or the ward rounds. He had to take pot-luck and might easily find an afternoon wasted by trailing along with the medical students in a ward round of doubtful value in his training. When the Dental School was founded consideration was given to teaching the general subjects in the Dental School but it was decided that for obvious reasons it was not a practicable possibility. (The problem was not really satisfactorily resolved, in fact, until the 1970s.)

Not only was the dental student a difficulty to the medical school because of his partial attendance, but in the early years his standard of general education was suspect because it had not been tested by the compulsory entrance examination to which medical students were subjected. However, this examination became compulsory for dental students as well after October 1877. Not all the medical schools would accept dental students and those which did were listed in the 1874 Calendar – the Middlesex, Charing Cross and King's College Hospitals (the latter then located in Lincoln's Inn Fields) – and the student was left to make a choice. In order to enable dental students to attend the courses at the medical school lectures, demonstrations and clinical sessions at the Dental School took place between 8 and 12 in the mornings and after 6.30 in the evenings.

The appointment of a Dean, to which reference has already been made, marks the beginning of the emergence of the School as an entity distinct from the Hospital, as does the production of a School Calendar. A further manifestation of this development was the first formal distribution of prizes, which took place in the new premises on 5th October 1874, setting a pattern which was to be repeated each October until 1985, except during the Second World War, when large gatherings in premises in the centre of London were discouraged. The style of the function was the same then as it was at the end of the life of the School – a distinguished visitor (Mr WS Savory, FRS, in this case) gave an address and the Dean reported on the activities of the School during the preceding year and announced the names of the prizewinners. Evidence that this developing separation of School and Hospital was apparent at the time is a proposal by a member of the Comittee of Management that the School might make some payment into Hospital funds for its accommodation. A sub-committee appointed to consider the matter concluded that such a charge would not be advisable, in view of the 'valuable services rendered by the pupils of the School to the Hospital' – a recognition of the amount of clinical work carried out by students and of the symbiotic relationship between the two institutions which was later to puzzle National Health Service administrators.

The amount of clinical work carried out by the institution and its value to the students under training there is referred to by Alfred Hill, writing in 1876:

> since its opening in the year 1858, no less a number than two hundred and fifty thousand cases of treatment have been entered upon its books. To have an opportunity of inspecting and studying from fifteen to twenty thousand cases each year of his pupillage is a gain which, although the student himself may not accurately estimate or appreciate its value, those who know from a long experience what dental practice demands will unhesitatingly admit. (*Reform in the Dental Profession*, p. 361.) (No doubt Hill did not mean to imply that a student could inspect 15–20,000 cases, but was illustrating the plethora of clinical experience available.)

An article in the *British Journal of Dental Science* (April 1874) describes the scene in the new premises, and their advantages over those at Soho Square (and incidentally reminds the reader of one of the harsh facts of Victorian dentistry that it is easy to forget in these days of painless treatment – that very often it hurt very much):

> A visit to the Hospital will show that if we were crowded at the old rooms in Soho Square we are crowded even now, but then the press was one of stagnation, now 'tis the press of progress, then we were crowded with loungers, our hall was filled with patients wearily waiting their turn, the operating rooms were filled with students anxiously looking out for a vacant chair and a chance of getting a small share of the Hospital practice; now the waiting hall is the most empty room in the house, so free is the circulation of the work. The filling room at the top of the building is still crowded, but it is with workers; a double, almost a triple row of chairs is filled with patients attended by earnest, industrious students; below again, the noisy operations of the extracting room are not hindered by the more quiet work of the anaesthetist, whose patients now inhale the soothing gas undisturbed by the shrieks of adjacent sufferers.

A later report in the same Journal refers to the inclusion in the new Hospital of all the recent improvements in dentistry, including 'the new American drill worked by a treadle'. In this connection, the editor of the Journal gave a warning – 'Notwithstanding our limited experience of this machine, we must caution the students against employing it too frequently to save time. We have seen the pulp cavity invaded before the operator knew where he was. The power of this instrument is so great that, unless used with great care, it may do much harm'. (It is of interest that Edward Sercombe, a Trustee of the Dental Hospital, whose partner, Morrison, had developed and patented the treadle drill in America, was the first to demonstrate it in this country in 1873.) In addition to this equipment the Committee of Management seem to have provided the Hospital Porter with a new uniform to mark the occasion of the move – the Accounts for 1874 show the expenditure of £3.18.6d for 'Livery'.

The first meeting of the Committee of Management in the new premises was held on 16th March 1874 and the minutes show that one of the troubles which afflicted the institution in Soho Square had survived the move. A subscriber had complained about the way two patients to whom he had given 'special orders' were dealt with – apparently the officers on duty at the time had noticed the superior style of dress of the two ladies concerned and had put questions to them to ascertain their fitness as objects of charity – 'but not', say the Minutes 'In a peremptory tone'. In an attempt to prevent such cases the Committee decided that the following notice be 'conspicuously exhibited' in the Waiting Room:

NOTICE

The Dental Hospital of London is intended to afford relief to the suffering poor and to them only. Persons not of the necessitous class will in all cases be refused admittance, and a ticket for special operation tendered under such circumstances will be forfeited.

A later Minute (February 1875) presents an intriguing insight into the sort of administrative detail which exercised the Committee of Management from time to time. It concerns the care of the donation boxes, for which an elaborate system was decided. The boxes were to be opened by the Secretary in the presence of Edwin Saunders or another named member of the Committee; the keys to the boxes were to be kept in a special box, together with the money removed from the donation boxes, the key to which was to be kept by Mr Saunders or the other Committee member. The box containing the keys and the money was to be kept in the 'iron safe', the key to which was to be held by the Hospital Secretary. The arrangement illustrates a proper concern by the Committee not only for the custody of money given to them for charitable purposes but also for the protection of their employees from the temptation which a more lax system might present. Evidence that the rising tide of financial activity had reached a level at which it was no longer feasible for the Committee of Management as a whole to scrutinise every bill presented for payment appears in 1876, when a Finance Committee was appointed to examine and certify them.

The campaign for the compulsory education and registration of dental practitioners was referred to briefly in Chapter 2. It came into being because, although since the foundation of the Dental Hospital and School it had been possible for those who wished to fit themselves properly for the practice of dental surgery to undertake a regular course of study and gain the Diploma of the Royal College of Surgeons, the condition of dental practice generally remained unsatisfactory. The early reformers had accomplished much; the Odontological Society which they had formed had done and continued to do much to raise the standard of scientific knowledge in the profession, and the institution which they had founded provided an excellent centre for the instruction of those entering it; and the LDS Diploma which they had persuaded the College to initiate had been accepted as a hallmark of proficiency. But the number of practitioners holding the Diploma was small in relation to the total number of 'dentists' (according to the *Chemists and Druggists Directory* of 1877 there were in practice in the country 1,808 dentists, of which 387 were Licentiates in Dental Surgery).

It was of concern to the qualified practitioner that the general public still had no ready means of distinguishing between himself and the unqualified and self-styled dental surgeon. More importantly, although the concession to those in practice before 1859 allowing them to take the examination for the Diploma without having gone through the prescribed curriculum of study and practice was generally accepted, neither they nor those entering the profession were obliged to obtain the qualification.

By 1876 a strong movement for further reform had developed and, as in the 1850s, it was split into two contending divisions: on one hand was the Association of Surgeons Practising Dental Surgery, a conservative group consisting exclusively of Fellows and Members of the Royal College of Surgeons, whose stated objective was the establishment of an improved ethical code and the encouragement of a higher standard of education and training for those wishing to practise. However, some of their statements suggested disapproval of the Licentiate as an inferior qualification and there is no doubt that they considered dentistry to be a branch of medicine and wanted it to remain so. On the other hand was the Dental Reform Committee, whose members wanted radical reform, advocating a separate status for the profession and a recognised legal status for dentists. In the middle was the Odontological Society, which maintained a neutral position and a non-political stance in contrast to the position adopted by its members 20 years previously, when they were the most ardent advocates of reform and the most successful politically. However, the Society's decision to stand aloof was doubtless wise; its members would have included members of both factions and an attempt to take sides might well have resulted in disastrous dissension within the Society. Interestingly, at one stage Samuel Cartwright found himself at the head of all three bodies simultaneously; he was Chairman of the Association, President of the Society and Chairman of the Committee, a situation which must have involved the exercise of almost superhuman tact and diplomacy. It was soon resolved, however, because in 1877 he and several others resigned from the Dental Reform Committee when the latter proposed that only Licentiates should be allowed to practise dentistry, and that surgeons be excluded from the profession.

In the event, against fierce opposition from the medical profession and the Royal College, the proposals of the Dental Reform Committee were embodied in legislation, but only after the Bill originally presented to

Parliament had been considerably modified to protect the right of those with medical qualifications to practise dentistry. The Dental Act 1878, with this proviso, made it illegal for anyone who was not registered to call himself 'Dentist' or 'Dental Surgeon' or to imply that he was specially qualified to practice dentistry. Under the Act, those entitled to be registered were holders of the Licentiate of the Royal College of Surgeons, and in deference to vested interests, anyone bona fide engaged in practising dental surgery on the date on which the Act was passed.

Apart from the fact that the Act permitted large numbers of unqualified practitioners to register if they were already in practice, its provisions were very difficult to enforce because there were so many loopholes:

> One could perform dental services either in his own home or office, and could even put a shingle or plate on the door marked 'Dental Surgery' if he did not term himself 'Dentist' or 'Dental Surgeon'. Any number of dental mechanics took advantage of this loophole. *(A History of Dentistry,* Luffkin, AW, London, 1948)

Having achieved its objective as far as politically possible, the Dental Reform Committee, on a proposal by Edwin Saunders, called for the formation of a national association of dentists; and on 27th October 1879, at a meeting at the Dental Hospital in Leicester Square, the Executive Council of the Committee dissolved itself and was reconstituted as the Representative Board of the British Dental Association. As has been shown, the reform movement of the 1870s cannot be said to have been entirely successful in reaching its objectives, but its results and particularly its outcome in the birth of the BDA, are significant in the history of the dental profession. The reforms of the '50s left dentistry very much tied to medicine and surgery; the effect of the agitation of the '70s was to set the profession on the road to independent status, to becoming a profession in its own right, with but not of the professions of medicine and surgery. It is pleasant to note that the Dental Hospital was the birthplace of the British Dental Association, even if only for the reason that it was the place in which mother happened to be at the time.

There was a considerable diminution in the number of students entering the School in 1879, there being only 17 new pupils during the year, against an average entry of 30. This, according to the editor of the *British Journal of Dental Science*, was a result of the passing of the Dental Act in the preceding year, which made it possible for anyone already in practice to be registered, even if only at the very commencement of his career. By 1881 the entry had risen to 27, but the situation at the National Dental Hospital and College in Great Portland Street was not so good – their intake in that year was only 11. It was probably this comparison which led to the resolution approved at the National Dental Hospital's Annual Meeting in 1882 that the two dental hospitals and schools should be amalgamated. By then, however, there had been a large increase in student numbers at

Leicester Square. The Minutes of the Dental Hospital's Annual Meeting record that this proposal was reported but no discussion of it is recorded, nor any decision about it. One assumes that it had no support which, in the circumstances, is not surprising.

The institution went, in fact, from strength to strength in its new home in Leicester Square. Patient attendances fell slightly to 19,261 in 1874, the first year in the new location; but they picked up quickly, reaching 29,242 in 1879 and 35,893 in 1882. Financially, too, the situation improved, to the extent that by 1882 the Trustees had been able, bit by bit, to set aside and invest a total of £1,790 – invested, of course, in that day and age, in 3 per cent Consols. But by 1882 there were once again complaints of overcrowding and lack of space and proposals were made for the acquisition of the Tower House, which adjoined the hospital premises on the eastern end, and of which Edwin Saunders held a 92½ year lease. This he was prepared to transfer to the Hospital. The price of his lease was put at £2,400 and the necessary alterations and other costs were estimated as £300 and in order to keep the transaction within the bounds of the Trustees' nest egg, Saunders most generously offered to contribute £1,200.

Simultaneously an opportunity occurred to purchase the freehold of the Hospital premises (40 and 41 Leicester Square) for £6,750. There was general agreement that this opportunity should not be lost and so the freehold was acquired, a mortgage loan of £5,000 at 4 per cent being raised towards the cost. This transaction wiped out the nest egg without adding to the space available; so Edwin Saunders, who became Sir Edwin in July 1883 – 'for many years Dentist to the Royal Family, and a liberal benefactor of the public institutions connected with his profession' – declared in a letter dated 31st July 1883 that he would make over his lease of the Tower House free of charge.

Sir Edwin, who had given the Hospital more than £4,000 since the move to Leicester Square, ended his letter with the following words:

> I have only to add that should my offer meet with acceptance at the hands of the Committee, I shall feel myself amply repaid by such acceptance, and trust that I shall not be thought ungracious in deprecating any more public recognition which might suggest itself to the minds of too partial and zealous friends and colleagues.

Despite Sir Edwin's protestations some of his friends and colleagues subscribed for his portrait by Mr Carlile H Macartney, which was presented at the Annual Meeting on 12th March 1884. This portrait, which shows him looking at a plan of the Tower House, hung in the entrance hall of the School Building in Orange Street for many years and is now displayed in the premises of the Royal Society of Medicine.

Looking back at all this from a distance of more than a hundred years and in the light of the financial records of the time, it seems doubtful whether this further act of generosity on Sir Edwin's part was necessary.

The Hospital's days of struggle on the edge of a financial precipice were over, at least for the next two decades – witness the nest egg already referred to and the fact that an appeal made in 1882 for donations towards a fund for extending the premises brought in over £1,100 in a year. By the time the Tower House and freehold transactions took place the fund had grown to nearly £2,300 and this covered the costs of buying the freeholds of Nos. 40 and 41 (after the mortgage) and of altering and furnishing the Tower House. So the £1,100 which resulted from the appeal remained, and was put towards a part repayment of the mortgage in 1884. And further repayments reduced it to £2,500 by the end of 1886.

The acquisition of the Tower House provided space and light for twenty-two more operating chairs, nearly doubling the existing provision. But the Hospital and School were now in a rising spiral in which their efforts to increase resources to meet increased demands resulted in increasing the demand even further – the raising of funds resulted in more governors and subscribers entitled to sponsor patients and so in more patients arriving for treatment. In 1886 patient attendances increased to 43,745, some 12 per cent over 1885, and nearly double the number of cases treated in 1874, the first year of operation in Leicester Square. As a result of this increase together with an unusually large entry of students (the intriguing reluctance to quote actual numbers persists) the Medical Committee reported that the work of the Hospital and School was carried out with great difficulty and noted with satisfaction that a scheme for providing yet more accommo-dation was in contemplation. This scheme involved the acquisition of No. 42 Leicester Square, at the western end of the premises, for £3,500 for the freehold plus £400 for the surrender of an existing lease. This addition, the Building Committee proposed, should be used to provide a good lecture theatre seating some 100 or 120 students, a patients' waiting room of sufficient size, and an addition to the 'Stopping Room' to provide 10 or 12 more chairs. It seemed to the Building Committee and their Surveyor that, since No. 42 was in fairly good condition and although there was a difference in level of some 2 feet between the first floor and the correspond-ing floor in the main building, all the alterations and adaptations needed seemed simple and practicable and not likely to involve ruinous outlay. A tender for the work was accepted and work was begun with the confident expectation that it would be finished by the end of 1887.

But not so. The approval of the District Surveyor and of the Board of Works was required – did no one think of getting it before starting work? – and this was not immediately forthcoming. Bowdler Henry tells the story:

> In 1887 there had been an extraordinary number of serious fires. Several lives had been lost in the burning of a theatre at Exeter and of William Whiteley's store in London. An even greater catastrophe was the fire at the Opera Comique in Paris in which more than 300 people had died. These terrible events had made the authorities very conscious of fire risks

– they had been subjected to great pressure from a panic-stricken press and from excited public opinion. The Hospital authorities had protested that restrictions which would be quite proper for a place of public amusement were not called for in a hospital. But all protests were in vain. The Hospital was a public building and as such was very properly made subject to the rules and regulations.

A great deal of further work would have to be done. The staircase to the first floor, which was in such good condition, was to be replaced by one of stone 4 feet wide and shut off by a brick wall from the building; it was to run straight from top to bottom without winding or doubling on itself – a difficult matter in so shallow a building. The party wall between the two buildings was to be replaced by a new wall 18 inches thick and carried down to a sound foundation.

These requirements added considerably to the original estimate of cost, and despite generous contributions to the Extension Fund (among others, the Medical Staff and Lecturers between them raised £1,000 and Messrs. Claudius Ash and Sons gave £500) there remained a deficiency of £5,700 when the extension was formally opened on 15th March 1888. Nobody seems to have had anything but good to say about the result at the time, but some twenty years later, defending the later move to bigger, better, purpose-built and even more costly premises, Morton Smale said:

> Our critics say we should not have moved at all, but been content with our old building. We were not only 'cribbed, cabined and confined,' but it was unclean; uncleanly and uncleanable, insanitary, unsavoury, undesirable and unfitted for its purpose, unworthy of the profession of which it was the leading hospital in the Kingdom. Every impartial visitor admitted our needs.

A significant event in the history of the Hospital and School was the appointment on 21st March 1881 of John Francis Pink as Secretary. He succeeded Captain HB Scoones, who had been appointed in 1874 and of his seven years service only two details emerge from the record. The first is that he was unable to attend the Annual Meeting in 1880 because of 'an accident in alighting from a train'. The second concerns his resignation and its aftermath. At the Annual Meeting in 1881, his resignation having been received, a vote of thanks to Captain Scoones was carried unanimously for the able manner in which he had performed his duties. Faint praise though this may be, the gesture turned out to be premature, because when the Committee of Management met in April it was reported that there was a deficiency of £32.45 in Captain Scoones' petty cash account – doubtless Mr Pink, who had been in office for a month, made quite sure that he was not going to be left holding this baby. The deficiency was a considerable sum for those days – the total bank balance of the institution at the time was only £245.35 – and the Committee took a serious view. Scoones was told of this – the phrase would have had threatening implications of arrest and imprisonment – and that he should consider the testimonial given to him withdrawn. He asked for 'a few days to arrange matters, the amount being so large' but paid up within a month. And so Captain Scoones disappears as far as our records are concerned (although, fifty years or so ahead, another Captain with a similar inability to keep his accounts in order, was to be sitting in his chair).

But Scoones' successor, John Francis Pink was certainly a man of a different stamp. He combined his post at the Dental Hospital with that of Secretary and Librarian at Charing Cross Hospital Medical School for many years and was also Registrar of Births and Deaths for the Parish of St Martin-in-the-Fields. From the outset he seems to have demonstrated drive and initiative. He set enthusiastically about the task of increasing the Hospital's income, having got the Management Committee to agree that he should receive 20 per cent of all he raised (the Committee shrewdly insisted that he met the costs of his appeals for funds himself) and regular records of the payments of his commission are evidence of his success. The Management Committee and, perhaps more significantly,the members of the Medical Committee were impressed by his zeal and ability. So much so, that when GA Ibbetson resigned as Honorary Secretary in 1887 it was agreed that it was unnecessary to fill the post vacated – 'inasmuch as they had in Mr Pink a thoroughly competent Secretary who did all that was necessary, who possessed such special knowledge of the work of the institution and showed as much zeal and energy in keeping it before the public, it was quite unnecessary to encumber the office of Secretary with that of Honorary Secretary.' This was followed, two years later, by his appointment as Honorary Secretary to the Medical Committee. The Annual Reports abound with his praises and Sir Edwin Saunders said publicly that the acquisition of the freeholds of 40 and 41 Leicester Square was largely due to the energy and application of Mr Pink.

The teaching of Prosthetic Dentistry became an issue during the 1880s; it is clear from the records that the matter was one of considerable controversy, but difficult to discern now precisely what the controversy was about. During 1881 the newly appointed Lecturer in Mechanical Dentistry, Dr Joseph Walker, told the Medical Committee that he had had numerous complaints that while dentists trained at the Hospital were able to extract teeth skilfully and make excellent fillings, as a rule they left the School without any experience whatsoever in the processes of applying artificial teeth to the mouth. Dentists in practice who obtained assistants trained in American Dental Schools, on the other hand, found they were were in most cases properly instructed in this field and it was understood that such practical instruction was also given at the dental schools in Edinburgh and Glasgow. The Medical Committee asked their Chairman, Alfred Coleman, with SJ Hutchinson, Dental Surgeon and Dr Walker to devise a remedy for this deficiency; and they produced a plan for a department, with Dr Walker as its Head, to give students 'the opportunity of constructing, adapting and inserting Mechanical Work, and fitting them to the mouths of Patients'. The patients who would benefit from this facility were to be 'convalescents from hospitals suffering from loss of teeth' and 'invalids with impaired digestion and loss of assimilative power', but restricted to people earning not more than £18 p.a., inclusive of any board and lodging received. The appliances so produced were to be charged for at rates, depending upon their nature and material, of from 7/6d to £1 per tooth.

When these ideas were reported to the Medical Committee the controversy began. 'After considerable discussion' – a phrase which minute-writers usually reserve for dissension and dispute – the Committee resolved that 'the Report in its present form be not received' and, after augmenting it by the addition of Mr Tomes and the Dean, asked the Sub-Committee to think again. The Medical Committee, in fact, wanted no part of the idea, but their reasons have not been recorded. It was perhaps politically injudicious for a newly-appointed Lecturer to propose the formation of a new department with himself in charge of it, and there is some evidence that Dr Walker may have been a rather abrasive colleague.

More cogent, perhaps, would have been the argument that it was inconsistent to propose that the supply of false teeth be restricted to the poorest members of society whilst suggesting that charges be made amounting perhaps to between £12 and £32 per full set – leading to the conclusion that given the restrictions imposed upon a charity and the cost of the appliances, legally the whole idea was incapable of implementation. But there is something more, although it seems impossible to put a finger on it. Why, one asks, in the 23 years of the institution's life, had it not been thought necessary to include these techniques in its teaching?

Whatever the reasons, the Sub-Committee, now with additional members, found themselves unable to draw up any scheme for meeting the objective (which had, after all, been set out by the Medical Committee itself) but said that they thought some form of teaching by demonstration might be practicable and valuable. On receiving this report, at a meeting of 19th January 1882, with Mr Coleman in the chair, the Medical Committee, again 'after considerable discussion' produced the following resolution:

> That in entire subservience to the interests of teaching Dr Walker be empowered to carry out a scheme whereby the students of his class shall have the opportunity of seeing the actual adjusting and wearing of artificial dentures, Dr Walker having kindly consented to provide a certain number of cases.

This resolution was to be referred to the Committee of Management but before the latter met, there was another meeting of the Medical Committee, at which the minutes of the meeting on 16th January were discussed – not, be it noted, approved. The discussion, it can be inferred, was about from whence the patients were to come. There seems to have been a suggestion at one stage that they would come from Dr Walker's practice, a proposal to which several objections are obvious. What seems eventually to have emerged was the idea that they would be selected 'without partiality' from people attending the hospital for treatment. The relevant minutes were not approved, in fact, until the following week, on 23rd February, at a meeting obviously called specially, at which Dr Walker was not present, and at which it was reported that the Committee of Management, having considered the resolution of 19th January, had referred it back 'for fuller details to be furnished'. The Medical Committee minutes record that 'Mr Coleman kindly consented to put the resolution in a different form for presentation to the Managing Committee'. On 16th March the Medical Committee, with both Dr Walker and Mr Coleman present, 'approved a detailed statement on the subject' which Mr Coleman proposed should be submitted to the Committee of Management and also gave him a 'cordial vote of thanks for the courteous and able way in which he had filled the post of chairman'. So Coleman was able to go to the Committee of Management armed with the expressed support of the Medical Committee for his 'detailed statement', which, after explaining the reasons why the subject needed to be taught and how it was proposed to do it, with an expression of gratitude for Dr Walker's offer, concluded with the words:

> but as the supplying any patients with artifical teeth was a matter not included in the present objects of the Institution they (i.e., the Medical Committee) deemed it right before taking any steps to submit the same to the Committee of Management.

The outcome, as was no doubt intended, was the response 'that this Committee cannot accede to the recommendation of the Medical Committee as to supplying mechanical work to patients' – and this response the Medical Committee pointedly agreed to record in its own minutes as if to mark the closure of the discussion.

All the evidence suggests a fundamental difference of opinion, but does not tell us precisely what it was about. Dr Walker – a forceful, determined and somewhat volatile character, as later events were to show – was up to something, perhaps, of which his collegues did not approve. Alfred Coleman, it can be hypothesised, was totally opposed, so much so that he was unable to be impartial and so resigned the chairmanship. He succeeded in carrying a majority of the Medical Committee with him and eventually in dishing the proposal when it came before the Committee of Management.

Whatever it was about, this row seems to have delayed the introduction of the teaching of prosthetic dentistry for nearly ten years, at a time when the making and fitting of dentures was a most important part of dental practice. That the subject was in the minds of members of the staff of the Hospital and School is evident from the rapid progress made once discussion started again, in 1889. By that time Coleman had gone to New Zealand and Walker had ceased to be Lecturer in Mechanical Dentistry.

The way in which this came about seems significant. In June 1888 the Medical Committee, in response to a proposal that in view of the great increase in the work done by the Hospital six additional Assistant Dental Surgeons be appointed, set up a sub-committee 'to consider the whole working of the Hospital and School and the further development of systematic teaching'. One of the recommendations of that sub-committee was 'that a Demonstrator of Mechanical Dentistry holding the dental qualification be appointed'.

It cannot be coincidence that in October 1888 Dr Walker resigned his appointment on the day before the commencement of his Winter Session course of lectures, causing considerable inconvenience – an apparently precipitate action indicative, surely, of considerable umbrage and ill-will. (This was by no means the end of Dr Walker, however; he was in 1888 a member of the Committee of Management and in 1892 became a Trustee of the charity and Honorary Treasurer to the Hospital and, as will be seen, contributed considerably in those capacities to the development of the institution.)

Dr Walker's place as Lecturer in Mechanical Dentistry was taken by David Hepburn, a man who had trained at the Hospital and served as a House Officer before becoming in due course one of the six Dental Surgeons, an appointment he resigned on taking up the lectureship. His father, Robert Hepburn, had been one of the founders of the Hospital and had himself been Lecturer in Mechanical Dentistry from 1859 to 1871. The situation was now apparently transformed. Immediately upon Dr Walker's resignation the Medical Committee, at the request of the new Demonstrator, Mr H Lloyd Williams, set up a sub-committee 'to enquire into the condition of the Mechanical Department', with the Dean and Hepburn among its membership. The sub-committee reported on 19th December with a fully developed plan for extending the teaching of prosthetic dentistry and supplying artificial teeth to patients, which set out to deal with all the arguments hitherto used against the proposal and included the telling admonition that so much was this teaching needed that rival schools were preparing to provide it, and that the Royal College of Surgeons had proposed to increase the stringency of its examinations in the subject. There was some detailed discussion, in particular of how to ensure that only poor people received the benefit of the artificial teeth and who was to pay for them, since by definition the patients would not be able to; the solution, it was decided, was that the patients' 'friends' should pay – in other words, a category of sponsored patients was created. And so the thing was done at last. In the Annual Report on 12th March 1891 appeared the following:

> The Managing Committee are pleased to be able to announce that the 'Dental Appliance Department' in connection with supplying Artificial Teeth, etc., is now complete and in working order.

Nobody is recorded on this occasion as having said anything about the compatibility or otherwise of the proposal with the institutional objects. In fact, the question very soon became redundant. The Appliance Department, under the control of the Appliance Committee, operated as a self-supporting unit within the institution, paying its own way from the contributions made by its patients' 'friends', its accounts kept separate from those of the rest of Hospital and School, so that none of the dentures supplied to patients were funded from donations made to the Hospital for charitable purposes. By June 1891 the appointments had been approved of a Mechanical Superintendent, at £100 p.a., a Laboratory Assistant at 30 shillings (£1.50) per week, and a Storekeeper at 12 shillings (60p) per week, 'all to be paid out of the Funds of the Appliance Department'. So it came about that the fitting of dentures for patients began to be taught to students at the Hospital. But students still did not learn the actual technical, as opposed to the clinical, work there. That had to wait until 1897, when it having been 'found convenient for certain students to obtain their mechanical training within the Hospital, rather than in the workroom of a private practitioner it had been decided to admit a limited number of students for this purpose.' This was the foundation of the Technical Laboratory, in which all students in due course spent a considerable period of time.

Since the foregoing was written there has come to light a Scrapbook in which David Hepburn collected documents and letters during his connection with the Appliance Department, with his own annotations and comments. The latter reveal more than do the official Minutes. For example, he complains of opposition and apathy. In October 1892, when he had proposed some alteration in the arrangements for the Department he notes:

> At this period a large section of the staff are most apathetic, only awakening to anything like activity when any progressive reform is organised, which they oppose tooth and nail. This Scheme ... was niggled over in the most puerile way and left on the table.

In the following year, in an effort to get away from the restrictions imposed by the Hospital's charitable status, Hepburn proposed that the Department be hived off as 'The London School of Dental Mechanics, attached to the Dental Hospital of London.' He notes:

> This Scheme ... being unanimously approved by the Appliance Committee was laid before the largest meeting of the Medical Committee I have ever known. It was never discussed but after a few irrelevant observations was left on the table.

Finally, Hepburn included in his Scrapbook a copy of a report he prepared setting out what he considered to be faults in the arrangements for the supply of dentures, including the fact that 'patients too often fail to regard the work done as an act of charity. The treatment involves a cash transaction which is not infrequently referred to; and thus a very distasteful element is too often introduced which destroys the good feeling which ought to exist as between Surgeon and patient'. One hundred years later the picture this quotation presents of the attitude of the nineteenth century Dental Surgeon, during his once-weekly attendance at the Dental Hospital, towards the 'objects of charity' presented for his attention there is itself distasteful. One has to remind oneself that David Hepburn and his colleagues were men of their time with the ideology of their time.

4

Dr Walker's
Great Scheme

The beginning of the century, when the move across St Martin's Street to Nos. 32 to 39 Leicester Square took place, was a turning point in the life of the institution. The acquisition of the site and the erection of the building presented administrative, legal and financial problems hugely greater than any which the Hospital authorities had so far encountered and the pressure upon the individuals responsible must have been considerable. It brought about the retirement from active involvement of Sir Edwin Saunders and at one stage created a rift between the Hospital and the School – not to mention a row with Governors and subscribers over the incorporation of a public house. That it was achieved despite all difficulties seems to be largely due to the initiative and drive of Dr Joseph Walker, lately Lecturer in Mechanical Dentistry and from 1892 Trustee and Treasurer in succession to Sir Edwin. This was acknowledged at the Annual Meeting in March 1896 when Mr FA Bevan said from the Chair that it was perfectly obvious that the Hospital had outgrown itself and that it was essential for the good of the patients and for the work of the Hospital that they should move as quickly as possible into better and more commodious premises; adding that gratitude was due to Dr Walker for 'his unfailing zeal and pertinacity in pursuing his great scheme'. The evidence suggests that John Francis Pink, whose appointment as Secretary now extended over two decades, also made a vital contribution; speaking at the 51st Annual Meeting in 1909, the Chairman said that 'to him and to Mrs Pink we are deeply indebted, and I doubt very much had it not been for them if we should have been in this building today.'

As one reads the records of the discussions starting in 1886 of the need for more space one is struck by the inadequacy of the premises into which Saunders so joyfully led his colleagues in 1874. Morton Smale's remarks quoted earlier (page 42 above) leave the impression of a thoroughly nasty and unsuitable building; and a sub-committee set up in 1891 to consider how the premises might be improved and extended to provide more space were advised that the state of the building was such that reconstruction was out of the question. It seemed unlikely that the Hospital would be able to acquire the property at the rear, which was the only way to expand and the sub-committee's advice was that the true interests of both Hospital and School would be best served by rebuilding on a new site; and they recomended that one of sufficient area and with ample possibilities of lighting be sought.

It is clear that when the management and staff designed their new building, their knowledge of the shortcomings of the one they occupied enabled them to avoid most of the pitfalls and remedy most of the faults, and to produce a purpose-built dental hospital (the first in the country) which gave good service for four-score years. The possession of the freeholds of 40, 41 and 42 Leicester Square gave the institution the means of raising loans to help launch the new project.

In the light of the report of the Extension Sub-committee the Management Committee decided to go for a new site, although it is clear that the decision was not unanimous. The following advertisement was published in The Times, The Builder and The City Press:

> Freehold site, with minimum area of 10,000 sq. ft., required. Neighbourhood of Leicester Square or Charing Cross preferred. Frontage if possible to the North, with ample access of light. Should be capable of being well lighted on two opposite sides.

Messrs. Young and Hall, Architects and Surveyors, of Southampton Street, were asked to deal with the replies and in due course they reported on five sites, variously situated, available at prices from £6 to £2.7s.0d (£2.35) per square foot. Unfortunately, in the same report, Young and Hall apologised for an error on their part as a result of which they had doubled their assessment of the area occupied by the existing premises; so that, as they said, the advertisement was for sites considerably larger than seemed to be required. They were instructed to re-advertise, this time for sites offering between 5000 and 7000 sq. ft.

Strangely, the second advertisement produced no response at all, and this provided the opponents of a move, of whom Sir Edwin Saunders seems to have been the leader, with an opportunity. At the meeting to which the failure of the second advertisement was reported, the Committee of Management agreed to ask Young and Hall to draw up proposals for extending the existing premises with the acquisition of 4 Spur Street, at the western end and Nos. 2 and 3 St Martins Street, adjoining the eastern end. At the same time, the Chairman was asked to enquire whether the owner of the premises at the rear of the Hospital would agree to an extension of the second floor on pillars over his property. It turned out that at least one of the St Martins Street houses was not for sale but in any case the discussion was overtaken by events. It was discovered, probably by Mr Pink, that somebody proposed to buy the entire site to the east of the Hospital, and he pointed out that if this happened any chance of extending

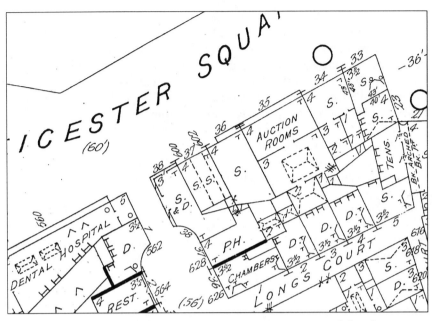

Plan (c. 1895) of the Leicester Square sites acquired by the
Hospital for the rebuilding project.

in that direction would disappear. Pink had found out that the owner of
five houses in Long's Court, which were part of the site in question, would
be prepared to sell them to the Hospital for £5000 if the deal was settled
quickly. Pink was proposing a pre-emptive strike and, with the Chairman's
permission, he called a special meeting of the Committee on 27th October
1892 to consider this scheme.

Sir Edwin Saunders had previously expressed himself very strongly
against proposals for moves to a new site and in favour of extending the
existing premises. On receiving the summons to the special meeting he
wrote at once to the effect that if it was decided not to buy the houses in
Long's Court he would not feel obliged to 'dissolve my connexion with the
Hospital' – otherwise, the inference was, they would have to find another
President. At the meeting, Dr Walker took the Chair, Dr Hare, the usual
Chairman, being unwell and, despite Sir Edwin's opposition, Pink's proposal was adopted unanimously. Walker immediately wrote out a cheque
for £100 on his personal account to provide a deposit for the purchase.

From that moment things moved quickly. At the next meeting, in
December, it was reported that the purchase of the Long's Court properties
was proceeding satisfactorily. So far, however, the intention seems to have
been to use them in some way to extend the existing Hospital – a bridge
across St Martins Street was talked about. But the Dean, Morton Smale,
had circulated a more radical proposal as a result of which it was agreed

unanimously 'that negotiations be opened with the freeholders of Nos. 35 to 38 Leicester Square with a view of purchasing this site for the smallest possible sum, upon which, and the ground already acquired, a new Hospital be built, this being the most eligible site obtainable through advertisement and private enquiry and that No. 35 Leicester Square be forthwith obtained for the smallest possible sum not exceeding £8,500; and that an appeal be made to the public forthwith to subscribe the necessary funds for the purpose'. This was the meeting which decided the development of the institution into its twentieth-century form and brought about a final breach with Sir Edwin Saunders.

The correspondence in this connection is worth reproducing in detail, because not only does it set out fairly concisely the considerations in the minds of the individuals concerned at the time, but it also says much about the strength of their feelings and their personalities. Saunders did not attend the meeting, but instead wrote the following letter to be read to the Committee:

> In view of the important – I will say – momentous, decision which will be asked of the Committee on 19th inst. – I have found it necessary to place my resignation of the offices of Treasurer and Trustee of the Dental Hospital in the hands of the Chairman. For though I can hardly believe that the Committee will sanction the destruction or abandonment of the present Hospital in which so much good work has been done yet we know that the unexpected does sometimes happen, and when one side of a question only is persistently presented votes are sometimes snatched, which would not be given on calmer reflection. I therefore in reply to a request would remark: that it does not appear to me that a sufficiently strong case for immediate further enlargement has been or can be made out to justify the large pecuniary responsibiity which the proposal involves.

Sir Edwin continued in his letter to maintain that sufficient extra space could be provided by extension into the Spur Street building, and said that he did not think that better accommodation could be provided on the new site which was proposed. He reminded the Committee once more of the size of the financial burden which would be incurred and ended:

> I will cherish the hope that the Committee will pause before sanctioning the abolition of the Dental Hospital of London, which has for so many years met with a well-deserved and liberal support from the public.

To this, after the meeting, the Chairman responded with a letter telling Sir Edwin how distressed the Committee was at his resignation and saying –

> Knowing your views on the subject (this was of course before the note of resignation was read) each member who spoke and who voted felt a real

diffidence and pain in differing from you in urging the case ... for a larger hospital ... But they felt that there was now very keen competition as regards dental instruction and they knew that the Dental Department at St Bartholemew's had been greatly augmented while Guy's Hospital had recently devoted £12,000 to buildings etc. in order to push forward a similar department. They thought that the Dental Hospital ought to maintain the foremost place in the promotion and teaching of Dental Sciences, and that this could not be done, at the present time and in the present condition of other schools, without a more ample, commodious and attractive hospital than the present one.

He added that the Committee thought they should take the opportunity of acquiring a site, which was not likely to occur again and concluded with the sincere hope that Sir Edwin would reconsider his resignation. In his reply, Sir Edwin declined, saying that he could not happily remain a Trustee with the burden of so great a debt – 'I must therefore leave it to those to whom the new arrangement commends itself'.

In January 1893 the contract for the purchase of 35 and 35a Leicester Square was signed, and it was decided to add Nos. 22 and 23 Green Street and No. 34 Leicester Square to the list of properties to be acquired. Next arose the question, to which Dr Walker had been giving attention, of funds pending results from the public appeal. At the Annual Meeting of Governors in March 1893 he was formally elected Treasurer and Trustee in place of Sir Edwin (he had been doing the job since the latter's resignation in the preceding October) and the Trustees were given authority to raise money by mortgaging the freehold property of the institution. The impression gained from the records that Walker and Pink, working together as a team, were largely responsible for what had been achieved so far and for the achievements which followed is supported by Walker's remarks in giving thanks for his election as Treasurer:

> were it not for the Secretary's energy it would be impossible for a private man to carry out the duties of Treasurer. As it was Mr Pink was really the Treasurer and he (Dr Walker) was simply a looker-on.

From this moment the energies of the Committee of Management were devoted to the problems of acquiring the properties required to provide the site for the new building, raising the large sums of money needed, and drawing up the plans for the premises. By the end of 1893 they had bought Nos. 35 and 36 Leicester Square, Nos. 22 and 23 Green Street and Nos. 1,2,3,4 and 5 Longs Court, and had put a deposit down for The Duke's Head, No. 37 St Martins Street, all of which were contained in one block of buildings. These acquisitions had entailed an expenditure of £20,398, three-quarters of which had been borrowed from the bank. The rest had come from a public appeal for contributions to the Building Fund, which totalled £9,721 – and it is noteworthy that 75 per cent of this had been given by members of staff and students, and by other members of the dental profession, in what must have been for the Committee of Management a remarkable and encouraging demonstration of loyalty and enthusiasm. But the response from the general public was, and continued to be, disappointing. All the properties were let, however, and the rents more than covered the interest on the loan from the bank.

By 1896 the whole of the the site had been bought, with the exception of No. 34 Leicester Square, the owners of which seem to have realised that their site was essential if the Hospital's plans were to be carried out and, not unnaturally, had decided that the longer they held out the better their price would be. (The Committee toyed with the idea of building around the site of No. 34, leaving a space to be filled up when opportunity occurred, but the architects thought this hardly feasible.) The bank advance was replaced by a loan on mortgage of the existing premises. However, in the middle of the year the process received an unexpected impetus. The Vestry of St Martins and the London County Council used their statutory powers to compel the Hospital to sell 22 and 23 Green Street to them in connection with street improvement plans. The demolition of these buildings by the Vestry rendered unsafe those adjoining them belonging to the Hospital and the London County Council obtained a magistrate's order for the clearance of the entire site – with the result that the Hospital was left with premises which everybody now agreed were inadequate and an empty site bought with a large loan and was deprived of the rents from which the loan was serviced. The Management Committee had no alternative but to rebuild as quickly as they could.

The task before them now had three main components, design, finance and compliance with the statutory requirements for the conduct of charities. They invited three architects to compete for the job of designing the new Hospital. After considering their submissions they appointed Keith D Young of Young and Hall, who had been the Hospital's building surveyors for some time. The question of finance was crucial and, as it turned out, troublesome. Sir Edwin Saunders had resigned partly because he was not prepared to accept responsibility for what he saw as an unwarranted financial burden, and it is clear from the minutes of the Committee that some members faced with proposals for raising large sums became concerned about their personal liability. Two alternatives which were suggested in an attempt to minimise this were that a firm of builders be asked to carry out the work on a speculative basis, being paid only when the building was handed over – Trollope and Sons had offered such an arrangement – or that the site be sold and a cheaper one sought. As the Chairman, Allen Stoneham, pointed out in a masterly memorandum circulated for the meeting of the Committee on 29th October 1896, these ideas were unsound – the first would increase the cost of the project by at least 50 per cent and the second was hardly likely to be worth the trouble since the purchase of the site was financed by a bank loan the repayment of which would use up most of the proceeds of sale. At the meeting FA Bevan, a Trustee of the Hospital and a Director of the Bank, explained that the bank was prepared to finance the building by advancing money in stages against architect's certification, at a fixed rate of 4 per cent, provided that the advances were repaid by mortgaging the property as soon as it was completed. There would, he was careful to explain, be no personal liability as far as members of the Committee were concerned, and the Treaurer had already reported that the Prudential Assurance Company had agreed to a mortgage loan on the building when it was finished.

The tension of the situation can be imagined. Although there can be little doubt that Stoneham, Walker, Bevan and Pink knew what they were about and had the situation well in hand, some members of the Committee must have felt that they had been led into a trap and were concerned that they might have bitten off more than they could chew. The relief of tension when the matter was resolved shows in the Minutes – there was 'a hearty vote of thanks to the bank for the generous manner in which they had met the necessities of the Managing Committee'.

The statutory obligations of the charity brought more problems. It was necessary to seek the permission of the Charity Commission for the disposal of the old premises and the mortgaging of the new. This was obtained in December 1896, but was subject to the conditions that no building work commenced until the site of No. 34 Leicester Square was acquired, that 20 per cent of the School's income was secured to the Hospital and that the mortgage loan was repaid in thirty years or less. The problem of No. 34 was swiftly and decisively dealt with. Having learned that the process would cost about £500 Dr Walker proposed that application be made for a private Act of Parliament for the compulsory acquisition of the property and, the Committee agreeing, advertised their intention in The Times, as the law required. The owners agreed to sell for £7000 forthwith, without the need for any further action.

The second of the Commission's conditions seems to have created considerable dissension, although, as so often where the affairs of the School are concerned at this period, the details can be discerned only vaguely through the curtain of discretion which surrounds them. The proposal was a matter for the Medical Committee, to the individual members of which, it will be remembered, belonged any excess of the School's income over its costs. The idea was not an entirely new one for the Committee, though – three years earlier, in October 1893, their Minutes record that the Dean, Morton Smale, with the support of Mr JF Colyer, proposed that all the profits from School fees for that year be paid into the Hospital Building Fund, and that in future years half of the profits be paid over to the Hospital until the debt incurred in rebuilding was repaid. Laconically, it is recorded that 'after considerable discussion the Dean withdrew his proposals'.

But he did not forget them. A year later, writing to the Chairman of the

Committee to apologise for his inability to attend a meeting, he asked for his views to be reported regarding a proposal that the practice of charging patients (or their 'friends') for appliances be discontinued, the resulting loss to be made up from School funds. In brief, his view was that it was wrong to give people false teeth for nothing, and he claimed the support of the Charity Organisation Committee for the view that such a course 'tends to pauperise and demoralise the recipient'. He went on, however, to remind the Committee of his earlier proposal (one senses that he probably took every opportunity to make the point): 'The money which it is proposed to pay from the Medical Committee's funds would I think be better employed if it with some considerable addition could be devoted to the New Building'. Despite the Dean's views the Committee decided the principle of the abolition of all payment by patients be adopted, (although there is no indication that this expression of principle had any practical effect) and no comment upon the Dean's alternative suggestion is recorded.

When the Charity Commissioners' requirements became known at the end of 1896 the Committee of Management referred the question of a contribution from School fees to the Medical Committee who, in turn, referred it to the School Finance Committee. The latter was a somewhat nebulous body with rather vague terms of reference whose main function was to draw up the School's Profit and Loss Account each year and decide how the profit should be shared among the honorary staff. Few records of its activities during this period exist but some details can be gleaned from the minutes of the Committee of Management. It seems that the School Finance Committee, in the person of Storer Bennett, reported to the Committee that they thought the required contribution too onerous and had said so at a meeting with representatives of the Commission. Subsequently CJ Tomes wrote to the Commissioners putting the case for the School and suggesting a contribution of 20 per cent up to a maximum of £300, (which, he said, was roughly 20 per cent of the preceding year's profit) so that the School would retain the full benefit of any future increase in profitability.

In this it would be wrong to assume that the motives of the honorary staff were entirely selfish. There is evidence that to some extent they were concerned for the future of the School, which was now operating in a competitive market – in addition to the School at the National Dental Hospital, which had been running almost as long as their own School, a Dental School had opened at Guy's Hospital in 1889. As Tomes said in his letter, the Dental School needed to attract and retain good teachers and to do this needed to be able to remunerate them adequately. In a letter of explanation which was read to the Committee of Management he said that this discussion with the Charity Commissioners need not delay proceedings – the School readily conceded an annual payment of £300, which was roughly the current value of 20 per cent of its profits, and the argument was whether or not this was to be a maximum. In the event, the Charity

Commissioners stuck to a contribution of 20 per cent with no maximum as a condition of their agreement to the mortgage and the School's representatives, somewhat reluctantly, agreed that if that was the decision there was not much they could do about it. As Storer Bennett said, it was in effect an ultimatum. (In the background to these exchanges, as Dr Walker pointed out to the Commissioners, was the expectation that the number of students and the income from them would increase significantly with the greater space and better facilities which the new building would provide.)

Thus the conditions imposed by the Charity Commissioners were met. But at the same time as they had to deal with the difficulties of meeting them the Committee of Management found themselves confronted by a number of problems arising from their ownership of property. One of these was Mrs Harris, who occupied the shop at No. 38 Leicester Square, on the corner with St Martins Street, when the Hospital acquired the property. What business she carried on there is not recorded; some of the businesses carried on in Leicester Square at that time were of a very doubtful nature indeed – one of the points made in the Hospital's appeals for money was that they would confer a great benefit on the neighbourhood by putting a respectable dental hospital in the place of a number of disrespectable houses and shops. She refused an offer of £600 to vacate the property and then failed to pay the rent. When the Committee asked Dr Walker to do something about this, he took counsel's opinion, which was that although the Hospital could distrain against Mrs Harris for non-payment of rent they had no power to evict her. She was still there when building operations started, threatening to sue the builders for trespass and for disrupting her supplies of gas and water, so they fenced her off and built around her, and she said she would sue them for that, too. In the end the Vestry of St Martins-in-the-Fields came to the rescue. They decided that half of her shop was in the way of their road-widening plans (a glance at the map shows that it certainly was) and, using statutory powers, gave her £300 and knocked it down. So she was left, presumably, with half a shop with no wall on one side. Her solicitors asked the Hospital for £500 in compensation (for what, they do not seem to have said). The Committee agreed to pay her £300 and remit 44 months' unpaid rent, and off she went at last.

A much more serious problem was the Duke's Head, at 37 St Martins Street. This public house had come into the Hospital's possession as a going concern, albeit a rather shabby and disreputable one. In planning the new building the policy had been adopted of providing shop accommodation on the ground floor to provide a rental income for the institution, and it seems that Dr Walker and his associates considered that a public house in such a situation would be, to use a phrase of today which seems appropriate, a nice little earner. So much so that they proposed to move it to the site next door, where it could be modestly extended. And so, in April 1897 application was made on behalf of the existing licensee for rebuilding on the site next door as part of the dental hospital complex and for the transfer of the licence. A barrister, Mr AH Bodkin, had been retained to handle the matter on behalf of the Hospital Trustees, but, having put in the formal application and a copy of the building plans, he decided not to attend the hearing because he expected no opposition.

In this expectation he was most severely disappointed. The proceedings were reported in detail in the *Morning Advertiser*. In addition to routine opposition on behalf of the landlords of The Stones and The Lord Belgrave together with 'several other gentlemen interested in the trade' there appeared counsel briefed by the Orange Street Chapel and the London Temperance Council. These two gentlemen, producing the plans for the new building, persuaded the magistrates that roughly half the Hospital site, on the ground floor, was to constitute the new Duke's Head, to provide a new super-pub, nine times the size of the present one with, they said, three entrances in Longs Court and one in Leicester Square, in addition to the existing entrance in St Martins Street. The three entrances in Longs Court they saw as particularly sinister; they would, the learned gentlemen said, be 'quite removed from police supervision'. And they dwelt upon the devious-ness of the Hospital Trustees in setting up the licensee of 'a small shanty facing a narrow court leading off Leicester Square' as a 'dummy' for themselves in an attempt to conceal their involvement in this doubtful affair. The justices, not unnaturally, were troubled by all this and rejected the application, saying that it was one for a new licence, not a mere transfer.

The unfortunate Mr Bodkin hastened to the court at the next oppor-tunity, which occurred a fortnight later, clutching a new set of plans. The *Morning Advertiser's* reporter was also there again. So too were counsel for the Orange Street Chapel and the London Temperance Council – unlike Mr Bodkin, they were leaving nothing to chance. At the conclusion of the morning's business, Mr Bodkin attempted to explain that the Hospital's proposals for the Duke's Head had been misunderstood and asked the magistrates to look at his new plans. But there was nothing doing. 'The Chairman observed that the matter was thoroughly gone into on the last occasion and they could not allow the case to be re-opened.' There is no record of Mr Bodkin being employed by the Hospital Trustees on a subsequent occasion.

When the Committee of Management met on 27th May 1897 they were told of these events and resigned themselves to waiting until the next full session of the licensing justices, in March 1898. But there was worse to come. When they assembled a week later the Committee had before them a copy of a pamphlet produced on behalf of the National United Temperance Council by a Mr Charles Pinhorn. This, headed 'A Scandalous Proposal', had been sent to all of the Hospital's Governors and Subscribers for whom Mr Pinhorn could find addresses, and contained an attack upon the members of the Committee for 'a very discreditable attempt ... to procure the extension of the Duke's Head for their own personal advantage at the expense of what we shall mildly term fair play.' It went with a letter from Mr Pinhorn calling upon subscribers to protest to the Committee of Management, and including the following comment:

> The neighbourhood of Leicester Square is unfortunately the notorious hunting ground of the debased and profligate and it is therefore an outrage upon decency to propose that an institution receiving generous support from the Christian public should provide a rendezvous for such persons as are nightly to be found in this locality and thus bring into sharp contrast the hollow merriment of the fallen with the cries of the suffering.

Mr Pinhorn, it will be agreed, applied his temperate principles to his use of punctuation but he did not extend them to the rest of his writing style.

It can be imagined that this broadside caused considerable consternation among the members of the Committee. The last thing that was needed in the middle of an appeal for funds for rebuilding was adverse publicity of this sort. A dignified response was drafted and sent to supporters of the institution pointing out that, far from getting any personal gain from their association with the Hospital, they, with the staff and other members of the dental profession had provided some £8,000 towards the cost of 'this public improvement and its charitable work.' They said that having acquired the public house in the process of acquiring the site for the new hospital they were in duty bound, as custodians of a charitable trust, to maintain and if possible to improve what was, whatever views might be held about public houses in general, a valuable asset. What they planned to do, therefore, was to transfer the licence 'attached to an inferior class of public house, in an obscure street, to a portion of the new building, with the capabilities of a first-class restaurant, the street being widened as part of the plan.' 'The Committee' their letter added 'will gladly concur in any arrangement the National United Temperance Council or other Temperance Societies may propose for the abandonment of the licence provided that the funds of the Hospital are guaranteed from loss.'

There are in fact no indications that Mr Pinhorn's efforts had any effect upon subscribers – the minutes refer to a few enquiries from some of those who received his pamphlet, but the flow of donations shows no signs of being influenced one way or another. He, and the other opponents may have influenced the licensing justices, however; when they had the application before them again in March 1898 they refused to allow the proposed transfer of the licence from its present site to the one next door. The Duke's Head was to stay where it was.

Convinced that it was their duty to maintain the license in being, the Committee now found themselves running a pub. They found it a worrying business and in August 1900 tried to auction a 50-year lease at a rental of £100 p.a., but there were no bids. They took on Mr WC Wiseman, at £2.50 per week 'to conduct the bar' but he complained that trade was poor and asked for more money or to be allowed to live in the premises. Remembering Mrs Harris, no doubt, the Committee were not creating any more sitting tenants, and refused permission. In 1901, they succeeded in letting the place to Trumans, the brewers, but next year the latter reported that their trade there had been disappointing and said they were prepared to give up their lease if it suited the Hospital for them to do so. Finally, after discussion with the Charity Commission, the Comittee of Management agreed to close the place down and, at the Annual General Meeting on 16th April 1903, the licence was ceremoniously torn up by the Chairman, Lord Kinnaird – 'amidst applause'. The hope was expressed that the space vacated by the closure might be put to more fitting use – in fact it provided accommodation for Mr and Mrs Pink and, no doubt, their daughter who was now working for the Hospital as Entry Clerk. The Committee decided, opaquely, that they should have the place 'free of any rent but on the understanding that Mr Pink makes a contribution to the funds of the Hospital of £50. p.a.' This contribution they agreed to remit in June 1905.

While dealing with these irritations and having solved the problems of funding and complying with the requirements of the Charity Commissioners, the Committee had to grapple with the matter of cost over-runs; it seems that our Victorian forerunners were no more immune to these afflictions than we were in our day. The project, it was reported, with much of the work completed, was running some £2,000 over budget. The desperation with which the Committee faced this news comes over in the Minutes; they decided that economies in the fitting out of the premises would have to be made and gave instructions accordingly. This alarmed the members of the Medical Committee, especially because the economies would fall mainly upon the parts of the premises to be used by the School and they produced an ingenious solution – at a meeting called dramatically at twenty-four hours notice they agreed that the School should pay £2,000 to the Management Committee, on condition that the original building plans were adhered to. To raise the money the School issued eighty bonds of £25 each, bearing interest at 4 per cent, and it was agreed that eight bonds chosen by lot were to be repaid each year out of the School's income. Since, as has been noted, any money which the School had left after meeting expenses was shared among the members of the Medical Committee, this contribution came out of their own pockets in reality – a recognition on their part of the future benefits likely to accrue to the School from the new accommodation.

These prolonged efforts received their reward in March 1901, when the new premises were taken into use, and the old building was sold for £18,000. The March issue of the *Journal of the British Dental Association* contained the following comments:

The past student of the Leicester Square Hospital, returning to the scene of his former studies, will open his eyes wide with astonishment. The old home of dentistry still stands, but close to it has arisen a new building, a building such as was never contemplated in the wildest dreams of those who loved and laboured at their studies in the confined area and amongst the unavoidable discomforts of the old school. Everything has been done to make the new Hospital the finest possible. There is abundance of room, every department is well ventilated and comfortably heated, and the sanitary arrangements are all that could be desired.

The article describes the mechanical laboratory, 'fitted with electric lathes', with seventy-six benches; the lecture theatre, with seating for 200; the 'prodigality in the matter of area' lavished on the metallurgical laboratory; and the 'Stopping Room' (i.e., the Department of Conservative Dentistry in modern terms) with 'pump-chairs of the most convenient pattern, saliva ejectors and all essentials, including plenty of elbow room, even should upwards of a hundred operators be at work at the same time.' The operating chairs, incidentally, were paid for by public subscription. Ash and Company, having installed them, agreed to wait for payment while a special appeal for the money was made, each of those who provided sufficient to pay for a chair having their name recorded on one of them. Some of these chairs were still in use after the Second World War.

An event which gratified the Committee of Management followed the accession of King Edward VII in 1901. The occasion was considered an appropriate time for the Hospital to apply for him to become Patron of the Hospital. This he agreed to do, as the General Keeper of the Privy Purse notified Mr Pink on 31st July 1901. Henceforward, at the Hospital's dinners and similar functions, the Loyal Toast was proudly addressed to 'Our Patron the King (or Queen)'. Patronage was a personal matter for the King and his advisors to decide, but the title of the institution, it seems, was a political question. Application to adopt the prefix 'Royal' had to be made to the Home Secretary, who wrote on 15th October 1901 to say that 'His Majesty had been graciously pleased ... to command that the Institution be known as the Royal Dental Hospital of London'.

The Annual Meeting of Governors on 28th March 1901 was held in the new building, although it was not yet formally opened. During the year, as the process of fitting-out and occupation proceeded, a number of administrative innovations were agreed to meet the needs of the enlarged institution. The Resident Porter and his wife, who were responsible for caretaking and cleaning, were provided with a full-time laundress ('to wash the Hospital's linen' and who was to have clogs supplied to wear at work) and a number of cleaning operatives (they called them charwomen, actually) who were to scrub the floors once each week. Between them the couple were responsible for the direction and supervision of this workforce, an arrangement which endured happily until the retirement of the last Resident Porter and Wife, Mr and Mrs Jack Knights, in 1964. An Engineer was appointed to look after the heating and electrical systems and to carry out routine plumbing and gasfitting. The appointments of two additional porters, a ward-maid and a messenger boy were also agreed. Finally Mrs Pink, who was already helping her husband with his work and receiving an annual honorarium in recognition of her services, was appointed Lady Superintendent and Assistant Secretary with the specific responsiblity of supervising all the domestic and engineering staff.

Another important innovation, implemented towards the end of the year, was the appointment of a Dental Superintendent. Under the direction of the Honorary Staff and the Medical Committee, his job comprised the control and administration of all the departments of the Hospital and School (except for the Secretary and Lady Superintendent and their specific areas of responsibility). He was to be present throughout the working day, and to examine all new patients and allot them to appropriate departments for treatment, drawing the attention of the Surgeon of the Day to any cases of particular interest from the teaching aspect. In the absence of any of the anaesthetists, he was to administer anaesthetics to patients and 'if required, to the surplus patients, both morning and afternoon, when the numbers exceed 20'. He was responsible for the allocation of patients to students and for seeing that students kept their appointments with patients. Finally, his Rules said, 'He shall in every respect endeavour to maintain order, decorum and professional behaviour within the building'.

5

Into the Twentieth Century

The Hospital emerged into the twentieth century in the shape and with the organisation which it maintained, more or less, for nearly seventy-five years. For the School the new century brought important changes.

In 1897 the College of Surgeons announced changes in the curriculum for the Diploma, effective from 1900, which necessitated changes in the School's arrangements. Practical courses in Dental Metallurgy and Dental Histology were established, together with a course for final year students in Dental Surgery Practice, which covered the field of what is now known as Conservative Dentistry with the addition of extraction and had tacked on to it the subject of Microscopic Pathology. In 1902 courses in Materia Medica in relation to Dentistry and Dental Bacteriology were added to the requirements. These developments, with those in the teaching of Dental Mechanics (which included components of the modern subjects of Dental Prosthetics and Orthodontics), and the introduction in 1900 of something very similar to a modern Phantom Head Course (except that they were then called mannikins) produced a curriculum similar to the modern one, if embryonic in some respects. The changes necessitated staff increases, and the Medical Committee debated whether students' fees should be increased accordingly. On learning that Guy's Dental School and the National Dental College had no intention of increasing their fees, the Committee dropped the idea.

The introduction of teaching the making of dentures ('mechanical teaching', as it was then called) is an interesting example of the way in which developments in the School came about as a result of a kind of semi-independent entrepreneurial initiative. In 1897 the Medical Committee set up a small sub-committee for mechanical teaching, which recruited four students, who each paid £105 for a two-year course, and a laboratory assistant at a wage of 30/- per week. Out of the students' fees they paid 20 per cent to the Committee of Management, the wages of the assistant, and an honorarium for the teacher, and bought the necessary instruments and materials. After three years this enterprise had accummulated a surplus of nearly £500 which, the sub-committee suggested, should be used to equip the teaching laboratory properly. The Medical Committee agreed to this suggestion, but ordered that any future surpluses be paid over to the School Treasurer – and appointed two of their number to audit the accounts of the sub-committee in future.

During 1899 the School began to consider the question of association with the University of London, which was itself undergoing radical change. Negley Harte *(The University of London, 1836–1986)* describes the University of the nineteenth century as 'in modern terms, an amalgam of an Open University and a Council for National Academic Awards. It had neither the technology of the one, nor the system of inspection of the other, but its functions were perceived as a sort of cross between the two.' Academic critics dismissed it as 'a mere examining board'. Nevertheless, it had the distinction of being, in 1880, the first British University to award degrees to women – it was forty years before Oxford and forty-three before Cambridge did so.

The changes at the beginning of the century were the result of the London University Act, 1898, one of the objectives of which was to enlarge the University by giving it a more powerful teaching side in order to promote research and the advancement of science and learning and to improve and extend higher education in the area within a 30 mile radius of the centre of London. The Act set up a Commission to frame the statutes for the reconsituted University, and the Medical Committee of the Dental Hospital discussed a joint approach to the Commission by the dental schools in London with a view to obtaining some definite recognition by the University. Guy's Dental School felt unable to take part in any joint action, possibly because they were constrained by their parent Medical School, but the Dental School of London and the National Dental College jointly petitioned for the institution of a dental degree. It was several years before the University discussed this proposal but when the new Statutes of the University were published in 1900 the London School of Dental Surgery (sic) was given the status of 'Institution with Recognised Teachers'. Three members of staff – CS Tomes, Morton Smale and WB Paterson – were appointed members of the Faculty of Medicine of the University and of the Board of Dental Studies.

Soon after, the University made an abortive attempt to centralise pre-clinical medical teaching in a proposed Institute of Medical Sciences to be established in South Kensington, for which some £70,000 had been raised by a public appeal. The scheme failed because of the inability of the London Medical Schools to agree upon any scheme of centralised co-operation and the University, no doubt with some embarrassment, had to return the money to its donors. A lesser degree of co-operation was achieved, however, by the Medical Schools at St George's, Westminster and Charing Cross Hospitals, who agreed to give up their pre-clinical teaching to University College and King's College; this arrangement led in due course to the association of the latter with the School at the Royal.

The University's Board of Studies in Dentistry considered the proposal for a dental degree early in 1902. A majority of the Board took the view that the LDS was all that was necessary as a qualification for registration, and said 'that it is undesirable for the University of London to enter into competition with the Royal Colleges and those provincial universities which propose to establish qualifying dental degrees'. The membership of the Board of Studies at that time included four members of the staff of the Royal Dental Hospital of London – CS Tomes, Morton Smale, G Hern and WB Paterson. Despite the fact that their School had been one of the petitioners for a dental degree only one of these, WB Patterson, with one other member of the Board, signed a minority report recommending that one be established. Naturally enough, the Senate of the University accepted the majority recommendation, the wording of which suggests that political rather than purely academic considerations weighed heavily in the minds of those who made it (the University had been offering a degree in Medicine since 1839).

It was not only in academic matters that the School was developing. Reference has been made to the somewhat informal arrangements for the School's financial administration; there are indications that during 1899 the Medical Committee became dissatisfied with them. At the suggestion of the Dean, they discharged the School Finance Committee, replacing it with one subject to annual election, comprising the School Treasurer, the Dean, two lecturers, three Senior Surgeons and two Assistant Surgeons, and instructed them to submit a financial report to the Medical Committee before any distribution of profits was made. The first such report was in respect of the year 1900, submitted on 24th January 1901. This, the first glimpse we have of the financial working of the School since its foundation forty-two years earlier, is interesting and the discussion of the report by the Medical Committee revealing. Income from students amounted to £2,418 and expenditure for the year, when a special payment of £1,000 for equipment for the new building is excluded, to £892. So, in a normal year, there could be some £1,500 'profit' to share out. In fact there was no share-out in that year; the Medical Committee reckoned that the £1,000 for equipment was only a first instalment and that more would be needed before long, and prudently decided to forego their personal shares.

This decision was not reached without a struggle. CS Tomes, who was a member of the Finance Committee, argued strongly in a closely reasoned letter that it was improper to charge the equipment expenditure, which was of a capital nature, upon a single year's income. He wanted it amortised over ten years, and a share of £35 paid out to those participating in the current year, £20 at once, with £15 held over for future consideration with a suggestion that any cash-flow problem resulting from such action be dealt with by borrowing the money needed for the capital expenditure. As an exposition of accountancy principle his argument is hard to fault; but the Medical Committee rejected it.

From the discussion of the accounts of the School for 1902 we learn that the number of shares into which the 'profit' was to be divided was 36, although this does not necessarily mean that thirty-six people participated – some were entitled to more than one share. In the same discussion it was agreed that in future the School's accounts should be audited professionally. In addition, the Treasurer presented another well-reasoned letter from Charles Tomes, who was about to retire, suggesting that profit-sharing as a means of remunerating those connected with the School was no longer suitable. Few nowadays would disagree with his views:

> It is now almost univerally recognised that the sort of volunteer system under which, at a number of medical schools teaching has been conducted without any adequate remuneration, other than the indirect advantages obtained by consulting surgeons and physicians by the, to them, indispensable connection with a hospital and its introduction to private practice, has been on average and in the long run a failure, and the present tendency is so to remunerate teachers, that teaching shall be in some measure an end and not merely a means to some other end.
>
> A survey of medical and science teaching and teachers will show that the most brilliant teachers are to be on the whole found where the remuneration is most adequate, and I strongly hold the conviction that it is a wrong policy, tending to the lessened sense of responsibility, to trust to volunteer effort.

Tomes failed to convince a majority of his colleagues because, after pondering the matter for two months, the Medical Committee decided to make no change in their arrangements. But his words remained in their minds, as later events showed.

The School's accounts for 1902, bearing the certification of JW Butcher and Co., Chartered Accountants, include a balance sheet for the first time. It shows an accummulated balance of £1,732. Charles Tomes' views on the inadequacy of the share as a means of remunerating teachers would seem to be borne out by the decision of the Medical Committee to pay £10 per share on this occasion. And soon the seed he had sown bore fruit, because when the School's accounts for 1906 were presented to them, the Medical Committee approved a recommendation by their Treasurer that for that year and in future the Dean and the Lecturers be paid set stipends, and that for 1906 no distribution be made to the Dental Surgeons and Assistant Dental Surgeons.

In 1910 the University made its first attempt at establishing a dental degree. What was decided upon was a Degree of Master of Science in Dental Surgery, entrants for which were required to have obtained MB, BS. The RDH Medical Committee gave the proposals for this degree their 'hearty support' despite the fact that one of their number, Norman Bennett, who was Secretary of the Board of Studies in Dentistry from which they emanated, strongly opposed them. His grounds, which he set out in a minority report to the University's Academic Council, were an objection to the main condition which made the degree contingent upon the possession of a MB BS degree 'or, in other words, offers a degree for dental students and practitioners to medical graduates only'. It would seem reasonable to expect that his views would be shared by his colleagues of the Dental Hospital and School; but not so. The explanation must be that they still did not really believe dentistry to be a profession independent of medicine. Bennett did, but in that company his seems to have been a lone voice – the Medical Committee's 'hearty support' could hardly have been more pointed. In the event it made no difference one way or the other. The first examination for the new degree was offered in 1911, but in October 1919 it was reported to the Board of Studies that no candidates had yet presented for it.

The existence of the degree did, however, provide a peg upon which the School of Dental Surgery was able to hang an application for its recognition as a School of the University. But the actual event which prompted the move as the Dean, WH Dolamore, readily admitted in his letter of application, was the announcement that the Board of Education was prepared to make available grants in aid of teaching at the School if it gained such recognition.

The Dean's letter of application seems lame and diffident, almost as if he had decided that it had to be written but he did not really expect much to come of it. If this was the case, he was very nearly right – the application came close to being turned down outright. In accordance with procedure when the application was received the Academic Council appointed Inspectors to visit the School and report upon its organisation and finance, staff, equipment and methods. They decided that the School was well equipped for clinical and theoretical teaching (although they thought the pathological specimens were badly displayed) and said that it was deserving of recognition. Notwithstanding, the view of the Academic Council was that since the School had no permanent endowment and its sole capital was a balance of assets over liabilities amounting to £1,328, its financial situation was not sufficiently stable to justify its admission as a School of the University. They recommended accordingly to the Senate.

Fortunately for the School the recomendation was referred back to the Academic Council apparently because two members of the Senate made the point that it was unfair to bar a School because of its financial situation when, so far as anyone knew, the financial arrangements of the medical schools already recognised had never been examined. Asked to think again the Academic Council took the point, although they also thought that before long the constitutions and financial arrangements of all the Medical Schools would have to be looked at, and agreed to support the temporary recognition of the Dental School. And so the Royal Dental Hospital and

London School of Dental Surgery was admitted as a School of the University for a period of five years from 1st October 1911.

Some interesting information about the School is contained in the correspondence published in the Senate Minutes of these proceedings. The number of students was given as 'about 150', which is the first definite statement of total numbers so far found. Regular salaries as distinct from shares of surplus were being paid to thirteen members of the teaching staff. The University authorities, after questioning the Hospital's solicitors and examining the Articles and Laws of the institution noted that 'it appears impossible to distinguish in any legal way between the Hospital and the Dental School, although the accounts of the Dental School are kept separate'; a fact which from time to time worried the University and many other people but never seemed to cause any difficulty for the two institutions themselves. Strangely enough, after their union had been dissolved by the National Health Service Act 1946 it became necessary to prove all over again that they had once been one organisation – as will be seen in due time. The School's expectation that money would flow from the Board of Education following their recognition by the University was not fulfilled. The Dean was told in July 1911 that there was no prospect of a grant from the Board to any dental school at 'the present time'.

The effect of the new premises upon the institution as a whole was profound. In 1902, the first full year in the new building, the Medical Committee reported a 22 per cent increase in the number of operations carried out – a total of 85,284. They noted, in passing, that in 1874, the first year in the old Leicester Square building, the total was 19,255. By 1909 the total had risen to 109,449. (It has to be said that the Medical Committee's statistical methods tended to make the most of the number of operations; each tooth extracted counted as one, for example, so that a patient who had five teeth removed at one go added five to the total; nevertheless, the comparison of one year's figures with another's remains valid.) The debt incurred in the acquisition of the building transformed the financial situation. The Annual Report for 1906 included an estimate that £6,000 was needed each year to keep the institution going, of which about half was expended in mortgage interest and repayment. The first year for which the published accounts included a proper balance sheet was 1907 and this shows that the total expended on the acquisition of the site, the building work and the provision of furniture and equipment was £101,216, (the equivalent, in modern money, of nearly four million pounds) and that the outstanding debt at the end of the year was £47,694. Interest on this debt was running at some £1,600 a year and annual repayments came to about £1,250; against this, rents from the shops incorporated in the ground floor of the building together with the contribution of 20 per cent of students' fees from the School provided a little over £2,000.

That the Managing Committee and officers of the Hospital were oppressed by this burden of debt is obvious from repeated reference to it in

Annual Reports, of which that of 1903 is typical, with its slightly wistful hope that somewhere there might be a charitable plutocrat prepared to wipe it out:

> The Committee are again thankful to be able to record that the half-yearly instalments of Mortgage, Principal and Interest, have been paid, but the responsibility of these payments for 30 years still weighs very heavily upon the Committee, and it appeals to its supporters for their continued help to meet it. The Committee ventured to appeal to those interested in the Hospital, and to the generous public, for the funds to discharge this financial liability, which would relieve the Committee of Management of much anxiety, and enable the charity to extend its usefulness.

There was criticism of the decisions which had brought this situation about, it seems clear, and at the Annual Meeting of Governors on 11th March 1909 Morton Smale from the chair set out to answer it. Unusually, his speech was reproduced in full in the bound Annual Report, no doubt to ensure that every Governor had a chance to read it. Morton Smale started by congratulating the Governors on their possession of a freehold site in the centre of London, easily accessible from every part of the city and its suburbs, occupied by a hygienic and sanitary hospital so well constructed that it would last for many years without serious dilapidations. He did not deny that it had been costly, both in money and in time and anxiety; but, he said 'it is not possible to purchase a Stradivarius violin or a Velasquez's Venus, or an American Liner, unless a large sum be paid for it, and as a 'strad' is to violins and the Liner to a penny steamboat so is our site to others that could have been obtained'. He pointed out that the sanction of the Charity Commission was a guarantee that there had been no extravagance, and that the support of the King's Hospital Fund and the Hospital Sunday and Hospital Saturday Funds, all bodies which investigated their beneficiaries carefully, was an added assurance – and the fact that the Prudential Insurance Company had granted a mortgage loan on the property showed that the underlying finance was sound.

> 'It is financially sound enough' he said 'but let us see what being so means. It means too few paid officials, one person doing two persons work, too little painting and decorating; it has had neither since it was built in 1900 and you all know what that means in smoky London.
>
> A second Anaesthetic Room only partially worked because we cannot afford a House Surgeon and a Nurse. No lift for either patients or staff, although the building has five stories.'

He returned to the theme of the hoped-for plutocrat, who could solve their problems at a stroke, but this time there was a hint of rancour – 'All these economies and many others could be dispensed with if some of those worth too much wealth would pay our debt and set the charity free to develop its full possibilities'.

Morton Smale's comments on the drawbacks of the 'old' Leicester Square building have already been quoted (p. 42 above). In his speech he goes on to sum up the work and aims of the institution after the first half-century of its life. His words make interesting reading, and the speech is reproduced in full as Appendix 3.

It seems evident that the burden of debt, which was not to be removed until 1930, and which in the earlier years was absorbing about half the institution's hard-won income, was a serious impediment to the development of the Hospital. Radiology is first mentioned in 1903, when arrangements existed for 'skiagrams' to be made at the Middlesex Hospital. In October 1907 a sub-committee appointed to study the subject of radiographs for patients reported that the system of sending patients to an outside institution was 'extremely unsatisfactory' and strongly recommended the establishment of an X-ray Department in the Hospital building, with a dentally and medically qualified person to run it. This, they estimated, would cost £100 to set up and about £50 a year to run.

The Medical Committee recommended accordingly, but the Management Committee, while recognising fully the desirability of an X-ray Department, at first said that they could not afford to provide one. But the Medical Committee pressed the issue strongly and the Management Committee eventually agreed, using part of a legacy of £1,000 from AJ Woodhouse (who also left £1,000 to the School to endow a prize and £1,000 to the BDA Benevolent Fund) for the capital expenditure (the Medical Committee's estimate of this was optimistic – it actually cost more than £300) and complaining that the annual running costs of the new department would be a severe strain. Without the legacy the needed development might well have been further postponed, and the Minutes abound with similar examples of extreme reluctance on the part of the authorities of the Hospital to accede to any increase in expenditure. In contrast, the School was relatively affluent during the period between the turn of the century and the First World War and there are several examples of the Medical Committee agreeing to expenditure from School funds on things which, they felt, should properly be paid for by the Hospital, in order to relieve the financial pressure on the latter.

Pathology came upon the scene at about the same time as Radiology, a Clinical Pathologist and Demonstrator in Bacteriology being appointed to the staff in 1907. The Pathologist attended for a few hours each week only, so that the amount of clinical work carried out must have been limited. As Demonstrator, interestingly, his duties included those of assisting 'any student (past or present) who, for the time being, may be carrying out laboratory work'; was this, one asks, a way of surreptitiously providing a rudimentary bacteriological service for practitioners who had trained at the Hospital? In 1908 the School started instructing students in the administration of anaesthetics, which was included in the LDS syllabus from 1909. A Lecturer in the subject was appointed and 'having satisfied the Lecturer of his knowledge and not before – each student was required to assist or be present at the administration of at least forty cases of nitrous oxide anaesthesia, under the instruction of the Honorary Anaesthetists'. In 1911 the School started teaching Chemistry and Physics and was recognised for the purpose by the College of Surgeons.

In spite of these innovations it is difficult to avoid the conclusion that after the turn of the century the institution as a whole was less forward-looking and innovative than it had been. Several examples come to mind. In 1905 the Medical Committee debated the advisability or otherwise of employing Lady Anaesthetists and decided solemnly that 'it is not desirable that a lady should hold the appointment of House Anaesthetist.' In 1906 the British Medical Association wrote to the governing bodies of all the medical charities with proposals for reforming the administration and management of hospitals in order to eliminate 'the widespread abuses which are generally admitted to exist'; their concern was the perennial one of patients who could afford to pay getting free treatment, which took the bread out of the mouths of the members of the Association, but they made the valid point that the practice reduced the resources available for treating the genuinely needy. Their proposals included the sensible one that almoners should be appointed to assess the eligibility of patients for charitable treatment, and they advocated co-operation between hospitals and the co-ordination of their work. The Medical Committee sent a detailed report upon these suggestions to the Committee of Management; and the minutes of the latter report that although the Committee had no time to consider the matter in detail, they asked their Chairman to attend the conference which the BMA was holding to discuss their proposals. Whether or not he attended is not clear; certainly the records contain no further reference to the subject.

The third example occurred in 1910. The London County Council, anxious to start a school dental service, having found that it was not possible for it to be provided on the premises of the Hospital, suggested an arrangement for establishing a clinic in premises provided by the Council, in Chelsea. The Council proposed to provide the necessary equipment and to pay the salaries of the dentists providing the service but asked the Hospital 'to control the surgery as part of the hospital organisation'. In return, they offered a fee for each case referred to the clinic by the Council. On the face of it, a generous offer and one giving the institution the opportunity of participating in the beginnings of public health dentistry. The Committee of Management expressed approval in principle and asked the Medical Committee what they thought of the idea. The answer was 'That the Medical Committee considers inadvisable the principles of the suggestions embodied in the Scheme'. That resolution was moved by Norman Bennett who was at that time Secretary of the British Dental Association and it has to be considered whether one of the principles with which he was concerned was that children who needed dental treatment should be taken to a dental practitioner and paid for by their parents, and not get free treatment in a school clinic. (A letter from the Metropolitan Branch of the BMA referred to the 'socialist' proposals of the LCC). The dichotomy on this subject between the two Committees persisted, however; at the Annual Meeting in March 1911 the Chairman spoke eloquently of the awakening interest in the dental health of schoolchildren and the establishment of school dental clinics, the results of which, he said, were marvellous.

Finally, there was the question of women students. At the Annual Dinner in September 1900 the Chairman, Mr FA Bevan, speaking of the opening of the new building, expressed the hope that 'possibly in the future a small corner might be found for lady students', adding ' – a very small corner indeed!' The matter does not seem to have recurred until October 1912, when the Dean (Dolamore) and Mr Gabell gave notice that at the next meeting of the Medical Committee they would put the motion 'That ladies shall be eligible as students and pupils at the Royal Dental Hospital of London.' The proposal was discussed at length on 28th November and again on 23rd January 1913 – when it was decided to defer consideration of the matter until the Report of the Royal Commission on University Education in London had been published, which rather smacks of an excuse to postpone a difficult decision. But with the outbreak of war in August 1914 the number of men coming into the School was reduced because so many of them were busy elsewhere, and views changed, particularly because of the resulting loss of income. Fees produced £3,452 in 1913/14 but only £2,217 in 1914/15, and were reduced to £898 in 1915/16. The Dean and Mr Gabell raised the matter again on 28th October 1915; and this time the Medical Committee were unanimous in recommending to the Committee of Management that ladies be admitted as students. The Report of the Medical Committee for 1917, referring to the decision and maintaining the apparent reluctance to quote actual figures, says 'A certain number have joined' and, lavish with faint praise, adds 'and as far as time has permitted they have shown themselves to be adapted to the work they have been called upon to do.'

We are now able to get a good idea of student numbers from The Students' Obligation Book, in which each student who entered the School was required to sign an undertaking to abide by its Rules, providing a continuous record from 1897 until the end of the School's life. This shows that the annual entry during the last few years in the 'old' building was around 40; it went up to fifty-odd during the early years in the new building and averaged 45 between 1900 and the outbreak of war in 1914. The effect of the War was indeed dramatic; 32 students enrolled in 1914, 17 in 1915, 9 in 1916 and in 1917, and 7 in 1918. Of the 25 who entered in 1916, 1917 and 1918, 10 were women. One of them was Doris Ada Grose, who in 1919 became the first woman to qualify at the School, gaining the Alfred Woodhouse Scholarship and the Robert Woodhouse Prize en route and who was also one of the the first two women House Surgeons. In view of the falling student numbers it is not surprising that in May 1916 the Students's Society was declared 'in abeyance'. Interestingly, wartime conditions led to the removal of the veto on lady anaesthetists in July 1916, when the Management Committee decided that ladies were now eligible for all hospital appointments. Some standards had to be maintained, however, come what might; in December 1917 the Management Committee refused a request from Mrs Sharpe, the Hospital's tenant at 35 Leicester Square, to be allowed to open her tea-rooms on Sundays.

One innovation which the Medical Committee did support was the introduction of research, in 1912, at the suggestion of JG Turner and W Warwick James; they agreed to allow the use of the Hospital's facilities in the evenings for the purpose, subject to their approval of the research subject and to due acknowledgement on publication. The historic significance of this event is enhanced by the stature of the two men who initiated it and by the names of two of the young men who were involved in their first research project – Stobie and Pitts. It is, perhaps, also worth mentioning that for the first time names have occurred in this record of people known personally, in later years, by one of the present authors.

On 15th December 1912 John Francis Pink died. This remarkable man had worked for the Dental Hospital and School for 31 years, during most of which period he had also been employed as Secretary and Librarian at Charing Cross Hospital Medical School, as well as holding the appointment of Secretary to the British Dental Association (a paid appointment, distinct from that of Honorary Secretary) for a number of years and the office of local Registrar of Births and Deaths. He managed to carry out all these duties to the entire satisfaction of the institutions concerned; their minutes abound with testimonials to his zeal, industry and tact, and expressions of gratitude for his services. What his colleagues at the Dental Hospital thought of him has been recorded here from time to time. An example of the personal feeling for him at Charing Cross Hospital Medical School occurs in 1905 when, because the Medical School was in financial difficulty, he asked them not to make the usual annual payment into his superannuation fund – but, the minutes record, a member of the School Committee who refused to have his name disclosed to Mr Pink, paid the premium himself. The Medical School's minutes show that in October 1910 Mr Pink was too ill to attend meetings and at the end of that year he resigned his post there on grounds of ill-health. He continued his work at the Dental Hospital, however – although it is clear that his wife Edith Pink, who had been appointed Lady Superintendent and Assistant Secretary in 1901, was largely doing it for him – and he died in office.

Mrs Pink continued in his post until 1918 and his daugther Florence, worked as a clerk in the Hospital until 1926. Together they spanned 45 years of the Hospital's life.

All attempts to find out something of Pink's personality have failed, but a codicil to his will gives some insight into his character. Edith was his second wife and his four children were from his first marriage. In his will he left all he possessed to Edith, with a small annuity to Florence; but, as an afterthought, he gave £25 to each of his children, to be invested in a building society, the interest to be used to buy each of them a 'new hat or bonnet' once a year in memory of their mother, his first wife.

The outbreak of World War 1 in August 1914 had an immediate effect upon the life and work of the institution. In September 1914 it was recorded that already 8 members of staff, including 3 house surgeons, 17 students and 4 pupils were absent on war service. As early as October 1914 the Management Committee debated the need to insure against the possibility of 'damage by hostile aircraft' and sought the advice of the police as to the need for 'darkening the windows and skylights' at night. Alfred Browne, one of the Hospital porters, was called up as an Army reservist and it was agreed to make up the difference between his Army pay of £1.05 per week and his Hospital pay of £1.25. By the end of 1915 fifty students had left to join the Army or the Navy and the students who remained were given permission to wear badges proclaiming that they were engaged in 'Hospital Service', in explanation of the fact that they were not, as every other right-thinking young male was supposed to be, in one of the fighting services. Mr A Fiveash, the School Porter decided to enlist at the beginning of 1915 and asked the School to consider making an allowance to his mother, to whom he gave 55p of his weekly wage of 85p, during his absence. (The Medical Committtee agreed to do this.) The Dinner and At Home were cancelled and a planned postgraduate lecture course was postponed. The departure of a large proportion of students to Flanders and France and the diminution of the flow of others to replace them, and the consquences for the finances of the School have been referred to. The five-year period of the provisional recognition of the School by the University of London expired in 1916, but the University agreed to extend it for the period of the War and one year thereafter.

The Hospital had offered its services for the dental treatment of Army recruits, and nearly 500 were dealt with in the first six weeks of the War. Former members of staff and former students had been asked to to help and the response was more than adequate, 55 people being named in the Annual Report for 1914 as participating in this work. Free treatment was also offered to Belgian refugees – the plight of 'plucky little Belgium' after the German invasion was one of the propaganda themes of the time -and two Belgian dentists were admitted to the Hospital practice without payment. The flow of military patients en route from the recruiting offices to the mincing machines of the Ypres Salient and the Somme Valley became a flood; they accounted for 7,737 attendances during 1914 and 17,510 of the 70,855 patient attendances in 1915 were by members of the Armed Forces. At first the Hospital assumed that this was an extension of their charitable work and appealed to their supporters for more money to help pay for it, but from April 1915 the War Office and the Admiralty agreed to pay for the treatment of their recruits on an item of service basis, and the Hospital received £1,737 from them in that year.

During the five years 1910 to 1914 patient attendances fluctuated little, averaging about 57,000 each year. The fact that the total varied very little from one year to another seems to indicate that this was very probably the practical capacity of the organisation; which makes the leap to 70,000 in 1915 all the more remarkable. Additional dental staff were taken on and remunerated at the rate of 50p per half-day of 3 hours; as a result,the bill for professional salaries in 1915 was three-and-a-half times those for each of the preceding five years. But, the figures for other salaries and wages indicate, no additional supporting staff was engaged, so the dentists doubtless earned their pay. It must have been very strenuous for all concerned, dealing with something approaching 250 patient attendances each working day; one imagines patients waiting for long periods in crowded waiting rooms, and the harassed and overworked staff. However, the arrangements were not to the entire satisfaction of the military authorities, although their reasons for dissatisfaction are not recorded, and on March 1917 the War Office, by agreement with the Management Committee, took possession of approximately half of the clinical accommodation. Mr EF Ackery who, as an Assistant Dental Surgeon had been supervising the clinics in which recruits were treated, was given a commission in the Royal Army Medical Corps and placed in command of what was in effect a separate military dental establishment which continued until 14th June 1919, when the premises were handed back to the Hospital authority.

The Hospital and School continued their normal work in the part of the premises which remained to them. Patient attendance numbers fell considerably during the four years of military occupation because of the restricted space. Wartime inflation hit hard, prices in 1918 being roughly twice those of 1914; but income held up, helped by revenue from the armed services, and the reduced throughput of patients made retrenchment possible. But the minutes of the years 1917 and 1918 transmit a gloomy picture of staff shortages, rising costs and, in some unexplainable but quite unmistakeable way, weariness; meetings fail to achieve quorums, proceedings are reduced to essentials and the records of them are brief and terse.

When the War ended on 11th November 1918 Leicester Square, like most of the other streets of the West End of London, was filled with rejoicing citizens. At the end of the year Mrs Pink resigned, worn out by her work, the records suggest. She was offered a choice between a pension of £100 a year for five years, or an annuity of £50 p.a. for life, and chose the former. In her place came Captain WJ Wadham, late Royal Horse Artillery, as Hospital Secretary and Miss Helen M Duncan as his Assistant.

An interesting development during the first two decades of the twentieth century was the drift of power away from the Medical Committee and towards the Management Committee. The latter, of course, had always had ultimate authority and responsibility constitutionally but during the first forty years or so of the institution's life the Medical Committee, which comprised the Honorary Staff, and the views of its members seem to have been dominant. Their precursors were, after all, the people who provided the initiative and the effort for the foundation of the institution and they provided the clinical supervision which validated the work of the Hospital and the instruction of the students. At first they were for practical purposes entirely in control of the recruitment of professional staff – including the replacement of themselves – because their recommendations were invariably approved by the Management Committee. But this changed in 1887 when a joint Election Committee was set up to consider applications for appointments, with members from both Committees. Appointments of Surgeons and Assistant Surgeons were at first held until retirement or resignation, but in 1907 the Management Committee made these posts subject to re-election after five years.

This change made significant inroads into the independence of the Honorary Staff, as the case of Norman Bennett showed. In 1912 he came up for re-election under the five year rule, being the first one to do so. When the proposal that he be re-appointed came to the Management Committee they responded that 'upon enquiry' they found 'that the length of time spent by Mr Norman Bennett has not been satisfactory and that before the re-election can be decided Mr Norman Bennett be required to promise to be punctual and to spend at least two hours at his duties on the days of his attendance.' This must have been a considerable blow to Mr Bennett's self-esteem and, it is recorded, he spoke to the Chairman of the Management Committee about it. What passed between them is *not* recorded, but it was reported to the Committee that he had said that he hoped in future to be able to attend as requested, upon which he was duly re-elected.

As the Management Committee asserted itself in its own house, other outside bodies were moving to restrict its authority. Increasingly during the early decades of the twentieth century there is evidence of efforts by a number of organisations to influence and direct the operations of hospital authorities, hitherto subject only to the ordinary law of the land and the supervision of the Charity Commissioners. Some of this effort was directed towards ensuring that patients treated at voluntary hospitals were suitable objects of charity – witness the work of the Charity Organisation Committee and the proposals of the British Medical Association already noted. As a result of these efforts the employment of hospital almoners to inquire into the ways and means of applicants for treatment was becoming general – although not at the Royal Dental Hospital, where the Management Committee imposed this task upon the professional staff, who carried it out – one wonders with what degree of zeal and efficiency – under protest.

As well, grant-giving bodies such as King Edward's Hospital Fund for

London, the Hospital Sunday Fund and the Hospital Saturday Fund began to concern themselves with the management of the institutions to which they gave money. The King's Fund in particular had considerable influence and authority. Morton Smale, it will be remembered, offered the Fund's approval of the rebuilding project as evidence of its soundness.

In 1913 there were two examples of the attempts of these bodies to influence hospitals. The Hospital Saturday Fund was (and is still) a fund to which work-people paid weekly subscriptions and from which they received financial help when they and their families needed medical treatment. When the Fund was founded in 1873, Saturday was pay day for the majority of workers, hence the Fund's title. (The Hospital Sunday Fund, an entirely separate organisation but with similar objectives, was so called because it derived its income from church collections.) The Saturday Fund contributed to a number of hospitals, including the Royal Dental Hospital, and its Chairman wrote to them all in May 1913 asking that patients sent to a hospital receiving support from the Fund should be exempted from the almoner's enquiries and medically treated as necessary without such investigation. The authorities of the Dental Hospital refused to accept any interference with their right of enquiry nor would they agree to give patients recommended by the Fund any preference over the generality of patients. In this case the majority of hospitals seem to have taken a similar view – which their status as charities probably obliged them to do – and the Fund had to withdraw its proposals.

The King's Fund had very early in the century successfully enforced a uniform accounting system in the hospitals it supported and its representatives had inspected the Royal Dental Hospital regularly for many years, without recorded comment other than general approval. But in 1913 we find them commenting adversely on the arrangements for monitoring the attendance and punctuality of staff and recommending that the Management Committee call for reports monthly instead of quarterly. Later, they commented on the inadequate fire precautions in the building, and asked the Management Committee to review them. In 1914 the Fund set up a committee to enquire into superannuation arrangements for the hospital officers – a move which was welcomed by the Management Committee of the Royal Dental Hospital – and, most significantly, in 1916, when wartime pressures had brought the King's, Saturday and Sunday Funds together under the title of The Three Funds, they felt powerful enough to insist that hospitals receiving support from the Funds should not undertake any work of reconstruction or extension of premises without consulting the Funds.

6

'We never closed'

After the War and the rejoicing, the country started to count the cost. In their report for 1918 the Medical Committee recorded that 57 students and 216 former students had served with the Armed Forces, 28 of whom had been killed – roughly one in ten. Since it can be assumed that a proportion of those who served did so in the comparatively safe role of dental officer the casualty rate among those who were in the trenches and gun positions was much higher. That numbers of them were in the trenches is evidenced by the number of gallantry awards they collected – two DSOs, one DSC, eleven MCs and one MC with bar, and five mentions-in-despatches. At home, it was calculated, during the War over 350,000 operations were carried out in the Hospital in Leicester Square and in 1919 The Prince of Wales agreed to become the President of the Royal Dental Hospital of London in recognition of the institution's services. During the same year Mrs Margaret Lloyd George, wife of the Prime Minister, unveiled the Memorial to those staff, students and former students who had been killed. The list (see Appendix 2) included the Dean's only son.

Almost as soon as the war was over, during the last days of 1918 and while part of the premises were still occupied by the Army, the authorities of the Hospital and School began to think of the future and to consider how best to develop the institution. Recognising that the need to service and repay the mortgage loan was a serious restriction it was decided as a first priority to make a special public appeal for funds to repay the debt and bring the Hospital and its equipment up to date. In the field of patient care, the appointment of officers with the special task of examining new patients and directing them to the appropriate departments for treatment was considered an urgent need, together with the provision of accommodation for in-patients. Very quickly staff returned from war service and resumed their work and students re-appeared in a flood – 160 enrolled in 1919, 98 in 1920 and 101 in 1921. Patient attendances were 26,420 in 1918, 31,573 in 1919 and 35,303 in 1920. In 1921, with a large force of students at work, the number rose to 59,292.

The need for a system for the examination of new patients was met at first by the appointment of four part-time Clinical Assistants, EF Ackery, who had, as a Major in the Royal Army Medical Corps, successfully commanded the wartime military clinic in the Hospital, AT Pitts, F StJ Steadman and H Stobie, all of whom subsequently had distinguished careers with the institution. The arrangement had the obvious disadvantage of a lack of continuity and uniformity and it was superseded in 1921 by the appointment of Mr Ackery as full-time Medical Registrar.

The proposal for a special appeal for funds does not seem to be referred to again in the surviving papers of the institution, but it appears that an appeal brochure was issued. A report in the *British Dental Journal* of 1st September 1919 refers to 'a tiny brochure – literally tiny enough to slip into an ordinary note-paper envelope' entitled 'A Spot of Historic Interest'. It is, says the BDJ, 'a model of what a begging letter ought to be – ingenious, pithy, pathetic, restrained' and is 'a charming bit of true literature, at once forcible and tender.' It is a pity that no copy of this remarkable document seems to have survived – and that, as far as can be told from the accounts, its effect upon the finances of the institution was negligible.

Financial problems and especially the pressing building debt harassed the Committee. By modern standards inflation in the United Kingdom was minimal between the two Wars, but the institution had to meet increasing expenditure in order to keep abreast of developments in treatment methods and more sophisticated demands from patients. Donations and subscriptions by the public fluctuated from year to year but the amount they contributed was not much greater in 1937/38 than it was in 1919/20. Help from grant-giving bodies such as the King's Fund, went down by a third during the same period. In this situation the Management Committee decided in 1922 that all patients who received operative treatment would be charged a fee, if they could afford it – it will be recalled that fees were already charged for the provision of dentures. In coming to this decision, involving a departure from what had hitherto seemed to be an important principle, the Committee were reflecting changes in public attitudes in favour of 'cheap' public service dentistry for the less well-off, subsidised by those who could afford to pay. This departure from precedent was regularised by the revision of the Laws of the institution effected in 1924; when they were drafted in 1858, the Laws laid down that one of the 'objects' of the Hospital was 'to provide the Poorer Classes with Gratuitous Advice and Surgical Aid in Diseases and Irregularities of the Teeth.' In the 1924 version this was replaced by the sentence 'To provide advice and treatment for poor persons in connection with their teeth.' – a development which had important implications.

The decision was a wise one, and timely. As receipts from other sources diminished so the amount paid by patients increased, more than doubling from £3,130 in 1922 to £7,617 in 1938. A suggestion that an almoner be appointed was rejected, it will be remembered, in 1906, so that the task of assessing patients' ability to pay remained that of the dental staff but the importance of the task and the unsuitability of this arrangement led in

1928 to the appointment of an Enquiry Officer. She was Miss D Brown, who continued in the post until 1948, when the inauguration of the National Health Service made it redundant. By 1934 the Dental Board was making its grants to dental schools conditional upon dental treatment being under the 'supervision of an efficient almoner's department, so as to secure that such treatment, apart from that which may be necessary for the proper training of students, shall be restricted to necessitous persons'.

The mortgage loan from the Prudential Insurance Company was paid off in 1931, precisely on time. It was an occasion for relief and rejoicing, the extent of which can be estimated from Morton Smale's remarks in 1909 (p. 69 above). After more than a quarter of a century of scraping and saving, frustration, tension and anxiety, it must have felt to those responsible for the administration of the institution like coming out of a long, dark tunnel into the bright sunshine. They are to be congratulated, and honoured for their achievement. It is easy, looking back from the viewpoint of 1995, to criticize or mock some of their views and decisions – how unenlightened, how old-fashioned they were! But why would they not be? – they were people of their time, as we of ours. Like the generations which preceded them in office they displayed as a body energy, determination, integrity and devotion to their subject. It behoves the generations which have followed them to allow them and their forbears appropriate respect, gratitude and admiration. They passed on to their successors more than bricks and mortar, bank balances and equipment. They endowed the institution with a life and spirit of its own, a sense of common purpose and co-operation, of being engaged in an undertaking of significance which influenced almost every person involved with it, and which survived until the end of its existence.

With the mortgage loan paid off the question arose during 1932 and 1933 whether or not the School's contribution to the finances of the Hospital should be continued. The two sets of auditors, Duncan, Allwork and Co. for the Hospital and Hilton, Sharpe and Clarke for the School, jointly produced a report which included the following quotation from a letter from the Charity Commissioners written in 1912, a question having then arisen about the calculation of the 20 per cent of fees payable by the School to the Hospital:

> The question (as to the twenty per cent of fees) is not stated expressly in the order authorising the mortgage. The payment is, in fact, made from funds over which the Commissioners have no jurisdiction, but there can be no doubt that the payment was made with the consent of the Committee of the Medical School and that it was an indispensable condition of the necessary sanction of the mortgage.
>
> I can add that the arrangement would seem to be binding upon the Medical School unless and until the Trustees of the Hospital are satisfied

that their financial position is so strong as to justify them in releasing the School from their undertaking.

This puts the arrangement in a somewhat different light to that in which it seems to have been seen when originally entered upon (p. 55 et seq). It was not, as the Medical Committee seems to have assumed in 1897, a contribution to the costs of the mortgage loan which would cease when the loan was repaid, but a contribution in aid of the general costs of the Hospital. This was probably not good news for the School and it seems strange that this important information had not been recorded before.

The auditors' report noted that from 1897 to 1931 the School had contributed £28,696.14.2d under the agreement, but also that there had been an underpayment. Because, over the whole period, fees for the Practical Metallurgy and Chemistry and Physics courses had not been taken into account when the payment was calculated, the School owed the Hospital £1,846.15.3d. Shown the figures, the Medical Committee accepted the debt but said that its payment would cripple the School and offered a 'contribution'. The Finance Committee agreed to settle for £1,200.

As a result of this examination by the auditors, following further research and much discussion, there emerged an agreement apportioning all costs between the Hospital and the School on the basis of usage and, for building maintenance and similar costs, areas of occupation.

Another morsel of financial history emerged a little later, in 1936. In a report to the Medical Committee the Secretary-Superintendent, Mr E Moore, said that because the School's balance at the end of 1935/6 had been better than estimated, an additional sum was available for distribution by way of 'clinical units'. He gave 'a brief resume of the circumstances which governed the position of these units'.

In 1910, he said, the University Grants Committee laid down that the grant to the School was intended purely for educational purposes and in particular for clinical teaching. The Grants Committee's requirements were laid down in a letter dated 24th May 1910, which Moore quoted as follows:

Having regard to the fact that the payment of the clinical staff of a Dental School is under modern circumstances largely hypothetical the Board would require that the payment be placed on some defined basis that would not indeed require that the clinical staff should be in receipt of salaries which were equal taking one year with another, but they would require the establishment of such a scheme for payment as would determine beforehand the method under which any payment of the staff should be calculated. They would also be required to be satisfied that the salaries were reasonable in all the circumstances of the case.

It was, said Moore, in order to meet these requirements that the unit scheme was originally evolved, whereby it was agreed that out of the balance of the School at the end of any given year a sum should be provided which would be divided up into units for clinical teaching – each clinical teacher to receive one or two units according to circumstances, and the unit not to exceed £50.

There is a mystery here, because what Moore says was evolved in 1910 is not markedly different from the way in which the clinical teachers (i.e., the Honorary staff) were remunerated from the School's first foundation. It is interesting, however, that the system of sharing the surplus was officially approved in 1910; and that the concept of a clinical unit of £50 survived the creation of the National Health Service in 1948, the School continuing to pay hospital consultants one or two units each year, in recognition of their contribution to clinical teaching. Until the mid-1970s, that is, when the Comptroller and Auditor General put an end to the practice on the grounds that NHS consultants in teaching hospitals were expected to contribute to clinical teaching and that payment for this work was already included in their NHS salaries.

As has been mentioned, the provision of in-patient accommodation was seen as an important priority in 1918, and a great deal of time and energy was devoted to the problem. Following the recommendation of the sub-committee the Committee of Management acquired for £2,500 an option to build on a plot of land in Orange Street adjacent to the Hospital, which belonged to the Orange Street Congregational Church – the plot upon which the Westminster Public Reference Library now stands. Space for expansion could be provided on this plot, it was suggested, and ambitious plans were discussed for accomodation for twenty-five in-patients with twenty-four hour medical and nursing cover and a resident matron. Attempts were made to raise money for the project; the Dean, WH Dolamore, had a letter published in *The Westminster Gazette*, entitled 'The Needs of the Royal Dental Hospital.' In the letter he said that the decision to admit women students to 'a Hospital where there is already a large and increasing number of male students' imposed a strain upon resources. Special cloak and common rooms were required and space for the additional patients which the women students would treat. He appealed to 'some of those interested in the education of women' for money for the acquisition and development of the Orange Street site, a project which, he said, 'is undertaken directly for and on behalf of women'. Dolamore seems artless in his use of what his successor in office later referred to as 'a wartime expedient' as the basis for his appeal. Like the work of literature referred to earlier, the appeal had no result which can now be detected.

The estimated cost of the suggested extension brought the Building Committee to the conclusion that it would be as well to rebuild completely. A vacant site of 10,000 sq. ft. in Malet Street was suggested for this purpose and University College Hospital Medical School was asked whether dental students would be able to attend there if such a move was made. The answer was no, they would not, the somewhat curious reason being given that the Dental School was not an integral part of the University of London. It was, perhaps, rather naive to have asked – the National Dental Hospital and its School, a rival of the Royal since its foundation in 1859, had amalgamated with University College Hospital in 1914 and its Medical School, apart from having no incentive to help the Royal, probably had all the dental students it wanted. In any case, it soon emerged that the Malet Street site was not available after all.

The Orange Street plot began to be something of a burden – it was costing £500 a year in rent, and the Congregational Church was pressing for a decision about building on it; as well, the King's Fund, when consulted about the plans for the extension there, said that they were too ambitious and that the Fund would not support a scheme involving more than twelve in-patient beds. Discouraged, the Management Committee sold the Hospital's option on the plot in 1921, and turned their attention to the possibility of adding an additional storey to the existing building. Again discouragement; professional opinion was that the foundations, although adequate for the building as designed, would not support the proposed addition.

The 1920s did, however, see one successful development, which was incidentally to help the achievment of a solution to the problem of in-patient accommodation. It was in connection with the Athletic Club. Sports activity at the Royal seems to have sprouted from the formation of a Tennis Club in 1884 or 1885, followed quickly by the formation of clubs for other sports, although many of the students joined the clubs of the general hospitals which they attended. In 1886, instigated by Frank Colyer, the individual sports clubs at the Dental Hospital joined together to form a single Athletic Club. This survived, with intermittent lapses into inactivity, despite two serious disadvantages – it had no ground of its own and so was compelled to find venues for its fixtures where it could, and it was not allowed entry to the Hospital Cup Competitions. Immediately after the First World War, however, the barriers were broken down and the medical schools began to agree to meet dental students at the Royal on equal terms.

In 1923 the Amalgamated Sports Committee decided that the time had come when they needed a sports ground of their own and asked the Medical Committee for help in their efforts to raise money with which to buy one. The Medical Committee responded to this request with enthusiasm. Within a month the Dean announced that two members of the Committee of Management had offered contributions – Sir Fisher Dilkes, who was prepared to lend £1,000 on mortgage and Mr H Haynes, who said he would meet 10 per cent of the purchase price. The Students' Club was able to provide £1,000, and the Medical Committee agreed to 'invest' £1,600 from the funds of the School. Members of the Committee themselves contributed £600, and the thing was done. A suitable ground was found at Colindale, which was bought for £4,200 and vested in trustees by a deed which set out the provenance of the funds and the interests of the parties.

Meanwhile, attempts to provide in-patient accommodation at Leicester

Square having failed, attention turned to the possibility of collaboration with a general hospital. Some members of staff, particularly Mr Warwick James, enthusiastically advocated association with the Middlesex Hospital in this connection, going so far as to suggest moving to a site nearer that institution to facilitate this. There was little chance of finding the money to make this possible and it became clear that Charing Cross Hospital, situated just across the Charing Cross Road, was the obvious choice. After all, the two institutions were close enough for Francis Pink, years before, to work for both. The Chairman of the Committee of Management and the Dean wrote jointly to the Chairman of the governing body of Charing Cross Hospital on 22nd April 1926 suggesting that there might be advantages in co-operation to both parties.

The wording of their letter suggests that there had been some informal exploratory talks. It referred to the additional space available to Charing Cross Hospital following the acquisition of the premises of the Westminster Ophthalmic Hospital; it set out the Dental Hospital's need – 8 to 12 beds, under the care of their own staff, with appropriate operating facilities and access to facilities for pathological investigation and research. In return, they offered Charing Cross the expectation that 'when closer co-operation exists, more of our students will choose to do their medicine and surgery at Charing Cross'. More importantly, as it turned out – and clearly the authors of the letter had been tipped off as to what the needs of Charing Cross Hospital were – the letter said that 'in the social and athletic life of the students we may be of assistance, being the possessors of a large and well laid out Athletic Ground, and some scheme of sharing could possibly be considered'. Charing Cross Hospital Medical School had no athletic ground of its own, a grievous deficiency at a time when inter-Hospital sport was an important part of student life.

This offer seems to have been decisive. Within two months a meeting took place of representatives of the two institutions, at which the principles upon which their co-operation might proceed were agreed. The minutes of this meeting indicate that the Athletic Ground question was of paramount importance to the Charing Cross Hospital representatives. 'This question' they say 'was very thoroughly gone into, but not finally settled as it was desirous that the students should be given the opportunity of discussing the matter freely among themselves'. The students' discussions were quickly concluded and with the concurrence of the two governing bodies the United Athletic Club of the Royal Dental and Charing Cross Hospitals came into being on 1st January 1927. But the ability of Charing Cross Hospital to provide in-patient facilities for the Dental Hospital depended upon their getting possession of their additional premises and this was delayed until January 1930.

At about the same time attempts were made to start courses for dental nurses at the School. The medical inspection of schoolchildren by local authorities, which had been compulsory since 1907, had disclosed the

1. Sir John Tomes, FRS, FRCS, LDS Eng., 1815–1894, a leading Memorialist.

2. Sir Edwin Saunders, FRCS, 1814–1901, Dental Surgeon to the Royal Family, an early pioneer of organised training for dentists and a benefactor of the Hospital.

3. T. Arnold Rogers, MRCS, LDS Eng., 1825–1913, the first Dean of the Dental School, appointed in 1874.

4. Dr. Joseph Walker, MD, MRCS, LDS, 1825–1908, a controversial character who was a prime mover in the rebuilding project of 1898 to 1901.

5. 32 Soho Square, occupied by the Dental Hospital and School from 1858 to 1874.

6. 40–41 Leicester Square, site of the Dental Hospital from 1874 until 1901.

7. The treatment clinic at 40–41 Leicester Square, c. 1885.

8. The 'Tower House' adjacent to 40–41 Leicester Square, incorporated with them to extend the Hospital's premises in 1882, through the generosity of Sir Edwin Saunders.

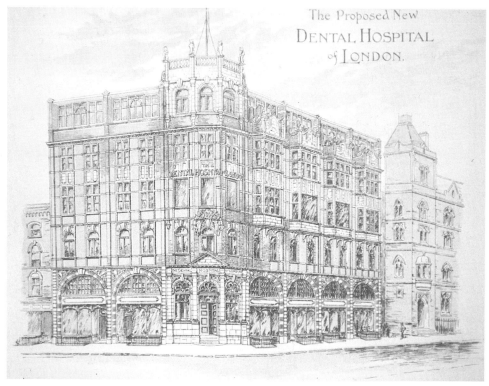

9. Artist's impression of the new premises at 32–39 Leicester Square, from the Appeal
Brochure issued in 1898 to raise funds for the Rebuilding Project.

10. The treatment clinic in the new building, c. 1901.

11. The Athletic Club's Pavilion at Colindale, acquired in 1923 and later shared with Charing Cross Hospital Medical School.

12. Professor Harry Stobie, FRCS, LRCP, FDS RCS Eng., 1882–1948 the longest serving Dean, in office from 1920 until his death in 1948.

13. Kenneth McKenzie Biggs, School Secretary from 1949 to 1972.

14. H.M. The Queen, who visited the Hospital and School on
3 June 1958, receiving a bouquet from a student, Angela Taylor.

15. The Athletic Club's pavilion at Stoke D'Abernon, built in 1968.

16. Jack Knights, Porter and Head Porter from 1924 to 1964.

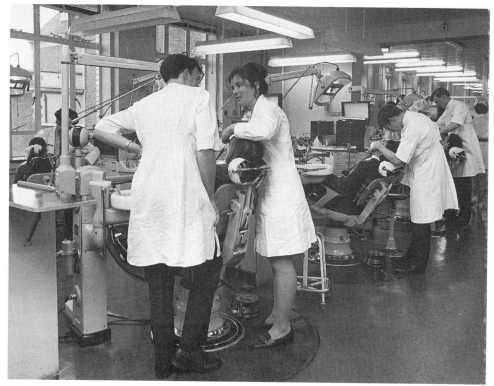

17. A treatment clinic of the 1960s.

18. Professor W.J.B. Houston BDs, PhD, FDS, D Orth, Dean from 1978 to 1985, and Dr. M.R. Gavin CBE, MA, DSc, F Inst P, FIEE, MIERE, Principal of Chelsea College and later Chairman of the School Council.

existence of a vast amount of dental disease among them. In an attempt to deal with this Medical Officers of Health set up school dental clinics and recruited dental practitioners to run them, thus establishing what became known as the public dental service. As time went on local authorities began to employ unqualified assistants to help their dental officers, under titles such as 'dental attendant' and 'dental nurse'. There was no recognised system of training or qualification for such people; in 1921, by which time their employment had become widespread, Middlesex County Council advertised for 'dental nurses to carry out treatment in connection with the dental inspection of schoolchildren' and specified only that they must have had some nursing experience.

The employment of such assistants was a matter of controversy. On one hand, the President of the BDA (Norman Bennett) said in 1920 in a Report for the Board of Education on School Dental Clinics that he had little doubt that more help could be given to the dentists and more of their time saved by specially trained assistants. On the other hand, the profession as a whole was concerned to define the role of such assistants and in the circumstances of the time their concern was understandable. Unqualified dental practice was not prohibited so that, as an article in the *British Dental Journal* suggested 'Any certified dental hygienist, dental dresser, or nurse, is but a potential unqualified practitioner let loose upon the public to complicate the issue in an already serious problem'.

The situation changed with the coming into force of the Dentists' Act in 1921, which marked a major step in the regulation of the profession, and in the drafting of which Norman Bennett had played an important role, in recognition of which he was knighted in 1930. The Act prohibited practice by people not duly registered as dental practitioners and allowed only those to be registered who were properly qualified (except that unqualified people who were *'bona fide'* in practice when the Act came into force were allowed to register, to the chagrin of the qualified members of the profession). In addition, the Act permitted registered dentists in public dental service to employ people to carry out 'minor dental work' under their personal supervision. The Minister of Health was empowered to make regulations for the training, qualification and employment of such assistants and when in due course he did so the title 'dental nurse' received formal recognition.

Official recognition or no, dental nurses were by no means universally welcomed by the profession. The possibility of training them was not considered by the Dental School until 1929 and when it was (apparently at the instigation of the Ministry of Health) there was displayed a marked lack of enthusiasm and a general sense of indecision. In July 1929 it was decided to try out a scheme for training dental nurses 'for one year only, as an experiment.' The course was to run from October to June. There were to be not more than ten students who would, it was assumed, be women.

For some reason not disclosed by the records the control of these ten young women was a matter of considerable concern – the Committee of

Management, although it approved the proposal for an experimental course, asked the Medical Committee 'to carefully consider the question of the training of students and dental nurses together and to ascertain what effect it might have on future entries of students'. The Medical Committee responded to this request by asking the Hospital and School Secretaries to report the measures they would propose 'to see that the dental nurses and the dental students are kept separate during the time they are in the Hospital'. Answer came there none; at least, none is recorded.

It seems likely that opinion in the Hospital was divided on the desirability of dental nurses and that those opposed took every opportunity to put obstacles in the way of their training. That there was still, eight years after the Act, firm opposition in the profession became clear when, in October 1929 the Ministry of Health tried to publish advertisements in the *British Dental Journal* headed 'A New Career for Women', giving details of courses for dental nurses available at dental schools, the list including the School at Leicester Square. The BDA wrote sternly to each of the schools concerned, saying that it was wrong to suggest 'that there is being introduced some new and desirable occupation in which numbers of women may obtain employment'. Such was not the case, the letter said, the employment of dental nurses being strictly limited to public clinics. Further, the letter directed the attention of the authorities of the schools concerned to the 'dangers associated with the creation of numbers of partially trained persons in connection with dental treatment'. The reasons for the strenuous opposition of the BDA were, it may be assumed, not only those given in the letter. This was 1929, when the Great Depression was beginning to bite, and retrenchment was the order of the day. Dental nurses, even with the limited scope allowed to them, would inevitably reduce the number of dentists employed in the public health service; the BDA, naturally enough, would oppose their introduction in the interests of its members.

The Medical Committee reacted firmly, however, resolving that the Dean be asked to go ahead and publicly invite applications for the course. They also asked the London County Council and the Board of Education for their views. They were assured by the latter that there would be no difficulty in finding employment for trained dental nurses, but the LCC took a different view. Inexplicably, and after a long delay, they replied that 'they regretted that they could not see their way to employ dental nurses'. Whatever the reason for this decision, this declaration by the major employing authority for the women likely to be trained at the Royal Dental Hospital was the end of plans to train them there. No course was held and nothing further was heard of dental nurses at Leicester Square until 1944.

The institution by the University of London of the M.S. Degree in Dentistry was recorded in Chapter 5 (p. 66) and the fact that no candidates for it were forthcoming. Although a number of universities did so much earlier, it was not until 1920 that the University of London decided to offer a degree of Bachelor in Dental Surgery. The School, however, showed no enthusiasm for the innovation. In this they reflected to a considerable extent the views of the dental students and their parents. Apart from the fact the the BDS course was longer and therefore more costly than that for the Diploma of the Royal College of Surgeons, a major difficulty was the standard of the University's entry requirements. Those applied by the Royal College were readily achievable by students educated at the grammar and technical schools of the period, but a degree student needed to have passed the Matriculation Examination, a much more difficult hurdle. It was not until the 1950s, after the adoption of the 'A' Level system at schools and its acceptance by the universities, that BDS candidates presented in large numbers so that eventually all dental students were expected to study for the degree.

In addition, the members of the Medical Committee were more orientated towards the Royal College of Surgeons than towards the University, and were particularly wedded to the idea that students who wanted to augment their LDS should be encouraged to aspire to a medical qualification. When, in 1930, the Royal College suggested that consideration be given to the establishment of a Higher Dental Diploma for Licentiates in Dental Surgery, opinion in the Medical Committee was evenly divided. Half of the members thought it unnecessary, the medical qualification allied with the LDS providing all that was needed. And even those who were prepared to welcome a higher diploma would do so only if 'the course of study would entail a high standard of medical and surgical principles comparable with that needed for a medical qualification.'

This aversion to the BDS qualification seems not to have been confined to the staff of the Hospital and School, but to have been general throughout the dental profession. In 1938, for example, the Dental Board made available grants to help needy dental students, but only to those studying for LDS. The University authorities tried to push the School into enrolling more degree students and in 1925 wrote to the Dean to say they 'would appreciate being told why, when the School has been admitted as a School at which courses may be pursued by Internal Students, there does not seem to have been at any time any Internal Students recognised at the School. It appears, therefore, that the question naturally arises whether the School has any claim to continue to be recognised as a School of the University'. The Medical Committee suggested that the Dean should tell the University that the requirements for BDS were so severe that no student would consider it. What the Dean actually said is not recorded, but the University seems to have taken no further action. The problem did not go away, however; in 1944 we again find the University asking the Dean why the School had so few BDS candidates and in April of that year the Medical Committee agreed 'in view of the attitude of the University and the Dental Board' that ways be examined of increasing their number. Not, it seems, to any effect, because in 1947, out of 86 students at the School, only 2 were studying for the degree.

Perhaps these were the reasons why the School delayed for so long its application for an Appointed Teacher post. The first Chair in Dentistry in Great Britain was established in 1920, at Liverpool, but it was not until 1938 that a proposal for a full-time Professor of Dental Surgery and Pathology was discussed by the Board of Management of the Royal. In due course the Board of Advisors of the University unanimously recommended the appointment of the Dean, Harry Stobie, to be effective from 1st October 1939. The Board of Management immediately concurred, arousing the ire of the Medical Committee; not that they objected to the appointment in any way at all, but they felt that they had a right to be consulted before the Board made a formal decision on such a matter, and registered the point for future reference.

For their part, the Board of Management noted a constitutional difficulty. The University had entitled the appointment 'Chair in Dental Surgery and Head of the School'. But according to the Laws of the institution the Dean was to be appointed by the Board. Although in discussion some strong views were expressed about this unconstitutional arrangement, the Minutes note mildly that the duties of Dean had become merged in the Professorship and that the Laws would have to be amended appropriately in due course. That was in 1939 and soon there were other things to worry about, and the matter dropped.

What would now be called orthodontic treatment began to be carried out in the Children's Department from the turn of the century, in the Regulation Room; the fact that such work was necessary treatment and not mainly a training exercise for students was recognised by the Committee of Management in 1905, when it was agreed that the School should no longer contribute to the salary of the Regulating Room House Surgeon. And in 1907 there first arose a question which became in later years a perennial problem, that of the storage of orthodontic models – cupboards in the Children's Department were modified for the purpose and 2,000 cardboard boxes were bought to contain the models. Although in 1905 it had been decided that it was undesirable to introduce the principle of payment in the Children's Department, in 1919 the Appliance Department reported an income of £10.85 for 'regulating appliances'.

When the school clinics were started their work brought to light a large number of cases in need of orthodontic treatment, as the British Dental Journal reported in January 1920: 'Some arrangements' the article said 'must be made whereby abnormalities in the position of teeth (of children attending school clinics) may be corrected. . . . We agree that education authorities might well arrange further treatment of difficult cases in dental hospitals.' The difficulty was that the charitable status of the dental hospitals seemed to inhibit the treatment of those children whose parents, although unable to afford the fees charged for orthodontic treatment by private practitioners, were better off than those whose children qualified as objects of charity. The writer of the article admonished those who took this view. 'These children ' he said sternly 'Should not be forced to be the recipients of charity, but equally the hospital authorities must not for pedantic reasons refuse co-operation. Those who refuse will have reason to regret it as the years go by'. This, presumably, is a reference to the increasing importance of orthodontics as a speciality within dentistry, its value to the practitioner as a source of income and the consequent demand from dental students to be taught how to do it; dental hospitals which did not develop an extensive orthodontic practice would, in the long run, fail to attract students.

The Royal Dental Hospital was not then one of those refusing co-operation, although not without much discussion of how best to co-operate. Since May 1919 children referred from the school clinics of Ealing Borough Council had been accepted for treatment for a charge of 7/6d per child, plus an annual donation of ten guineas to Hospital funds by the Borough Council. This arrangement continued until May 1924, when the Council withdrew. A month later the *British Dental Journal* reported the commencement of a postgraduate course of 6 lectures in orthodontics offered at the University of Birmingham. The dental schools could render great service in organising such courses, said the Journal, but those who want to attend them should expect to pay sufficient to reward the considerable effort needed to prepare them – 'We take it that they will not attend from altruistic motives'.

Something of the spirit behind this remark must have motivated the members of the Medical Committee when, in July 1924, they instigated a letter to the Board of Education drawing attention to the difficulty of arranging orthodontic treatment for children, which was 'not specifically excluded from the work of the School dentist but does not form a regular or usual part of it . . . due to lack of time, or the difficulty of diagnosis, treatment and the manufacture of appliances'. The letter suggested that the most valuable way in which the Hospital might help was by making arrangements for members of staff to give opinions on cases sent to them for the purpose. The Children's Sub-committee suggested in this connection, 'as the work was additional', when members of staff acted in a consultant capacity in this way a fee of half a guinea should be charged. The Sub-committee did not suggest who might pay the fee but they had very clear ideas as to who should receive it; one shilling, they said, should go to the Hospital and nine shillings and sixpence to the consultant. The Medical Committee however, declined to approve this interesting idea in its entirety, on the grounds that its adoption might imperil the honorary status of the members of staff concerned, and suggested instead that the consultant's share of the fee be paid into a Staff Benefit Fund.

Under these arrangements orthodontic cases flowed into the Hospital and something had to be done to provide treatment for them. An expedient was adopted whereby qualified practitioners attended for one or two sessions per week for three months, paying for their instruction and carrying out the treatment under the supervision of a member of the senior staff, their numbers being restricted to five per session. Despite this, by June 1925 there was a waiting list of 200 patients, a full-time technician had been taken on to meet the demand for appliances and steps were advocated to attract more 'unpaid clinical assistants', as they were called. This arrangement was rather similar to that in force during the 1960s and 70s,when practitioners were enrolled by the School as half-time postgraduate students of orthodontics and simultaneously appointed by the Hospital as half-time Registrars in Orthodontics.

At the time, however, all these activities were carried on by the School rather than the Hospital. No doubt the reason for this was that many of the patients were not strictly 'objects of charity'; although the Hospital could not in theory treat them, the School could, as part of a teaching exercise, and was able to raise funds for the work by charging fees to patients according to their means. As well, orthodontics was an important and growing component of the practices of many of the senior staff and their expertise was saleable by the School to the postgraduate students who attended, as the quotation from the British Dental Journal suggests, for the very reason that they wanted to acquire so valuable a set of skills.

On the other hand, the amount of orthodontics taught to undergraduate students up to 1927 was negligible. It was dealt with in the lectures on Dental Disease in Children, given then by Mr F St J Steadman. The Medical Committee gave attention to this deficiency in 1927, when it was decided that in addition a course of Demonstrations in Orthodontics should be given during the six weeks preceding the Final LDS Examinations. In 1930 Miss KC Smyth was appointed Demonstrator in Orthodontics, with funding from the Dental Board and this development was followed by the inauguration of a full course of lectures in Orthodontia in 1931. (It is significant that the inauguration of this post, it was resolved by the Medical Committee, was not to infringe the existing rights of members of staff to teach orthodontics and treat orthodontic cases.) Norman Bennett was the first Lecturer in Orthodontics and by the end of 1931 plans were under discussion for the establishment of a Department of Orthodontics.

During 1930, 1931 and 1932 there occurred a struggle between the Management Committee and the Medical Committee over the control of the funds of the School, in which the grant towards Miss Smyth's salary played a catalytic part and in the course of which the Medical Committee seriously considered resigning en masse. There was an intriguing precursor to it in 1926, when the Staff Dining Club was formed. The Club, which was to meet on the days of the Medical Committee's meetings in February, May and July, was intended 'to afford members of the honorary staff and lecturers together with the Medical Registrar an opportunity to meet one another in a social environment and for the informal discussion of matters relative to the current business of the Royal Dental Hospital and School'. Its Chairman was the Chairman of the Medical Committee for the time being. Minutes were kept of the proceedings at the Club's meetings, although they were often fairly perfunctory, recording only the names of those present and the menu – occasionally the jokes with which the members amused each other. But the inference must be that the members of staff concerned felt that they needed to be able to discuss institutional policy without the presence of any representative of the Committee of Management; the Club was, in fact, a caucus and its existence suggests the apprehension of conflict.

Conflict there duly was. It began innocently enough, in April 1930, with the establishment by the Management Committee of a sub-committee 'to enquire into the general administration of the School and Hospital and the duties of the secretarial staff'. The Sub-committee reported in June, raising questions about arrangements for patient treatment and supervision of students, details which hitherto had been left to the Medical Committee, together with the question whether the School should have a Secretary and Assistant Secretary of its own, and a censorious comment upon the failure of the School to report to the Management Committee the receipt of £500 from the Dental Board and the Medical Committee's proposals for its use. (The grant, £500 p.a. for five years, had been made to support the appointment of two additional demonstrators, one being Miss Smyth. The Medical Committee received it 'with gratitude' on 15th May 1930 and agreed to advertise the new posts forthwith.) These questions were accompanied by a pointed reminder that constitutionally the Management Committee was ultimately responsible for running the School, as well as the Hospital.

The Report was referred to the Medical Committee, who commented peevishly that there was nothing secret about the grant from the Dental Board, full details of which were in their Minutes, as anyone who cared to read them would know. Coincidentally, being also concerned about the administration of the School, they recommended that a Sub-Dean be appointed to ease the Dean's workload. An indication of the rising temperature is that the Management Committee's reaction to this was to resolve that the Medical Committee be *instructed* not to implement the appointment until the Administration Sub-Committee had completed its work. Normal usage was for the Management Committee to request, suggest or recommend a course of action to the Medical Committee.

In July the Sub-committee submitted another report, saying that they had studied the finances of the School over the past ten years and had formed the opinion that the financial arrangements were unsatisfactory. In their view the time had come to consider setting up a College Board to run the School, consisting of members of the Management Committee and the medical staff. The Management Committee did not adopt this recommendation, probably because the Chairman was reminded that such an arrangement was not possible under the existing constitution of the institution. That the members of the Sub-committee felt strongly that here was a wrong which had to be righted is clear – undaunted, they set about the task of designing a new Constitution and a new set of Laws, maintaining meanwhile a running fire of questions and comments upon the Medical Committee – was the latter aware that in two months time the Research Department would be bankrupt and what did they propose should be done about it? Is not the Chemistry Department redundant and should it not be closed down?

The feelings of the members of the Medical Committee when told that their financial arrangements were unsatisfactory, and their dismay at this unprecedented interference in the details of the running of the School, can be imagined. They stood their ground, responding to the Sub-committee's questions at length with reasoned proposals, but the movement for change had an impetus of its own. In April 1931 the Management Committee received the draft of new Laws prepared by the Sub-committee. Among other things the draft proposed a Finance Committee responsible for the financial affairs of both School and Hospital, a School Committee on the lines of the College Board suggested earlier, and representation of the Management Committee on the Medical Committee. The Management Committee's consideration of these proposals was quickly concluded. They approved the draft at the meeting at which they received it and agreed to forward it to a Special Court of Governors with a strong recommendation that it be adopted. They asked their Chairman to attend a special meeting of the Medical Committee to explain to its members 'those parts of the draft which affected them'. There was a strong reaction to this offensively *de haut en bas* attitude and the Management Committee eventually agreed to supply each member of the Medical Committee with a copy of the complete draft.

For several months the Medical Committee fought a desperate rearguard action. Their representatives discussed amendments to the proposals with the Sub-committee, but on the main point at issue there was no ground to be gained. In November 1931 the Administration Sub-committee reported on the negotiations, saying that control of the financial affairs of the School was a matter of principle on which they could not give way, and recommending that as discussions had reached an impasse the Management Committee should proceed with the implementation of the new Laws without further delay. In response, the Medical Committee, at a special meeting on 25th November 1931, said that if the new Laws were to be passed 'over their heads in their present or any similar form' they would be obliged to recommend to the Honorary Staff that every member should resign forthwith. The Chairman, Norman Bennett, it seems, had misgivings and consulted lawyers – the fact is referred to only obliquely by a decision that the cost of the legal opinion 'recently obtained by the Chairman' be paid by the Staff Dining Club. One can guess, however, that his question was whether the proposed changes were within the powers of the Court of Governors and that the answer was that they were, because during

December the Medical Committee agreed to re-open negotiations to try to effect a satisfactory compromise.

Perhaps the threat of action by the Medical Committee made an impression, because the new negotiations achieved some concessions for them. The proposed School Committee was dropped, and the running of the School was left in the hands of the Medical Committee, but the Committee was henceforward to include three representatives of the Board of Management, as the Committee of Management was now retitled. The Finance Committee's role *vis-a-vis* the School's finances was maintained, but it was now agreed that the Committee would consist of three members from the Board of Management and three from the Medical Committee, with the Honorary Treasurer. Attempts by the Medical Committee to increase their membership of the Board of Management were unsuccessful – it was limited to the Chairman and the Dean. On 10th March 1932 the Medical Committee hauled down the flag. They accepted the amended proposals 'with some reluctance' and said that 'they would watch the outcome with interest and some concern but with a desire to play a useful part in promoting the success of the Hospital and School.' The new Laws were formally adopted by the Court of Governors at their Annual Meeting on 31st March 1932, and peace was declared at the Annual Dinner in November of that year when the Dean, Stobie, spoke of the close co-operation *now* existing between the School and Hospital which, he said, was largely due to the work of the Honorary Treasurer, Mr Ellis Richards. One of the by-products of the administrative review which produced the new Laws was the creation of a separate administration for the School – Miss Helen M Duncan, who had been Assistant to the Hospital Secretary since 1919, was appointed as the first School Secretary on 1st April 1932.

In the same year it was decided to cease admitting women students. The decision to admit them, it will be recalled, was made in 1915. Their number was not great – 59 were enrolled between 1920 and 1933, just over 8 per cent of the total. Exactly why it was decided to stop is unclear – no minutes have been found of discussion of the subject – but it seems likely that the decision was forced upon the School by the medical schools with which it was associated for the teaching of the general medical subjects. There seems to have been concern in the medical profession that the supply of doctors was outstripping the demand; one of the reports in the *British Dental Journal* in 1925 of the proceedings of the Royal Commission on the Health Insurance Acts contains a statement by a witness that 'numbers of women rushed into it (the medical service) at a great rate and the demand was not equal to the supply'. Whatever the reasons, in April 1928 Charing Cross Hospital notified the Committee of Management that they had decided to admit no more women students. The School decided to take no action at that stage, although it was agreed to point out to prospective women dental students that arrangments for them to study the general medical subjects were a little doubtful. By 1932 they seem to have become impossible and at the Prize Distribution on 3rd October in that year the Dean referred to the decision of 1915 as 'an experiment, a war measure' and said that 'after much anxious and careful thought' it had been decided to admit no more women students after March 1933. Six years later this decision was reversed, and women students were admitted once more from 1st May 1939.

Certainly the School's decision to stop admitting women was not made because there were too many students – numbers declined drastically between the two Wars, from the post-war boom years of 1920 and 1921, when 96 and 101 were registered, to lows of 20 and 22 in 1928 and 1929; and from 1930 to 1938 the average annual entry was 27. So serious did the situation seem that in 1935 the Medical Committee unanimously recommended to the Board of Management that amalgamation with a medical school be considered. Their fear, set out in a confidential memorandum by their Chairman, AL Packham, and the Dean was that the decline in student numbers, if it continued, threatened the very existence of the institution because without sufficient students the work of the Hospital could not be carried on. The number of dental students in the country as a whole was decreasing and the provincial dental schools were attracting an increasing proportion of them – of the London Schools, only Guy's was full to capacity. In a passage which foreshadowed events of the 1980s, the memorandum said that it was arguable that five dental schools in London were too many and that, if a reduction was felt necessary, the University would sacrifice the one independent dental school rather than one attached to an influential medical school. The University was known to look upon the isolated situation of the School with disfavour – 'our grant from the University has been precarious for some time and though it has been renewed from year to year we have had an uneasy feeling that its continuance hangs on a slender thread'. If the grant was lost the School would be unable to continue.

Discussions about the possibility of amalgamation followed with each of the London medical schools which had not already a dental school of their own, but without success, although for a while it seemed that agreement might be achieved with St Bartholomew's Hospital Medical College. They would welcome the addition of a dental hospital to complete their service to the public and seemed willing and able to provide suitable accommodation and facilities. However, the King's Fund, which expected to be consulted about such proposals, urged consideration of the needs of West London; and, more importantly, it proved impossible to agree financial terms between the two institutions. In the end, every eligible medical school in London having been approached, the idea was abandoned.

The appointment of Captain WJ Wadham as Secretary at the end of the War was mentioned in Chapter 5. He was a man with theatrical connections and in 1922 was instrumental in the formation of the Royal Dental Hospital Dramatic Society, and was its first President and Chairman. He organised several concerts and performances on the West End stage which raised substantial contributions to Hospital funds. The programmes of two of the performances have survived and they testify to the strength of Wadham's stage connections.

The first performance recorded was on Sunday, 5th October 1924; 'A Grand Concert under the patronage of His Royal Highness the Prince of Wales' at the Alhambra Theatre, Leicester Square. The programme included performances by an impressive string of stars of the West End stage – Gracie Fields, Jack Buchanan, Will Fyffe, Stanley Holloway and George Robey, all of whom, the programme records, gave their services free to aid the Hospital. The programme contained a rather plaintive appeal, eloquent of the extent to which the building debt burdened the institution:-

> The Hospital owes about £20,000, and it is the earnest desire of the Board of Governors that this should be reduced. Unless money is forthcoming the work of the Hospital will have to be cut down, and this would fall very hardly upon the little children, the mothers who are expecting babies and men and women whose living depends upon their work and who cannot keep their health if their teeth are bad.
>
> The Hospital cannot in humanity send these people away whilst at the same time it cannot treat them without getting deeper and deeper into debt. An earnest appeal is therefore made for regular subscriptions to cover maintenance expenses and Donations towards wiping off the existing debt of over £20,000.

There was another similar performance, on 28th March 1928 – also a Sunday, chosen obviously because it was a day on which the performers would have no professional commitments. This was at the Victoria Palace Theatre, and those appearing included Leslie Sarony, Norman Long, and Debroy Somers and his All-British Band. The appeal this time was for money to provide a lift, as well as for help in paying off the debt.

There is anecdotal evidence that his theatrical connections and the wish to keep up with a 'fast set' of acquaintances led Captain Wadham into financial difficulties. In 1928 and 1929 he was given permission to sub-let his flat in the Hospital, an indication of his need to raise money on his own account, which an alert employer might perhaps have recognised. Indeed, the Board of Management may have been uneasy about him, because in 1932 when his appointment was changed from that of Secretary to Secretary/Superintendent he was made 'Acting' only in the new appointment, which he was to hold 'during the pleasure of the Board' – confirmation of the appointment, said the Board, would be deferred until 'he had sold his hotel in Faversham and could devote his whole time to the Hospital'. It seems that he never did this, because when in 1934 the Medical Committee asked him if he had fulfilled these conditions 'the answer was in the negative'. It signifies some concern and mistrust, perhaps, that the question was asked and the answer minuted.

If concern there was, early in 1935 it was shown to be justified. In February the auditors wrote to the Chairman of the Board of Management saying that they believed that Captain Wadham had misappropriated about £392. He was immediately suspended from duty and in due course, having admitted the offence, formally dismissed. The question of prosecution was deferred while ways of recovering the loss were examined, but in June the question was resolved. On the 20th of that month, in a brief Minute, the Board of Management noted 'with regret' the death of Captain Wadham, apparently during surgery at Charing Cross Hospital.

Meanwhile, on 11th April 1935, Mr E Moore had been appointed Secretary/Superintendent in Wadham's place, the shortlist of candidates from which he was selected including the name of Mr WJ Ickeringill. The salary for the post was not inconsiderable for the time – he started at £450 p.a. with free accommodation, and in 1936 he was put on a scale starting at £600 p.a. and rising to £750 p.a., and an extension to his accommodation was promised. In January 1938, however, financial irregularities again became apparent, and Mr Moore was suspended from duty – and forbidden to enter the Hospital premises – pending a report from the auditors. On 3rd February the Chairman of the Medical Committee reported that Mr Moore had been found in a coma, a suicide attempt being suspected, and that he was in a mental institution under observation. His defalcations, which he admitted, were found to amount to £1,498. This time the loss was recovered from the Hospital's insurers.

To have one dishonest chief administrator may be put down to bad luck but to have two in succession suggests that the system of financial control needed examination. In fact, there is evidence that it was only the vigilance of Miss Duncan, the School Secretary, which brought both these defalcations to light in the first instance. However, the Board of Management did not make the same mistake a third time. Mr Ickeringill again applied for the post, this time successfully. He was appointed on 2nd June 1938 and served the institution loyally and with honour until his retirement in 1961. He was a qualified accountant and an experienced auditor, as well as being a competent and devoted administrator. No doubt with his advice, the Board put its financial house in order. Henceforward, all cheques were to be signed by two members of the Finance Committee as well as by the Secretary/Superintendent, and the auditors were instructed to make, unannounced, a monthly check of the books and cash balances.

The development of research as an institutional rather than an individual activity was a feature of the 1920s and 30s, although discussion of the establishment of a research laboratory in memory of John Hampton Hale, Chairman of the Committee of Management from 1902 to 1911, started in 1913. A Research Fund was set up and Hale's widow gave £1,000 to buy research equipment. It is evident that there was enthusiastic interest and it was agreed to equip the laboratory for research in Bacteriology, Chemistry and Physics, Histology, Dental Mechanics and Anthropology – a mixture of subjects which reflected the interests of the members of staff active in research.

Development of the project was suspended soon after the outbreak of war in 1914, but was resumed in 1926 with the stimulus of a grant of £1,000 from the Dental Board for structural work and equipment. It had been decided that research in Bacteriology should have priority so that the John Hampton Hale Laboratory was able to provide clinical pathology for the Institution and was the progenitor of the Department of Pathology.

The Research Laboratory was very much a function of the School, administered by the Medical Committee, and as such it became involved in the constitutional struggle between the medical staff and the Committee of Management which has been described. In 1929 it was recorded that expenditure in the Laboratory exceeded income by about £468, the greater part of the deficiency being provided by Dr (later Sir) Wilfred Fish from his private research grant. In June 1936 an unsigned report to the Board of Management said that the Laboratory had an overdraft of £880 and that 'the Department had been enlarged without any examination of the likely costs and the prospective income to meet them'. Research, although desirable and advantageous, the report continued, was not 'a direction in which funds for charitable purposes can be utilised'. On this somewhat doubtful premise the anonymous writer recommended that the Hospital should divorce itself from any liability for or connection with the Research Department.

The writer of the Report went further, drawing attention to experiments upon animals in the Department. Public knowledge that operations were carried out on living animals, he said, would be prejudicial to the Hospital. So, since the experts he had consulted had said that research was not possible without such operations, the Report concluded, 'the Research Department as at present constituted should not continue to work within the present premises'.

Dr Fish needed animals for his research and the background to the Report was that a dog being exercised on the roof fell into Leicester Square and was killed. The Board of Management was alarmed by the resulting publicity and so took these comments very seriously. They agreed to allow the Laboratory to continue for a further year, as the responsibility of the School, on the understanding that Dr Fish guaranteed the School against loss, and provided that only rats or guinea pigs were used for experiments. This combination of restrictions, particularly the last, completely inhibited the work of Dr Fish who, before long, resigned his posts of Lecturer in Dental Prosthetics and Honorary Dental Surgeon and transferred his research activity to St Mary's Hospital. In the privacy of the Staff Dining Club, its minutes record, he said that the School was unlikely ever to prosper academically so long as it remained under the control of a charity administered by a committee of laymen.

His departure was followed by that of W Warwick James, for similar reasons. So were severed connections with two highly distinguished clini-icans and research workers – Dr Fish had started the first periodontal department in the country at the Royal in 1935. The John Hampton Hale Laboratory continued to function, however, under the control of the School, until its accommodation became incorporated in the Department of Prosthetic Dentistry in the post-1948 reconstruction and its functions were subsumed in those of the Department of Pathology.

The outbreak of war in September 1939 took very few people by surprise. The likelihood of war with Germany had been obvious for months, if not for years, and some preparations for it had been made. In March 1938 (roughly the time of the Czechoslovakian crisis and the Munich settlement) Westminster City Council strengthened the vaults beneath the Hospital building to provide shelter during air raids. Arrangements were made for general hospitals in London to evacuate their patients on the declaration of war to places thought less likely to be subjected to air attack, leaving their premises available to deal with the large number of casualties expected in London. It must be realised that most people, including the Government, expected massive air raids upon London and other cities to follow – or perhaps to precede – the outbreak of war. The Dental Hospital, having no in-patient facilities, was not included in these arrangements. What took place there was reported to the Medical Committee by the Dean on 23rd November 1939, some twelve weeks after the war commenced.

The Board of Management had decided early in July 1939 that in the event of war the Hospital and School should close down completely for a period of from three to six weeks while future policy was worked out. In the event, although war was declared on 3rd September 1939, it was clear to everyone during the last week of August that it was coming. In London, schoolchildren were evacuated to country areas and the dispersal of hospitals started; air-raid shelters were established in the streets and buildings were protected by sand-bags, their windows criss-crossed by adhesive paper tape to minimise danger from flying glass, street lighting was abolished and windows and doorways were 'blacked-out' at dusk. Gas masks were issued to the entire population.

The School and Hospital were closed for the Summer recess, only a skeleton staff being in attendance. They, said Professor Stobie, were busily occupied in improving the protection of the building and providing more effective shelter for its occupants. When war was declared students and staff were asked to stay at home and await further instructions (it will be appreciated that only those doing essential work were encouraged to stay in London).

All the London general hospitals (the Dean's report continued) moved forthwith into the country, those that had dental schools attached either taking them with them or closing them down, so that patients requiring special dental treatment had nowhere to go. During the first few days after 3rd September some students and members of staff who, in Stobie's words, 'turned up voluntarily' , were able to give treatment to alleviate pain to a few patients 'in the intervals of strenuously completing protective measures'. All the valuable and vulnerable equipment of the Conservation Room, Mechanical Laboratory, X-Ray Department and Electro-therapy Department was dismantled and removed to the basement, where a reinforced shelter for 150 people had been provided.

It soon became publicly known that some sort of dental treatment was available at the Dental Hospital in Leicester Square, and the numbers applying increased rapidly. On 5th September, therefore, arrangements were made for a skeleton service to provide urgent treatment. On 8th September the Prosthetics Demonstrators, the staff of the Mechanical Department and the students due to take their First Professional Examination were asked to return on the 11th, when revision classes in Dental Mechanics were started. Students due for Finals in November were recalled on 14th September, some of the conservation units being reinstated for their use, 'by which time the Hospital was assuming something of its usual activity'. 1st and 2nd Year students were recalled on 15th September, and all remaining students on 2nd October, when the School resumed was fully operational again. A normal intake of new students took place on 9th October.

In his report the Dean expressed appreciation of the work of Mr Ackery, Mr Ickeringill and Miss Duncan 'for their unflagging labour and valuable direction and attention to the many details associated with this effort to enable our Hospital and School to keep unbroken its record of succour and instruction'.

It is difficult to express adequately one's admiration for this achievement, in which Stobie, however ably supported by his colleagues, must have been the leader and the driving force. As an administrative exercise it is remarkable; the more so because it was carried out by so few people. One can imagine, perhaps, the meetings, discussions and consultations which would be required in order to do such things – or, perhaps, to fail to do them – in the modern hospital service. The task was carried out under threat of imminent attack by the German Air Force which, although it did not materialise, must have been very often in the thoughts of those concerned. And it was done, as Stobie's words make clear, in the maintenance of a tradition of service.

It was this achievement at the outbreak of the War that inspired the institution's proud boast 'We never closed!' – borrowed from a neighbouring institution, the Windmill Theatre, which also continued to provide its services throughout the War.

Other difficulties had to be overcome. Because the general hospitals had left London the courses in Anatomy and Physiology for dental students were in jeopardy – but the Royal Free Hospital came to the rescue. Although they had moved to Scotland their laboratories in London were available for use and they were able to help the Dean recruit teachers.

While all this was going on the staff and students were not, as it turned out, exposed to physical danger, but it was not long before they were. The London Blitz – the continuous air attack upon the metropolis – began in September 1940. Ickeringill reported to the Board of Management on 17th October that at 3.25 a.m. on the preceding day a land mine – a huge container of high explosive dropped by parachute, which detonated on impact – had exploded in Panton Street, severely damaging the front corner of the Hospital building. Staff and students had worked to clear away debris and a week later all essential repairs had been completed and the Hospital was providing a full service once more.

Wartime conditions created other difficulties. Air raid damage to the shops on the ground floor put some of their occupants out of business, reducing the institution's income from them. Staff shortages made the work of Hospital and School difficult and by April 1944 it had become necessary to discourage the referral of patients for consultant opinion. Patients continued to be subjected to a means test and those entitled to benefit under the National Health Insurance Scheme were sent to private dentists.

The Hospital and School *did* close (except for emergency treatment) for the official celebrations of Victory in Europe on 8th and 9th July 1945.

7

O Brave New World

A month after the end of the war in Europe the Board of Management notified the tenants of the shops attached to the institution that their rents, reduced because of wartime conditions of trade, would go up to the full peacetime rates as soon as their leases permitted. The nation elected a Labour Government committed to the establishment of a welfare state; and, soon, two atomic bombs brought the war in the Far East to an end. But peace did not bring plenty. On the contrary, the wealth of the country had been spent in sustaining its military effort for nearly five years and the nation was bankrupt. The men and women released from the Army, Navy and Air Force returned to a life of shortages and restrictions; food, clothing and furniture were rationed, and materials for rebuilding the bomb-shattered and neglected homes and factories were strictly controlled. Yet despite all, there was a general optimism, a sense of change and improvement, a belief in the future.

Planning for the new peacetime Britain had started well before the end of the War and it was more or less accepted by all political parties that among the changes needed was the establishment of a national health service, although there were differing opinions as to how such a service might operate and how it should be funded. It is typical of the time that in 1943, with total war raging throughout the world and no end to it in sight, government organisations, political parties and individuals started planning for the new better Britain which, most believed, would be created when the War was won. In that year the Royal started its own forward planning, establishing a special committee 'to consider the best scheme for the School and Hospital in the post-war period'. The chairman of the committee was Professor Stobie and the members were Messrs. Ainsworth, Greenish, Bowdler Henry and Packham.

The report of this committee, dated 30th September 1943, makes interesting reading, giving as it does a concise summary of the objectives and aspirations of the institution at the time. After rehearsing the history of its foundation by the Odontological Society the committee set out the seminal principles around which debate was to centre during the formative years immediately after the end of the war and upon which were laid the foundations for the policy of the institution during the next four decades. They were –

– that the Hospital existed to serve the School by providing 'a supply of patients for students to practice upon'
– that dentistry was a branch of general medicine, a principle to which the School 'had proclaimed its adherence by preferring to appoint to its honorary consultant staff dental surgeons fully qualified also in medicine'
– that the institution was foremost in the field of dental teaching and that this was 'in no small measure due to its isolation and autonomy. It is not conceivable that it could exercise the same freedom of thought nor expression of its views if it were incorporated in a general medical school.'

Nevertheless, association with a general medical school was necessary to preserve the link with general medicine, provide facilities for teaching the pre-clinical subjects and to give students the necessary experience in general medicine and surgery. Means needed to be found, therefore, of retaining such an association while preserving this essential autonomy.

Among many bodies set up by the government in that year to consider the requirements for a health service was the Inter-departmental Committee on Dentistry (the 'Teviot Committee'). The Teviot Committee produced an interim report in 1944, recommending inter alia that the health service should include a comprehensive dental service from its inception, with freedom for both patient and dentist to participate in the service or not at their own wish. By 1945 the Committee had turned its attention to the means of providing such a service, including those for training the men and women needed to run it, and asked individuals and institutions with experience in the field for information and advice. Accordingly, in September the Medical Committee at the Royal Dental Hospital prepared for them a statement on the resources, requirements and aims of the School.

Despite the existence of the report made two years earlier by Professor Stobie's committee (which seems to have been forgotten) the Medical Committee started from scratch, basing their submission upon a detailed questionnaire which each member was asked to complete. They too, started from basic principles, re-affirming the conviction that Dental Surgery was a branch of General Medicine. Their forbears, they said, had 'fought for this conception against considerable opposition, from men who wished to keep Dental Surgery as a profession on its own account.' However, while acknowledging that the uniquely autonomous position of the independent Dental School had advantages, the Medical Committee felt that on balance they were outweighed by the disadvantages. The report continued

The Royal Dental Hospital does not favour the establishment of a completely autonomous dental school; the dental school must be closely associated with a college of the university or a medical school providing the requisite pre-clinical teaching. In particular the student must be taught to approach the subject of dental disease with a medical outlook.

The writers of the report were careful, once again, to stress that close association in this context did not imply 'absorption or amalgamation'. They said that provision should be made for postgraduate training and for the training of dental nurses and hygienists 'should such be encouraged by official action to improve the dental health of the nation'. The Hospital would need 'stipendiary staff' to deal with 'the excess of clinical material' and full-time teachers should be appointed in Dental Surgery and Pathology, Operative Dental Surgery, Prosthetic Dentistry and Orthodontics, with a view to the establishment of Chairs in those subjects. The present building, the report continued, was out-of-date and had many disadvantages and could not accommodate the 300 students envisaged or the clinical departments required to provide modern dental treatment.

The Medical Committee approved this submission at their meeting on Thursday, 13th September 1945, and insisted it be considered by the Board of Management at their meeting on the following day, because the timetable required it to be sent to the Teviot Committee without fail by the end of that week. Anticipating that the Board might be reluctant to decide so important a matter at such short notice the Medical Committee resolved that the Teviot Committee should have their 'considered report' even if the Board did not adopt it, and they empowered their Chairman or the Dean to send it forward whatever the Board said.

At the meeting of the Board of Management on the following day the Chairman, Sir James Donald, protested that the short notice gave insufficient time for examination of the report, which he found defective in some respects. In particular, it seems, he and some other members of the Board were strongly in favour of continuing the association with Charing Cross Hospital; the Medical Committee were not, because it was known that Charing Cross Hospital proposed to move to Harrow. If the Royal were to accompany it, thought the Medical Committee, the important advantages – accessibility to patients from all over London, and proximity to the University – gained from its central position would be lost. Pressed by the Chairman of the Medical Committee, Mr BW Fickling, the Board agreed to send the report forward, with a rider to the effect that the governing body, which alone was responsible for policy decisions, 'had come to no decision which can at present be communicated'. This disclaimer did not satisfy Sir James, who, in protest at the Medical Committee's appropriation of the Board's policy-deciding function, resigned all his offices in the Hospital forthwith, as did his Vice-Chairman.

Quite apart from the constitutional issue and the irritation of a committee asked to deal with an important and lengthy document at short notice and with a pistol at its head, the submission contained much in addition to the question of location that must have seemed controversial. The view that dentistry was a branch of general medicine was by no means shared by all members of the dental profession. When, in 1945, Glasgow Dental School wanted to advertise for a Dean and Director of Dental Studies specifying 'a qualified registered dental practitioner with a medical qualification' the Editor of the British Dental Journal refused to publish the advertisement. The suggestion contained in the report that the institution was so restricted by an old-fashioned and cramped building that it was unable to provide modern dental treatment probably took the Board by surprise. As for the view that an independent dental hospital and school was not viable, there is evidence that some members at least thought otherwise. The new Chairman, Brigadier-General FG Lewis, for example, at a meeting a month later, said that his personal view of the future of the institution was as a Dental Centre, with a school for training dentists, hygienists, nurses and mechanics, under the direction of a Dean; postgraduate teaching; research under the control of a Director; clinical work under the control of a Medical Registrar, an in-patients department and consulting rooms for use of specialists; together with a large hall for meetings. This specification seems to ignore the need for facilities for pre-clinical teaching and the teaching of medicine and surgery and hindsight shows it to have been an extremely optimistic vision; it remains a praiseworthy one, nevertheless.

Brigadier-General Lewis seems to have been a forceful and sometimes controversial personality. He introduced a system of monthly inspections by members of the Board of Management and on one occasion referred at a meeting to the need for greater control of the students. The Dean, the Minutes record, 'emphatically disagreed' and said that the subject was one 'on which he did not consider the Brigadier-General competent to judge'. Brigadier-General Lewis was concerned to restrict the role of the Medical Committee, pointing out in 1947 that at no other Hospital did the Chairman of the Medical Committee as well as the Chairman of the Governing Body sign the Annual Report.

The election of a Labour Government and the promise of a comprehensive National Health Service had put the medical and dental professions in a ferment. In particular, the London teaching hospitals, so long accustomed to financial stringency, saw opportunities for the realisation of their dreams of rebuilding, modernisation and expansion. In this turmoil the Dental Hospital, as the Medical Committee had suggested, was a pigmy among contending giants. Through the United Athletic Club and the provision of in-patient faciities there was an association with Charing Cross Hospital and Medical School, But, as has been seen, the Royal Dental Hospital and School did not want to join them in the move to Harrow, saying that the public service the Dental Hospital provided made it unlikely that the authorities would support a move from its central position. In return, Charing Cross Hospital gave notice that facilities for dental in-patients would be withdrawn at the end of 1945.

The National Health Service Act became law in November 1946 and the fact that it would come into operation on 5th July 1948 was announced in June 1947. During the hiatus, while the medical and dental world awaited the advent of the Service some of the Royal Dental Hospital's links with its past slipped away. Mrs Pink, long retired, died in 1946, severing a family connection extending back some sixty years to the days of Saunders and Tomes. Professor Stobie died in 1948, having been Dean since 1920, holding the office longer than any other Dean before or since. New times and new ideas brought changes to old practices. When Sister Morgan of the Surgical Department married in 1947 the Board of Management decided it was not necessary to ask her to resign; and in January 1948 the practice of issuing tickets to governors, subscribers and donors for the treatment of patients was discontinued. But many of the old ways remained, even after five years of warfare. For example, when the Annual Dinner for members of Staff and Past and Present Students was revived in November 1946, Mr EDD Davis was invited to take the chair, on the grounds that he would have been Chairman if the function had been held in 1939; and the privilege of a reduction in tuition fees for the sons and daughters of former students was reiterated. Meanwhile, patients continued to pay for treatment; there was a registration fee of 2/6d for adults and 1/- for children. The Enquiry Officer graded them A, B or C, according to their means and they paid for their treatment accordingly. And Mr Ickeringill remained as Secretary/ Superintendent for many years, a skilful and devoted pilot into the uncharted waters of the National Health Service. But there were signs that reluctance to change with the times was hampering the work of the institution; in May 1947 Ickeringill reported that he was unable to recruit clerical staff because the salaries offered by the Hospital were too low, and working on Saturdays was unpopular, as was starting work at 8.45 in the morning.

Not everyone thought that the new world to be created by the National Health Service Act would be a brave one, or approved of the policies of the Labour Government. The Medical Committee agreed to ask Aneurin Bevan, the Labour Minister of Health, to attend the School's Prize-giving in 1946. It was usual to ask the distinguished guest on these occasions to 'preside'. Significantly, the Committee decided that Mr Bevan should be invited only 'to present the prizes'. Heaping coals of fire, the Minister said in his address that he would do all he could to further the schemes upon which the institution was working.

In 1947, perhaps to maintain balance, Sir Ernest Graham-Little, Conservative Member of Parliament for the University of London, was invited. Although most of what else the Minister said at the function in 1946 seems to have been lost, Sir Ernest's speech in 1947 was reported in full in the *British Dental Journal* and it provides an example of the extent of controversy. In what is described as a spirited address he warned that in its efforts to meet the manpower needs of the Health Act the Government might allow unqualified practice – a statement guaranteed to raise the hackles of the profession. He went on to advise prospective graduates to 'consider wherein their duty lay in relation to this great problem and to consider the advantages in those Dominions where the regulation of medical services was not contemplated'.

In fact many members of the dental profession, like many of their medical colleagues, watched the development of the new arrangements very warily. The feeling after the end of the War that radical changes were impending made them apprehensive and concerned to defend their interests as they saw them and this concern was reflected in the actions of the British Dental Association and the Dental Board. The latter, when announcing its grants to the School in 1945 introduced a new condition to the effect that as far as practicable students should not treat patients except where the treatment was a necessary or desirable part of their training. This condition, one assumes, was imposed so that the Board could avoid the accusation that it was financing competition against dentists in practice.

These feelings of concern and suspicion, fostered no doubt by statements such as those made by Sir Ernest Graham-Little, led the British Dental Association into a confrontation with the Government in which they overplayed their hand and misjudged the true feelings of their members. Their demands regarding the arrangements for dentists taking part in the health service, as an editorial in The Times pointed out, were unreasonable and the Government rightly resisted them. When, in consequence, in June 1948 the BDA advised its members not to join the general dental service, the advice was ignored by the majority.

This was a time of anxiety for the Hospital and School. It had become clear that in the new health service small teaching hospitals would be grouped with a larger one for administrative purposes and the question which group the Royal should aim to join was difficult to decide. Future location was a consideration, as has been seen; whichever general hospital was to be the partner had to be capable of providing the in-patient and operating facilities needed by the Hospital and the teaching of the pre-clinical subjects and general medicine and surgery which the School needed – and to be willing to provide them. In addition, the nature of the relationship with the larger partner was particularly important to the School. There was a fear that dental hospitals and schools which were integrated with medical institutions tended to become poor relations, receiving a less than appropriate share of resources. Hence all the references to these arrangements spoke of them as associations or alliances; it was considered important to maintain for the Royal as much independence as possible. After the divorce from Charing Cross Hospital minds turned at first to the Middlesex and University College Hospitals. When the decision to plump for St George's was made is not revealed by the records, but it seems to have been a last-minute one. In February 1948 the Minister of Health announced that the Royal would be grouped with Charing Cross

Hospital, together with the Harrow Hospital and the Wembley Hospital. In March the Board of Management asked to be transferred to the St George's Group and in May the Minister concurred.

The question was complicated by the urgent need to replace the in-patient facilities lost following the breach with Charing Cross Hospital. A number of approaches were made to other hospitals, but all failed; in desperation, in 1947, the Medical Committee turned again to Charing Cross who, with an eye perhaps to the future NHS grouping of the dental hospital, offered six beds at Mount Vernon Hospital at Northwood. This was considered too far from Leicester Square for convenience and, pressed, Charing Cross offered two more beds in the main Hospital. This was in March 1948, when the Royal was once again seeking to repudiate the association with Charing Cross Hospital and, sensibly, the Board of Management stepped in to suspend negotiations until the question of affiliation within the NHS was settled.

Before the National Health Service Act 1946 came into effect hospitals were operated and governed in a variety of ways. The vast majority were either unincorporated charities – the voluntary hospitals, like the Royal Dental Hospital of London, managed by committees representative (at least in theory) of their subscribers – or were owned and operated by local government authorities, the members of which were elected by the local voters. A small number of hospitals had been established to serve the needs of special groups, such as Freemasons, or members of a trade union. On 5th July 1948, most of this was swept away, only the latter group being left untouched. All the voluntary and local authority hospitals became part of the National Health Service, and were formed into groups for administrative purposes under Hospital Management Committees (HMCs), whose members were nominated by the Minister of Health after consultation with local representatives, including the former managing bodies. The country was divided into regions under Regional Health Boards (RHBs), with members similarly appointed, from which HMCs received their funds and to which they were accountable. RHBs received their funds from and were accountable to the Minister of Health. Hospitals designated by the Minister as teaching hospitals, of which the Royal was one, were treated differently. They were grouped under Boards of Governors, which were outside the regional system, dealing directly with the Ministry.

The ownership of the land, premises. and other property belonging to voluntary and local authority hospitals and used for hospital purposes immediately before 5th July 1948 was transferred forthwith to the Minister of Health. By this process the Royal Dental Hospital of London found itself in the hands of the Board of Governors of St George's Hospital, its property and premises transferred to the Minister of Health, and its Board of Management, Medical Committee and the very Laws and Constitution upon which its legal existence was founded, abolished.

The School, on the other hand, at the same moment found itself a free self-governing institution. The legislation had required medical and dental schools associated with the University of London to prepare in consultation with the University a scheme for constituting a new governing body for their schools, which was to be 'a body corporate, having a perpetual succession and a Common Seal'. These schemes came into operation on 5th July 1948, when the Royal Dental Hospital of London School of Dental Surgery (University of London) became, from the legal point of view, independent of the Hospital and responsible for its own management and control. The independence of the School was made manifest in 1949 when the School Council obtained a formal Grant of Arms from the College of Heralds. In contrast to the arrangements for Hospital property, property used immediately before the appointed day for purposes of the School was vested in the newly constituted Governing Body of the School.

It seems symbolic that the transformation of the School brought about by the National Health Service Act was accompanied by a complete change of command; Professor Stobie's place as Dean was filled by Mr HL Hardwick and Helen Duncan, who retired at the end of 1948, was replaced as School Secretary by Kenneth McKenzie Biggs, who had been appointed Deputy School Secretary on 1st September 1948.

The question who owned what, so far as the premises at Leicester Square were concerned, was, it turned out, one which it proved impossible to settle until 1985, when the premises came to be sold after the closure of the Hospital. There was no difficulty as far as the institutions themselves were concerned. Soon after the War, in order to allocate expenses fairly, the auditors for the Hospital and School had apportioned the premises as to three-fifths occupied by the Hospital, and two-fifths by the School. Later Ickeringill and Biggs agreed a plan of the premises showing which areas were occupied immediately before the appointed day for Hospital purposes and which for School purposes. The plan also recorded the areas – the revenue-producing shops – which were not occupied by either party, because the legislation decreed that such 'endowment' property vested in the Board of Governors. This plan, and the proportionate ownership of the premises derived from it were agreed by the Board of Governors and the School Council in due course, together with the fifty-fifty apportionment of the Endowment property and the income from it.

There was no difficulty over the latter – the simple agreement between the Board of Governors and the School was sufficient to settle the matter; for convenience the Board continued to administer the property, allocating half the income from it for the benefit of the School for the rest of the life of the institution.

But settlement of the ownership of the functional part of the premises proved to be exceedingly difficult, although it should not have been. The 1946 Act was a model of clarity and, every lawyer consulted on the subject agreed, left no doubt that the part occupied for Hospital purposes immediately before 5th July 1948 belonged to the Minister of Health while that occupied for the purposes of the School belonged to the School Council. The Minister's officials were unwilling to accept the implications of this fact particularly, one suspects, that since the Minister was not the sole owner of the building he could not dispose of it without having regard to the School's interest. There ensued a legal wrangle which, unbelievable though it may seem, lasted for thirty-seven years.

At first the Ministry suggested that they recognise the School's rights by granting a lease for ninety-nine years at a peppercorn rent. The School pointed out that its tenure of its share of the property was the equivalent of freehold. So is ours, said the Ministry, and our legal department is unable to suggest any way in which there can be two freeholders of one building. Lawyers for the School were not so inhibited, whereupon the officials turned their attention to the basis of apportionment. Was division of the property on the straightforward basis of area occupied right, they asked. Surely space on the ground floor was more valuable than space on the first floor, and so on – should there not be a weighted formula for the split?

It seemed to be the case that the Royal Dental Hospital came to attention at the Ministry at roughly five-yearly intervals – it was believed at the School that these coincided with the rotation of officials on posting, and that each new appointee found the file left by his or her predecessor, seized it with the zeal of the the newcomer, and called a meeting of the interested parties. These meetings were usually followed by a prolonged silence at the end of which would emerge, if anything did emerge, a suggestion for a more abstruse method of measurement, or a recalculation of areas or both.

A Dickensian flavour was added to the proceedings when, during the 1960s, it was realised that since no agreement on the apportionment of the property had been reached – nor, indeed, did any seem probable – no transfer of ownership under the Act had been effected and it remained vested in the Trustees of the Unincorporated Charity known as the Royal Dental Hospital of London. The last individuals to hold these offices were Lord Churston, Colonel Walter Churchill Hale and the Hon. PC Kinnaird. Everyone, themselves included, had assumed that their office and functions had been abolished by the NHS Act of 1946. Not so, agreed the lawyers, and a search was made for such of them as had survived and new trustees were appointed in the places of those who had not, to keep the trusteeship in being. These and similar operations exercised the administrators of the School and the Board of Governors from time to time throughout much of the remainder of the life of the institution.

To return to 1948, St George's Hospital welcomed the affiliation of the Royal Dental Hospital. Sir Walter Monckton, Chairman of the Board of Governers said, when he presented the prizes for the Dental School in October 1948, that he considered St George's lucky in having the Royal in its Group. The Board of Governors met for the first time on 28th June 1948. At the meeting the administrative structure for the group of hospitals was decided, and a House Committee was set up to deal with the affairs of the Royal Dental Hospital. Its members were Mr AH Clarke, a long-standing member of the former governing body who had been appointed to the Board of Governors, and Brigadier General Lewis and Dr D Greer Walker, Chairmen of the Board of Management and the Medical Committee respectively before the demise of those bodies. HJJ (Harry) Blackwood, who had been appointed Medical Registrar at the Hospital in 1948, was to attend the meetings of the House Committee.

To the consultant staff, who were responsible for providing the clinical service at the Hospital, the disappearance of the Medical Committee was a severe blow. Based upon the premise that all the honorary consultants were entitled to an equal say in the running of the institution, it had been been the mainspring of its teaching and clinical work since its foundation, and the House Committee was a totally inadequate replacement. For a brief period the School's Academic Board – of which several consultants were members by virtue of their teaching duties – attempted to exercise the functions of the defunct Committee, making recommendations to the House Committee for the appointment of house officers and registrars, but this was obviously an unsatisfactory and unconstitutional arrangement. In November 1948 the House Committee itself recommended that the Medical Committee be resuscitated 'to report to and advise the Governing Body on any matters referred to them by the Body and to make any suggestions and recommendations in the general interest of the Hospital'. The Board of Governors acquiesced, and the Medical Committee rose from the grave and once again became the the forum in which Hospital policy was decided, surviving successive National Health Service re-organisations until the Hospital was closed. Unfortunately, it seems that its minutes for the period 1948 to 1964 did not.

In their report to the Teviot Committee the Medical Committee had emphasised the inadequacy of the accommodation of the Hospital and School. The Royal was not alone in this situation. In September 1948 the President of the Odontological Section of the Royal Society of Medicine said 'If we are to be frank about the facilities provided for the clinical instruction of dental students in this country we must admit that they are second-rate and it is a depressing experience to travel round our dental schools'. The School at Leicester Square, justified though the Medical Committee's criticisms may have been, was probably better off than its sister dental schools in London. The latter were without exception appendages of large and influential medical schools and their circumstances justified the belief at the Royal that dental schools so situated inevitably came to be treated as poor relations. During the 1950s this fact was recognised by the University Grants Committee who started to include in their allocations of funds to medical schools with dental components sums 'earmarked for dentistry' to ensure that dental education really did benefit from them.

St George's Hospital and Medical School had agreed before the War that they needed to rebuild their premises and had planned to do so on the Hyde Park Corner site; after the War, prompted by the Ministry of Health, they transferred their attention to the Springfield site at Tooting. The Board of Governors set up a New Hospital Committee to deal with 'the planning and construction of the new St George's Hospital and the Medical and Dental Schools. Its membership included two people nominated by the Council of the Royal Dental School, but the Dental Hospital as such was not represented.

The New Hospital Committee, under the chairmanship of Sir Malcolm Trustram Eve, set to work with enthusiasm and optimism. The Minister of Health, Aneurin Bevan, who visited the proposed site in 1948, also examined the site of the Fountain and Grove Hospitals and in due course instructed the Board of Governors that the latter was the site to be used. Accepting this change of site with reluctance, the Board agreed to proceed with planning for an 800 bed teaching hospital there. They also agreed to include the Dental Hospital and School in their plans, but only on condition that its inclusion did not prejudice their plans for the new St George's Hospital and Medical School, saying that a new Dental School would be included ('with the small number of beds such a school requires') *if the site allowed.* They made the same point when reporting these developments to the University of London: 'I should mention that if sufficient site is made available a dental school will be included with an annual intake of up to 70–75 students'. In fact the caveat was redundant, because in September 1949 the architects reported that the site would accommodate the dental school as well as a teaching hospital of the size specified.

The project seemed to be progressing merrily; early in 1950, after a meeting with representatives of the Ministry of Health and South-West Metropolitan Regional Hospital Board the Committee approved rebuilding on the Grove site in instalments, the first to consist of 400 new beds, the Out-Patient Department, administrative and residential staff accommo- dation, the Medical School and the Dental School; the rebuilding and move of the Royal Dental Hospital, said the Committee, should be completed at one time and as soon as possible. This stage of the project, the Committee was led to believe, might well start in 1952.

The Dental School, however, did not believe that a transfer to a distant site would be as easy as the New Hospital Committee seemed to think. In April 1952, when these proceedings were reported to the Academic Board, the point was made that because it took time to build up a dental clinic with a throughput of patients sufficient for the teaching requirements of a school of the size contemplated, it would not be possible to close down the Leicester Square premises as soon as the new accommodation at Tooting became available. It would be necessary to operate on both sites, thought the members of the Academic Board, for something like ten years until the number of patients at Tooting reached the required level. At the same meeting members of the Board raised the question of the degree of autonomy to be retained by the Dental School when associated with St George's Hospital Medical School and the Board recorded the view 'that the best interests of the School and dental education would be served by the retention by the School of control over its own affairs'. In this connection the Dental School Council suggested that the two Schools should together constitute St George's College, with separate faculties of Medicine and Dentistry.

In the background to these proceedings the country was trying to deal with the economic consequences of the War, as well as those of the creation of the Welfare State. After the surrender of Japan the abrupt withdrawal of 'Lend-lease', the arrangement whereby the United States made essential supplies available without immediate payment, had been a severe blow. Resources were scarce and many commodities continued to be rationed until the middle of 1950 – sugar until 1953. The era of peace and plenty failed to materialise; the spread of Communism caused alarm, especially in America. Not only were Communist regimes established in those countries occupied by the Red Army at the end of the War, but, much nearer home, the Communist Party made tremendous electoral progress in France and Italy. The Russian government instigated the Cominform, an international Communist organisation, the United States sponsored the Atlantic Pact and urged its allies, especially the United Kingdom, to re-arm; early in 1950 the American Air Force began to establish Super-fortress bases in Great Britain and the Iron Curtain divided Europe.

On 25th June 1950 Communist troops from North Korea invaded the US-sponsored Republic of South Korea. American troops landed to support the South Koreans on 2nd July and British troops were in action there on 6th September. For the British government the over-riding consideration became the need to finance the increase in defence expenditure. In the previous year what Bevan called the 'gorged and swollen defence estimates' amounted to £740 million; on 1st August 1950 the Cabinet was asked to agree to annual expenditure of £950 million for the next three years; in November the figure was increased to £3,600 million in three years. The threat to social service expenditure was obvious and, despite Bevan's protests, it was slashed.

To a considerable extent the decision of the British Government in 1950 to increase defence expenditure hugely set in train the series of economic events which had as one of its many results the demise of the Royal 35 years later. Most commentators agree that the rush to re-arm begun in 1950 denied to Britain the opportunity to rebuild the exporting capacity upon which the country's economic well-being depended, enabling other countries – notably Germany and Japan – to take over the export markets which Britain needed. Other factors were relevant too and it may have been unlikely that Britain would have recovered from the economic effects of the Second World War in any event; after July 1950 it was certain, as subsequent events showed. The strain on the economy resulted in a continual demand for the reduction of non-defence expenditure extending over more than a generation, which resulted in 1979 in the election of a government committed to doing something positive about it. The Royal was one of the early victims of the policies of that government.

In July 1950 the New Hospital Committee asked the Minister of Health for confirmation of the start date for rebuilding at Tooting. It is not surprising, having regard to the timing of their request, that they were given what Sir Malcolm described as an indefinite and non-committal reply. The impression he received, he reported, was that the project was deferred indefinitely. Feeling that years of hard work in planning for it had been thrown away Sir Malcolm resigned in disgust and the Board of Governors asked the New Hospital Committee to suspend operations. The Dental School Council, however, took a more positive view, urging that whatever delays were imposed in the rebuilding of their parent Hospitals it was still open to the two Schools to press forward with their plans – such as the provision of facilities for pre-clinical education – which were the concern of the University authorities rather than of the Ministry of Health.

This attitude of the Dental School Council, one feels sure, stemmed from the advice of the School Secretary, McKenzie Biggs. From the very beginning of his appointment his constant concern was to advance the School as a University institution and to enable it to enhance its academic status; he advocated advance, on every front possible and with all resources available; and his motto when encountering a setback was 'When one door closes, another opens'.

With his guidance, and the co-operation of Ickeringill, the School and Hospital prepared plans for supplying the deficiencies in resources for teaching and clinical treatment. Stobie's place as Dean was taken by Lionel Hardwick, as has been noted; but his replacement as Professor of Dental Surgery proved difficult. In 1947, when he was due to retire, the only applicant for appointment to his Chair, was considered unsuitable by the University's Board of Advisors, so Stobie was asked to stay on for another year. He died before the year was up. When Biggs took office at the end of 1948 the situation of the School was serious. The failure to find a replacement for Stobie placed the only Chair in jeopardy, and facilities for research, essential if the School was to have any academic standing, were lacking. The number of students had increased and the need to update and extend the facilities for them was pressing. Numbers of staff and patients had increased in proportion, increasing the strain on what resources there were.

Biggs had joined the staff, after his release from the Army, from Senate House, where he had been aware of the difficulties which the School and Hospital faced. On appointment, it is recalled, he said that his aim was to rescue the School from these difficulties, and he set about the task in short order. In February 1949 the Academic Board approved a comprehensive plan for progress. With the concurrence of the University the vacant Chair was to be converted into a Readership in Oral Pathology; the Library was to be reconstructed, with facilities appropriate for the increasing number of BDS candidates; common room accommodation for students was to be improved, and clinical services for radiology, prosthetic dentistry and pathology augmented. Most importantly, the search for additional accommodation outside the existing premises was to be intensified.

It is fascinating to read the minutes and papers of the period and to watch the steady implementation of this plan. It could not have been done without the co-operation of the Board of Governors of St George's Hospital, because much of it involved the provision or extension of clinical facilities, for which the Board and the Ministry of Health were responsible. The Medical School, too, took part in this collaboration, agreeing that their Professor of Pathology, TC Crawford, be appointed Director of the Dental School's Department of Pathology in order to facilitate the appointment of a Reader there. Dr RB Lucas took up the Readership in January 1950, the word 'Oral' being omitted from its title at Professor Crawford's suggestion. The new department of Pathology headed by Professor Lucas assumed responsibility for the teaching of general pathology and bacteriology; and the research activity of the John Hampton Hale Laboratory, which had been in abeyance since the beginning of the War, was renewed. Soon after the University agreed to the establishment of a Readership in Orthodontics, to which Miss KM Smyth was appointed in October 1951.

The Board of Governors and the School Council used their funds and those they were able to get from the Ministry of Health and the University Grants Committee respectively, and their resources of administrative and technical skill in collaboration to maximum effect to the benefit of the institution as a whole. The need was modernisation and expansion, the difficulty was the constraint imposed by a building which was now too small for all it should contain. But despite this, the late-Victorian architects who designed it had conferred upon its occupants an inestimable advantage; it was in fact a shell, the external walls and those of the inner light well supporting the entire load, so that the internal arrangements could be altered and re-altered as circumstances required. As indeed they were, throughout the last four decades of its life as a Dental Hospital and in its metamorphosis into an hotel.

By April 1952 accommodation had been created for the new Department of Pathology on the second floor, together with the Photographic Department and a Seminar Room, and much needed storage space had been provided in the basement. By the end of 1954 the Refectory and Staff Dining Room had been installed on the first floor and a Common Room for women students provided on the ground floor in shop accommodation belonging to the Endowment Fund. Other improvements had to await the acquisition of new space, but in the meantime the Board of Governors was able to salve from the wreck of the major rebuilding project at Tooting a most important development for the Dental Hospital.

The Board of Governors carried on the tradition of monthly members' visits revived after the War by Brigadier-General Lewis and in March 1949 the Visitors to the Royal Dental Hospital reported that it was impossible for the Hospital to function properly without in-patient facilities. The Board had included provision for dental beds in their rebuilding plans but, as has been noted, these plans collapsed in the 1950 public expenditure cuts. As an alternative, at the suggestion of the Ministry, proposals were agreed for the refurbishment of buildings on the Tooting site to provide two additional wards for St George's Hospital and 12 beds for the Dental Hospital. This plan became the victim of another round of public funding restrictions in 1951, only the dental beds surviving – probably because it was the cheapest single component which a cash-starved Ministry of Health could afford. The twelve-bed unit was opened on 15th April 1952. The Board of Governors called it the St George's Hospital RDH Unit – a cumbersome title which was soon dropped for the more felicitous and very appropriate Tomes Ward.

Thus, at last, was made good a deficiency which had been a prolific source of debate and difficulty over the lifetime of the institution. The new resource became part of the Hospital itself, administered from Leicester Square, and was used by the consultant staff with an enthusiasm which overcame its remoteness and the inconvenience of the journey to and from Tooting.

The proposal for the improvement of the School's library facilities was implemented by the establishment of the Stobie Memorial Library, funded in part by an appeal to former students in memory of the late Dean. It was opened in November 1949 by Dr Lilian Lindsay, the first woman to qualify LDS in Great Britain and an important dental personality. She enrolled at Edinburgh Dental School in 1892, having been rejected by the London dental schools – refused entry quite literally in one case, being interviewed by the Dean on the pavement outside the entrance, her presence inside the building being, apparently, quite intolerable. (The London medical and dental schools were not entirely to blame for this reluctance to admit women students – at the time the regulations of the Royal College of Surgeons of England, unlike those of its Scottish counterpart, did not permit women to enter for their examinations.) Dr Lindsay went on to become the first woman President of the British Dental Association and her name is preserved in the title of the Lindsay Society for the History of Dentistry.

During 1951 the Dental School and St George's Hospital Medical School agreed to suspend discussions about arrangements for closer association because the probability now seemed to be that they would have to remain geographically separated for some time to come. The University of London, however, anxious to relieve pressure on the pre-clinical departments of Kings College – which were attended by students from both schools, among others – continued to press the authorities for a new pre-clinical school at

Tooting. This, it was agreed, when it materialised, should be run by the Medical School in consultation with the Dental School.

The search for additional premises in the Leicester Square area bore fruit in due course. In April 1954 Mr Bowdler Henry drew the attention of the School Council to the closure of Ciro's Club, which occupied a building at the rear of the Hospital. It was agreed to try to buy the premises, which belonged then to the Crown Estate Commissioners. They were not willing to sell the freehold but offered a lease for sixty years, and the School applied to the University Grants Committee for funds to buy it. Like his predecessor, Francis Pink, sixty years earlier, Biggs found that speedy action was necessary if the premises were to be secured for the School; the need to pre-empt competitive bids for what was a prime West End site was pressing and without waiting for the UGC to make funds available the School acquired the lease in July 1955, with the aid of an interest-free loan of £20,000 generously made by the University Court. The UGC grant was not announced until the following October. At about the same time the Board of Governors acquired the freehold of 21 Irving Street, a three-storey building adjoining the main Hospital building on the east side. These acquisitions promised to make possible the much-needed expansion, but planning for their use was interrupted by an alarming onslaught upon the lifestyle of the institution as a whole and of the School in particular.

The occasion was the Quinquennial Visitation of the University Grants Committee to the School, which took place on 14th March 1956. The comments of the Visitors, after they had carried out the customary discussions with members of staff and the governing body and representatives of the students, were summarised by the School Secretary in a personal note which he submitted in due course to the School Council:

> In general the Visitors were not happy that the School was moving in the right direction. They felt that wrong decisions on policy had been and were being taken; that space was being wrongly allocated; that the attitude to work and in particular the multiplicity of class examinations was unhealthy; and that teachers who devoted their services wholly to the School should have a much larger say at the level at which policy was made. This was what made the difference between a University School and a technical institute.

Speaking to representatives of the Court and Senate of the University, the Chairman of the UGC, Sir Keith Murray, was blunt. 'Of all the Schools visited and, indeed, one might say of all the University institutions so far visited throughout the country,' he said 'The Royal Dental Hospital of London School of Dental Surgery was the least satisfactory. The School was under the control of part-time teachers and there seemed to the Committee to be little about it to suggest that one was in a university institution. It was a matter for serious consideration whether the continuance of financial support should not be conditional on a radical re-organisation, giving control to full-time teachers, abolishing the repeated class examinations and encouraging research.'

The concern of the UGC, obviously, was to ensure that proper advantage was taken of the administrative and legal separation of the Dental School from its parent hospital brought about by the National Health Service Act to enable it to become a university institution, a centre of scholarship and research, as well as a training centre. And not only the Dental School. Similar considerations applied to medical schools and dental schools up and down the country and it is difficult to avoid the conclusion that one of the reasons why the RDHLSDS was so severely censured was *pour encourager les autres*. Before 1948, as has been shown, the School was administered by the consultant staff (the part-time teachers whose influence was so strongly criticised by the UGC) in the form of the Medical Committee. Their approach to dental education and training was that it was still in a sense an apprenticeship; the teacher passed on to the pupil his practical skills and theoretical knowledge and was responsible for ensuring that before the pupil exercised them on patients he was competent to do so safely and successfully. Hence the 'multiplicity of class examinations', the majority of which were designed to establish the student's readiness to move on to the next stage of training.

This point was made by Mr AL Packham, a part-time teacher and Chairman of the School Council at the time of the Visitation, in response to Sir Keith Murray's strong condemnation of the system. Sir Keith said that they made students too examinations minded and that students subjected to them tended to cram, and to cram the wrong things, concentrating upon their lecture notes instead of broadening their reading. There were other ways, he said, of getting students to work, by seminars and tutorials and there were ways of making students develop their subjects as university students should. Be that as it may, was Packham's response – where a class examination imposed a test on a student of his fitness to proceed to treat patients it should be retained. The Visitors were critical of the School's initial plans for the use of the new space which the Ciro's Club building would provide, asking why a lecture hall with 250 places was needed. The response, on behalf of the School, that it would provide a venue for class examinations was not calculated to assuage their concern.

It is difficult to disagree with Packham and his colleagues on this issue. Sir Keith seems to ignore the point that as a university discipline Dental Surgery cannot be equated with English Literature or Greek History, because the dental student has to master difficult manual skills in addition to assimilating the academic background of his subject. These skills and the ability to apply them to patients can only be developed by practising them under the guidance of an expert. The employment of the part-time teachers – dental consultants acknowledged to be leaders of the profession – was an economical way of providing expert guidance, just as the system of class examinations was an economical way of monitoring the progress of the students. The process can now be seen as one capable of turning out numbers of competent dentists as quickly and as cheaply as possible – an objective difficult to criticise in the context of a newly-launched health service facing a huge demand for dental treatment.

Sir Keith Murray and the UGC took a conflicting and longer view. They wanted an output of dentists of an academic standard such that they were capable of developing and extending their subject throughout their professional life, educated in establishments which were centres of research, actively engaged in extending the range and scope of the subject. They accepted that this necessitated full-time staff with a good academic background as well as a sound professional experience, and a higher staff-student ratio, and that this would be more costly. To do them justice, subsequent events showed that they were prepared to provide the additional resources needed to implement this change.

The UGC realised that such a change could only be brought about if control of the School was removed from the hands of the part-time teachers. The extent of the domination of the latter was considerable – indeed, it could not be otherwise given the structure of the staff of the School at the time of the Visitation. Of seven clinical departments, five were headed by part-time teachers; the senior full-time academic staff consisted of one Professor, one Reader and five Senior Lecturers. The Chairman of the School Council was a member of the consultant staff, as were 10 of its 18 members. The Dean was a part-time consultant, and so were thirteen of the Academic Board's 17 members.

After the Visitors had departed, leaving, it can be assumed, a certain amount of consternation in their wake, the School was asked to send representatives to Senate House to discuss the outcome of their report with officials of the University. Those selected to go were the Chairman of the Council, Mr Packham, Professor RB Lucas and the Dean, Mr HL Hardwick. They were told that the School must move quickly in appointing Appointed Teachers, and that its Development Policy for the forthcoming quinquennium, which had been submitted in 1955, should be reviewed forthwith. This was quickly done, the revised statement of policy being approved by the School Council in the September following the Visitation.

A number of other changes were made rapidly. When BW Fickling resigned as Head of the Department of Periodontology in 1956, a post he had held since 1938, he was replaced by a member of the teaching staff, AB Wade. NJ Ainsworth, who had been in charge of the Department of Dental Prosthetics for a similar period was replaced by AO Chick, Professor of Dental Prosthetics, from the beginning of 1957. Similarly, JNW McCagie replaced Dr D Greer Walker as Director of the Department of Oral Surgery in the same year. So the control of the School's major teaching departments passed from the part-time consultants to the teaching staff; thus, in order to meet some of the criticisms of the UGC there occurred, quietly and amicably, a peaceful revolution. In the same vein, Professor RB Lucas replaced HL Hardwick as Dean in 1958.

The revised Statement of Development Policy for 1957/62 included a number of other proposals designed to meet the criticisms of the Visitors and its successful implementation can be judged from the achievements recorded in the preamble to the *next* Statement of Development Policy, that for the 1962/67 Quinquennium, prepared in 1960. During the Quinquennium following the Visitation of March 1956, the School had appointed five full-time teachers, one being a Reader in Oral Anatomy, and had augmented the technical and clerical support for the clinical teaching departments. During the remaining two years of the Quinquennium it was proposed, if resources permitted, to appoint a Professor of Oral Surgery, a Reader in Periodontology, and a Senior Lecturer in Dental Prosthetics, and to upgrade to Professors the existing Readers in Conservative Dentistry and Orthodontics.

The acquisition of the former Ciro's Club premises and 21 Irving Street had made possible a major replanning of the accommodation in the main Hospital building, providing another outstanding example of co-operation between the School and the Hospital and the University and the Board of Governors in the joint planning and funding of a scheme to the advantage of the institution as a whole. The lecture theatre, students' common room, library, School offices and the dental materials unit had been moved into the new premises in Orange Street, and seventeen rooms there had been equipped as laboratories for use by individual teachers. 21 Irving Street had provided a seminar room, and accommodation for the technical laboratories associated with the Department of Orthodontics.

The space in the main building freed by these decantations made possible a major replanning of the clinical departments in the Hospital building, providing for the extension of the Children's and Orthodontic Departments so that the former would become an administrative entity for the first time, new and larger accommodation for clinical records, and a staff common room. Consultants' clinics were to be moved from the Conservation Department to the second floor and the Department of Oral Surgery on the third floor was extended, as were the Radiology and Photographic Departments and the Department of Dental Prosthetics; and the Department of Conservative Dentistry was to be replanned to give more space between chairs. As a result of these alterations, which would improve facilities throughout the institution, there would be an overall gain of fourteen in the number of chairs available for treatment and clinical teaching. This, said the Statement submitted to the University and the UGC, would make it possible for forty students to qualify each year, on average. In a rather artful use of statistics the writer of the Statement compared this figure with the average of twenty-eight per year during the period 1925–1959, 'excluding the War and post-War years'. The building alterations to give effect to the replanning were carried out during 1961, funded by the Ministry of Health and the Board of Governors.

It would be a mistake, however, to assume that the School waited until it was jolted by the UGC before it began to move with the times. As early as 1955 the Dean asked HM Pickard, Reader in Conservative Dentistry and AO Mack, Assistant Director of the Department of Prosthetic Dentistry to undertake an informal review of the undergraduate curriculum. They enlisted AB Wade, Assistant Director of the Department of Periodontology and DP Walther, Reader in Orthodontics and the four presented proposals for new arrangements based primarily upon the requirements for the BDS Examination, designed so that teaching would always keep the student abreast in all his subjects instead of disposing of them in sequence. They proposed that there should be one entry of students only each year, so as to simplify teaching (there had been as many as three each year since the end of the war). They also invented the institution known as 'the clock', which governed all student activity throughout clinical training – more precisely, a system which they called Rotational Clinical Practice, by which students were divided into groups which were allocated to clinical departments in rotation so as to meet the requirements of the new teaching system.

This scheme was in being before the visit of the UGC, although it was not approved by the Academic Board until July 1956. Even then, its implementation was not possible until the completion of the re-planning exercise, because more space was needed for it. The restriction of student intake to one in each year was instituted in October 1957.

The UGC sent their Visitors to the School again in October 1960, in accordance with their five-yearly programme, and were impressed by what they found. In their formal report the Visitors said that they had been encouraged by the developments since their last visit and that the work of the School had been transformed 'partly by the good use to which they have put the Ciro's Club accommodation and partly by a complete change in the inter-relationship of the governing body, the staff and the students'. When these remarks were reported to the Academic Board members agreed 'that now that the salient points made by the UGC's Visitors in 1956 had been met and the School's facilities so vastly improved, the policy for the next Quinquennium must be to achieve in all departments the balance of teaching and research which would be expected of a university institution and reflected in the published work of its staff'.

This recovery in so short a time from a situation of potential disaster demonstrates the innate vitality of the Royal Dental Hospital and School. Its members were able to overcome the destruction of the system which had existed since the institution had been formed and to adjust immediately – the Dean's proposals for the changes needed to meet the UGC's strictures were issued within weeks of the Visitation in 1956 – to the new require-ments. Without diminishing the contribution of anyone else it would be wrong in this context not to mention that of Mckenzie Biggs, the School

Secretary. His scholarly appreciation of the situation and how to deal with it, and his experience of university administration and especially his academic approach to administration, must have been invaluable to the School in developing its policy; and without his indefatigable energy in working to implement that policy it is doubtful whether the thing could have been achieved so quickly.

The administrative burden of those five years must have been tremendous. The key to the solution was the acquisition of the Ciro's Club premises, because from that sprang the ability to take on more full-time teachers and provide them with the resources necessary to enable them to function, to improve and extend the Library so that it became an academic asset and to provide proper accommodation for the students. That in itself was a major task, involving negotiating the purchase, raising the funds, planning and allocating space and overseeing the work of building and equipping. At the same time there was the extensive committee work and lobbying in getting agreement to and implementing the necessary organisational changes – including the introduction of a new curriculum.

Taken as a whole, the operation ranks in scale and significance in the history of the institution with the the acquisition of the Leicester Square sites and the erection of the Hospital Building at the turn of the century.

While this transformation of the School into a university institution was in progress a similar change was taking place in the composition of the student body. In 1949/50 students enrolling for the BDS Course comprised 28 per cent of the total, a considerable increase over their pre-war percentage. The proportion continued to increase steadily, so that in May 1959, in a year in which the proportion of BDS students was 95 per cent, the Dean, Professor Lucas, was able to announce to the Academic Board that 'for all practical purposes it may now be said that no LDS candidates present themselves'.

These events marked for the School the final stage of the swing in orientation away from the Royal College and towards the University. A similar trend was evident in the profession as well, although not everyone approved of it. The Bill which preceded the Dentists' Act of 1955 contained a proposal, subsequently enacted, for the establishment of the General Dental Council to take over the General Medical Council's responsibilities for the regulation of dentistry in the United Kingdom, causing concern among the staff of the Hospital. So much so that during the period of consultation before the Bill became law a joint meeting of the Medical Committee and the Academic Board 'viewed with concern the implications of such a step, namely the establishment of Dental Surgery as an entity in itself and its separation from its parent, General Medicine', a change which would 'retard the advancement of knowledge and research and generally create a retrogressive atmosphere for the student and the qualified practitioner'. Significantly, when the Academic Board, the majority of whom were dentally rather than dentally and medically qualified, met on its own to decide whether or not to add its authority to this pronouncement, different views prevailed. The Board agreed, tactfully, that the matter should 'lie on the table'; in journalistic jargon, it was spiked.

Notwithstanding, the bond between the Hospital and School remained strong. In 1958 a suggestion was made that the School should apply for the title 'The Royal School of Dentistry'. The School Council was not enthusiastic, expressing grave concern that such a change 'would sever all titular connection between the School and its Associated Teaching Hospital'. In fact, when asked, the Home Secretary turned the idea down and the Council, perhaps with relief, agreed to take no further action in the matter.

Not only did the numbers of BDS students increase during this period. The numbers of women students did, too. In 1949/50 they formed 13 per cent of the entry; by 1958/59 the proportion had increased to 40 per cent. The minutes of the Academic Board record concern about this proportionate increase, without giving any reason for the concern, and asked the Dean to find out what the British Dental Association and the Dental Education Advisory Committee thought of the situation. Neither had much to offer. The Association said, in a strangely vague and unhelpful letter, that a government committee had recommended in 1955, when there were 15,895 registered practitioners of whom only 1,231 (7 per cent) were women, that the number of women dentists should be increased. This, the writer thought, was difficult to achieve because of the tendency of women dentists to become housewives and mothers and to cease practice. The DEAC thought that the increase in the number of women students was not undesirable when this wastage was taken into consideration. This seems to amount to an official view that the number of women dentists should be increased and that sufficient should be trained to achieve an increase despite wastage.

Despite these views, the Academic Board remained vaguely worried about the proportion of women students entering the School, deciding to take no further action provided that it did not increase. In fact it did not, averaging about one-third fairly consistently throughout the remaining lifetime of the School.

Unlike some medical schools the Royal did not operate a quota system restricting the number of women entrants, but whether or not the selection process was prejudicial to them seems impossible now to determine; the necessary statistics no longer exist. Certainly the system for many years contained no safeguards against prejudice, whether class, race or gender, because selection was made, subject to educational attainments, following interview by one individual, usually the Dean or the Assistant Dean.

The Centenary Year of the Hospital was celebrated in 1958. Her Majesty the Queen visited the institution on 3rd June and toured the Hospital building, being received there by the Right Honourable Viscount Ingleby, Chairman of the Board of Governors, who presented the Chairman of the School Council and Senior Surgeon of the Hospital, Mr C Bowdler Henry, the Chairman of the House Committee, Mr AH Clarke, and the Dean of the School, Mr HL Hardwick. Next, she formally opened the new extension to the School's premises – 'the former Ciro's Club', where she unveiled a commemorative tablet and received a bouquet from Miss Angela Taylor, a West Indian student. Afterwards, the Minutes of the School Council record, 'the Queen took tea with guests' in the Library.

The Centenary Year of the School, 1959, was marked by the attendance of Her Majesty the Queen Mother at the Annual Dinner for staff and former students held at the Dorchester Hotel Hotel on 8th May 1959. Dr Wilfred Fish, the controversies of the thirties set aside, proposed the toast of the Hospital and School.

Also in 1958 the National Health Service reached its tenth anniversary. Dentists who were in practice before the Second World War have spoken of the changes the Health Service made to their profession, recalling how competitive they were required to be to make a living in the 1920s and 1930s, and how meagre that living often was. FFV Manfield, writing in the *British Dental Journal,* spoke warmly of the improvements from the point of view of the general dental practitioner:

> Twenty years ago suspicion and antagonism were still widespread within our ranks and men working in the same district often neither knew each other nor wished to. The most favourable trend of the present has been the development, which started during the last war and has continued ever since, of a spirit of understanding and friendship between the individual members of our profession. It is one of the brightest auguries for the future.

Apart from this the advent of the National Health Service had an immediate effect upon the work-load of the dental profession as the pent-up demand for dental treatment made itself evident. This was especially the case in the demand for dentures. The number of dentists was insufficient to meet this demand and in 1956 the McNair Committee concluded that a register of at least 20,000 practising dentists was required. The actual figure was 15,922 (1958), the number increasing slowly each year. The Government had accepted the Committee's recommendation that the annual output of qualified dentists be increased to 800.

Reference has been made to the examination of the curriculum of the School in 1955 and the changes which resulted from it. Other changes became necessary as a result of the switch of emphasis from LDS to BDS, which was more or less accomplished by 1957. The examinations for the degree dealt with individual subjects in greater detail and placed less emphasis on the technical work related to prosthetic dentistry. The need to co-ordinate the pre-clinical and clinical courses and to ensure that the best use was made of the limited time available for the study of basic sciences led to the conclusion that the pre-clinical course should be designed specifically for dental students and under the direction of a senior teacher with dental interests and commitments. For this reason the School had by

1975 established its own Departments of Oral Anatomy, Physiology in relation to Dentistry, Biochemistry in relation to Dentistry and Physical Sciences. These new Departments provided undergraduate and postgraduate teaching and quickly established research links with almost all of the clinical departments of the School, adding considerably to its academic potential. When the Dental Pre-clinical School at Tooting opened to students in 1977 there came to an end complicated arrangements for other institutions to provide the pre-clinical course, in which the dental students were divided between St Bartholemew's Hospital Medical College, King's College, The Royal Free Hospital and University College. Latterly, of course, the teaching in these locations had been under the direction on the Dental School's own teachers of pre-clinical subjects.

The School took full advantage of the inclusion in the UGC grants for 1962/67 of funds to promote research in dentistry to appoint three lecturers with principal duties in research. Speed was necessary, because the availability of the money would result in strong competition among dental schools for people to fill such posts; the grants were announced on 17th May 1982 and by 1st October two of the new posts had been filled.

In 1962 the Ministry of Health announced that the rebuilding of St George's Hospital and its Medical School, together with the Dental Hospital and School, at Tooting would start some time during the period 1966 to 1968. There would be 850 hospital beds and provision for annual intakes of 80 medical and 70 dental students; subsequently reduced to 64, because for some reason now forgotten it was considered necessary to have numbers divisible by 8.

The question whether it was in the interests of the institution to move to Tooting with St George's was one which aroused contention throughout the period from the end of the Second World War until the irrevocable move of the Dental School's pre-clinical departments in 1976. In fact both Hospital and School were committed to the move from the outset, but there remained a powerful body of opinion within the institution which opposed it; so much so that to the Board of Governors, the University and the UGC the Royal must at times have seemed a most reluctant participant in the project, constantly looking elsewhere for a better arrangement.

One example among several of this apparently grudging acceptance followed the visit of the General Dental Council to the School in February 1961. Taking advantage of the occasion, the Dean of St Bartholemew's Medical College asked Professor Lucas 'informally' whether the Royal would consider rebuilding in conjunction with Barts, which was considering the inclusion of a dental school in its plans for the future. Professor Lucas replied to the effect that the request might be opportune because some members of the senior staff of the School and Hospital felt that the question with which hospital to associate might be re-opened, 'informal conversations' having suggested that association with St Mary's Hospital might be feasible; and, anyhow, many felt Tooting to be geographically remote.

Professor Lucas discussed these ideas with the Vice-Chancellor and Principal of the University and although the results of his discussion are not recorded it can be imagined that something was said about the inadvisability of changing horses in midstream. So, advised by the Dean, the School Council decided to stay with St George's, but not without including in their Minute recording the decision that 'doubts had been expressed as to the suitability of the geographical location of the site'.

The reasons for this reluctance – as opposed to the reasons given for it – were related to the Dental Hospital's situation in the centre of the West End of London. For the part-time senior and junior staff who had their practices to run elsewhere, Leicester Square was a convenient place to get to; the prospect of an additional three-quarters of an hour on the Northern Line to Tooting did not appeal. The argument advanced by the opponents of Tooting, however, was that patients would be equally reluctant to go there, with disastrous results for student teaching.

This issue obstinately refused to go away. When the UGC next visited the School in 1965, the School Secretary recorded them as expressing their general impression that the School was a place where the spirit was splendid and the teaching sound, and which was obviously a first-class dental school; sentiments most gratifying to those who recalled the dire Visitation of 1956. But beneath the surface was ticking away a little time bomb.

It had been planted by the representatives of the Junior Staff of the School, who had an unhappy knack of unintentionally creating rods for the backs of their seniors. Earlier, at the GDC Visitation when the question of association with Barts surfaced, the Junior Staff representatives had been briefed to tell the Visitors that the Junior Staff considered the dental training curriculum devised by the GDC to be deficient in several serious particulars. Whether they were insufficiently explicit or the Visitors unusually obtuse is not known; but the remarks were construed as an attack upon the curriculum of the School. The subsequent report by the GDC to the School Council included a remark to the effect that they were disturbed to find that the Junior Staff had little confidence in the curriculum of the School.

With the UGC, in 1965, however, there was no question of a misunderstanding. The Junior Staff said that they were worried about the move to Tooting because they were afraid that there would be insufficient patients there for the requirements of clinical teaching. The Visitors heard it, understood it, and went away and brooded on it.

It was a year before the results of this remark became manifest. The UGC referred to doubts expressed about the supply of patients at Tooting and said that officials of the Ministry of Health had similar doubts and had advanced a number of reasons why. They had, they said, analysed the details of patient attendances at Leicester Square and the places from whence they came, and concluded that of the 141,000 each year at present only 35,000 could be expected to travel to Tooting. They thought that the general dental service at Tooting was already adequate and that the planned expansion of King's College Hospital Dental School would absorb a lot of the patients who might otherwise go to Tooting. In the opinion of the Ministry, the smaller the dental hospital at Tooting the better.

At Leicester Square this was seen as potentially menacing the future of the institution. A meeting of all concerned was called to discuss the matter, and the importance which the School attached to it is indicated by the composition of its party of representatives – Lady Monckton, the Chairman of the School Council, Fickling, as senior surgeon of the Hospital, Hardwick and Lucas, the Dean and his predecessor, and Pickard, a senior teacher. Briefed by the School Secretary, they demolished most of the arguments advanced and pointed out that out-patient attendances at the Dental Unit at Tooting had increased from 7,000 in 1962 to 28,000 in 1965; availability creates demand, they said. The representatives of the UGC and the Ministry of Health said they would go away and think about the matter; perhaps, they suggested, a statistical survey of the Tooting area might be helpful.

Eight months passed. In February 1967 the UGC announced that they had dropped the idea of a statistical survey because whatever it revealed now would not be valid in the late 1970s, when the new Dental Hospital would be in being. They had reached the conclusion, with the Ministry, that 'there are over-riding advantages in continuing the association of the Royal Dental Hospital with St George's and its re-development at Tooting, where there is already a nucleus of hospital dental activity which is forming links with the local community and will provide a basis for future expansion'. An annual intake of 64 students was approved for the School when it was rebuilt at Tooting. Stewart, the Clerk of the University Court, in passing on this information, commented drily that this indicated that the arguments put by the School had in the end prevailed.

(Here, incidentally, is an example of the phenomenon of the receding building date which, like the mirage in the desert, moves away as the thirsty traveller advances towards it. It seemed to be the rule that whenever the Ministry mentioned a date for the rebuilding of the Royal the date was later than that mentioned when the subject had last been discussed.)

This diversion had repercussions elsewhere. The United Athletic Club had been dissolved in 1959, Charing Cross Hospital Medical School and its students having decided to go their own way, leaving the Athletic Ground at Colindale, which belonged to the Royal Dental Hospital Trustees, for the sole use of the dental students. In 1962, at the suggestion of the School Secretary, who was aware of the likelihood of suitable land becoming available at Stoke D'Abernon, the School Council agreed that the possibility should be explored of acquiring a larger athletic ground than the one at Colindale, which could be shared with St George's Hospital Medical School. It was three years before the site actually became available; it was adjacent to the grounds of Charing Cross, St Thomas' and Westminster Hospital Medical Schools, and the School Council agreed to try to buy thirty acres, inviting St George's Hospital Medical School to associate themselves with the project. The latter's response, however, was less than enthusiastic; to recycle a well-known saying, they offered all aid short of help. They said that although the project would seem most suitable for meeting the needs of the two institutions in the future they were not able to make any immediate contribution to it.

McKenzie Biggs was convinced that the right thing to do was to go ahead and in this he was strongly supported by Fickling, then Vice-Chairman of the School Council, who threw the weight of his authority in the institution behind the project and contributed to the detailed planning his experience of and enthusiasm for student sport and a meticulous attention to detail.

Their task was a difficult one, Biggs in particular having to carry out a complex negotiation to raise the money for the project, hampered by the lack of real help from St George's. Through the University the UGC was asked about the chances of a capital grant towards the cost. Their immediate reaction was discouraging because, they said – harking back to the unfortunate remarks made by the Junior Staff representatives at the 1965 Visitation – there was doubt whether the School would in fact move with St George's to Tooting, because of worries about the availability of patients there. Biggs, the most urbane and diplomatic of administrators, must have ground his teeth in private at this unnecessary and untimely obstacle.

It was overcome as has already been related but other obstacles remained. Fortunately, Westfield College needed an athletic ground and thought that the one at Colindate would suit and the prospect of a deal which would benefit two of their institutions simultaneously (three, if St George's be included) brought the enthusiastic help of the staff of the Court Department of the University. An interest-free loan financed the initial purchase of forty-three acres, seven of which were sold on to Charing Cross Hospital Medical School; the transfer of the ground at Colindale to Westfield College brought £45,000; and the trustees of the Centenary Fund and the Endowment Fund made generous grants. When all was bought and built, there was left £15,499 to be met by a capital grant from the University. The School Council was well aware that they were parting with the Colindale ground at less than its full value and had, in fact, applied for outline planning approval for house-building on the site in order to maximise it. But, the Deputy Clerk of the University Court pointed out, 'any action by the School to up the value of the ground will price it out of the market for Westfield College'. The School Council took Biggs' advice and agreed to accept £45,000 without further negotiation, out of loyalty to the University.

This brought its reward when the UGC questioned the plans for the pavilion to be built at Stoke D'Abernon, saying that the accommodation proposed exceeded their norms – a paradigm which soon became familiar to those engaged in trying to plan the new School and Hospital – and insisting that the changing room and social areas be reduced by nearly 30 per cent. This, Fickling pointed out to the School Council, would provide a lower standard than existed at Colindale. The UGC's need to keep down the cost of acquiring the Colindale ground for Westfield College encouraged them to see reason and a compromise was achieved enabling the School to retain the pavilion as planned on the theoretical understanding that appropriate reductions would be effected when the building was extended at some time in the future to serve St George's Hospital Medical School as well.

So was acquired the Athletic Ground and Pavilion which, under the skilled and conscientious control of Jim Coleman, the Head Groundsman appointed in 1968, became what many believed to be the finest in the University. It was sold to St George's Hospital Medical School when the Royal Dental Hospital and School closed.

8

Ambitions and Frustrations

The tale of the last fifteen years of the Royal's existence is one of hopes and disappointments, ambitious plans frustrated, disaster and demise. But before embarking upon it, note should be taken of several people who made particular contributions to the life and work of the institution but did not remain to see the events of the final decade-and-a-half.

Jack Knights, the Hospital Hall Porter, retired in 1964 after 40 years' service. For many years, including those of the German air attacks upon London, he lived on the premises with his wife, Lilian, who was House-keeper. She was, incidentally, a daughter of the Hospital Engineer appointed earlier in the century. Jack Knights died in 1969.

Miss Jan van Thal, Speech Therapist at the Royal for 40 years until her retirement in 1962, died in 1970. At the time it was made, her appointment was an innovation. An outstanding pioneer in her field, she was remembered as a kind and enthusiastic teacher, who took a great interest in the welfare and progress of the patients referred to her.

Mr WE Earle, Consultant Dental Surgeon, died suddenly on 4th August 1968. He had qualified at the School and had been a member of the staff since 1936; he had always taken a keen interest in the affairs of the Athletic Club, whose President he was at the time of his death. He was one of the kindest of men, whose consideration, gentleness and honesty of purpose was felt by all who knew him; the affection and esteem in which he was held was expressed in his nickname of Uncle Bill.

Sidney Blackman, Consultant Radiologist from 1931 to 1966, died in 1971. He qualified in medicine in 1920 and was interested in radiology in its therapeutic and diagnostic roles from the outset. He joined the staff of the Royal in 1931 and became concerned to extend the scope of dental radiology to keep pace with the expanding role of dentistry itself, especially in the fields of orthodontics and maxillo-facial surgery. He helped to found the British Society of Dental Radiology in 1958 and was its first President. He was undoubtedly helped in his work by his extensive knowledge of the workings of x-ray apparatus and of the techniques of radiography. His work on the standardisation of the lateral skull view, rotograph and pan-oral view of upper and lower teeth in particular were important contributions. He was an enthusiastic teacher and his interest in the welfare of students led him to accept responsibility, as Chairman of the Refectory Committee, for the establishment and operation of the refectory for staff and students – a bed of nails if ever there was one. Apart from this, Dr Blackman was impatient of committee work and bureaucracy and sometimes upset his colleagues by his refusal to adhere to 'the usual channels'. After his retirement from the Royal in 1966 he was appointed to the Chair of Radiology at the North Western University in Chicago, where he remained until his death.

Kenneth McKenzie Biggs, School Secretary from 1948, whose contribution to the success of the institution has been recorded, retired in 1972. He set standards of meticulous administration, service to the institution and to the individuals of which it was composed, and leadership and devotion to duty which those who came after him remembered and tried to emulate. His predecessor, Helen M Duncan, died in January 1974, aged 81. She had joined the staff of the Hospital in 1915, became Assistant Hospital Secretary in 1918 and School Secretary in 1932.

Between Nellie Duncan's retirement in 1948 and the end of the '60s the institution had changed greatly. Research activity at the Royal had proliferated, both by students and members of staff registered for higher degrees and research not necessarily related to the award of a degree. A notable addition to the institution's research facilities and potential had been the acquisition in 1963 of an electron-microscope with grants from the Wellcome Trust and the Nuffield Foundation, helped by the Royal's Centenary and Endowment Funds.

As well, the School had extended considerably its activities in clinical postgraduate education. By the beginning of the decade courses were offered leading to higher diplomas, as well as refresher courses for general practitioners under the aegis of the British Postgraduate Medical Federation. Courses for the Diploma in Orthodontics of the Royal College of Surgeons of England and MSc Degrees of the University were run in collaboration with the Institute of Dental Surgery, where the students attended for lectures, clinical and other supervision being provided at the Royal.

Through this activity the influence of the Department of Orthodontics became widespread. As the demand for these courses increased arrangements were made for some students to undertake their clinical work at centres outside London; a Study Day each week brought them together at the Royal for tutorials and discussions. At undergraduate level, the Department of Children's Dentistry arranged attachments for students for a week at a time at local authority clinics in the outskirts of London, whose practitioners were appointed Honorary Lecturers at the Royal.

The Hospital, too, led by the consultant staff through the Medical

Committee (which, after the National Health Service re-organisation of 1974 became the Dental Advisory Committee, although – *plus ça change* ... – with its vigour and authority unaltered) had progressed, both at Leicester Square and at Tooting. Patient attendances in 1972 were just under 100,000, with another 40,000 at Tooting. Training schemes were established for dental hygienists, dental surgery assistants and dental technicians, and programmes organised to enable junior clinical staff to gain experience and training in the dental specialities.

As important as the development of the Royal as a clinical and academic institution was the way it matured as a community during the 1960s. The place always had a strong corporate spirit. The people who worked and studied in the Leicester Square premises, whether they belonged to Hospital or School, formed a group small enough for each to know all; and the ambience was in general sufficiently informal for friendly relations irrespective of rank. But with the acquisition of the former Ciro's Club in 1958 there flowered a rich social life which benefitted the entire community. For the first time the students had a proper Common Room with a Bar, to which all members of staff were invited, providing a venue for informal gatherings and refreshment after work.

For a while the new premises were referred to as 'the former Ciro's Club' until the Academic Board asked how long this usage was to continue. It then became 'the School Building', or 'No. 39 Orange Street'. Students, however, invariably referred to the building, and especially their Common Room within it, as 'Ciro's'; the original coat-of-arms which had adorned Ciro's Club was installed behind the Bar.

Ciro's also provided the venue for more structured activities. The annual Inauguration and Prizegiving Ceremony took place there, with gowned staff and students, speeches by the Dean and a distinguished visitor, and Tea upstairs in the Library. Each year, too, in the week before Christmas, came the Christmas Show; this started as an event which gave students an opportunity to display musical, dramatic or comical talent, but very soon became an opportunity for satirical comment upon the beings and doings of School and Hospital. Members of staff, especially those with readily reproducible and recognisable idiosyncracies, were skilfully and mercilessly guyed, to the considerable enjoyment of all.

The new Athletic Ground and Pavilion at Stoke D'Abernon provided a further impetus to the social life of School and Hospital. It was a place of considerable beauty, with well-maintained grass beside the tree-shaded river Mole, frequented by herons and kingfishers. Apart from its obvious functions, it was used by students and staff and their families as a place for picnics in the summer; the Royal Dental Hospital Angling Society tried to catch roach and dace there; and several successful all-night dances took place.

A less successful innovation during the decade was the Department of Restorative Dentistry. During the early '60s a number of senior teachers had advocated the establishment of a combined clinic in which the work of the Departments of Conservative Dentistry, Dental Prosthetics and Periodontology could be co-ordinated, allowing students to experience work of the kind they would be likely to be doing in practice. After plans to provide accommodation for such a clinic by building on the 6th Floor had failed it was decided in 1965 to embark on the project using existing resources. Accordingly the Department of Restorative Dentistry was established, with the intention of integrating the work of the Departments of Conservative Dentistry and Dental Prosthetics, 'whose activities' said the report recommending the project to the Academic Board 'tended to be separated by tradition though not by logic'. The new Department was seen 'as an experiment in unifying two branches of dentistry which both had the objective of restoring the mouth to its proper functions, and was to be instituted on the understanding that if experience showed the traditional organisation of this work in distinct and separate departments is preferable it would be possible to revert to that arrangement without difficulty'. In any event, it was thought, valuable experience would be gained upon which to base the departmental planning for the new School at Tooting.

The idea, which to the layman (and to many clinicians) seemed self-evidently sensible, turned out to be an administrative disaster, mainly because of the incongruent personalities, ambitions and academic views of the senior teachers involved in putting it into operation. After some five years of guerilla warfare it was decided that enough was enough. In 1971, by which time the Department of Periodontology had been added to the brew, the Dean reported to the Academic Board that the senior teachers in the Department of Restorative Dentistry were 'seriously at variance over the way the Department was run'. In the light of this, the Board decided that the Department of Restorative Dentistry should be replaced 'by an association of independent Departments of Conservative Dentistry, Prosthetic Dentistry and Periodontology, co-ordinated by a Restorative Dentistry Committee'. The Committee, which was created as a gesture in the direction of the original idea, has left no record of its activities which were, in any case, minimal.

At the same time a new department was created, that of Preventive Dentistry, with which was associated the School of Dental Hygiene; a good example of the way in which Hospital and School functions meshed smoothly – the Head of the new Department, Dr (later Professor) W Sims, was a full-time member of the academic staff of the School and also Director of the Hospital's School of Dental Hygiene.

The 1960s had been a period of unrest and turmoil in university institutions, with students asserting a right to be involved in decision making and engaging in demonstrations, sit-ins and lock-outs in places up and down the country (and especially at the London School of Economics) intended to impress the fervour of their beliefs and the justice of their cause upon the public generally and the university authorities in particular.

Medical and dental students seemed to remain aloof, although there did arise at the Royal a demand for students to be allowed to examine their personal records; students generally being convinced at that time that their teachers collected and filed voluminous malignant comments upon their individual activities and prowess, to their serious detriment and prejudice. Those few students at the Royal who expressed a wish to 'see their file' were allowed to do so without discussion; most must have been quite disappointed at the mundane nature of its contents.

It was not until 1970 that the students at the Royal raised the question of student membership of the School Council, pointing out that this had been granted at many, if not at most, other university institutions. When the idea was first discussed some members of the School Council were concerned that although the School's students were without question a body of responsible, level-headed adults, when it came to the election of representatives 'agitators' might take advantage of apathy to gain seats around the table in the Council Room with the support of a politically motivated minority – during the '60s the press had frequently attributed manifestations of unrest among students to the presence of 'agitators'. In order to minimise this danger the Council stipulated that the representatives should be selected by means of a properly conducted secret ballot at which not less than 50 per cent of the electorate voted. In practice the annual election of student Council representatives was combined with that of the officers of the Students' Society, the ballot being organised and supervised by the School Secretary. In no case, incidentally, was a result declared invalid because of an insufficiency of votes.

A further difficulty arose from the view of the Council that some subjects were unsuitable for discussion in the presence of students; they proposed to exclude students from 'business concerning the appointment, promotion and personal affairs of members of staff, and the academic progress and assessment of students *whether in general or* in any particular case and, (the 'variance' between members of the Department of Restorative Dentistry much in mind) *business relating to differences within and between Departments of the School or with and between committees*'.

These ideas were submitted to the University because the inclusion of student members in the Council involved a formal amendment of the Constitution of the School by the Privy Council. The officials of the University had been down this road before and knew that the Privy Council would not agree to such wide restrictions upon the participation of student members. Only the personal affairs of students and staff could be withheld from them, and the advice the School Council received was to strike out the words italicised in the preceding paragraph. And struck out they were.

Student members first attended meetings of the School Council in October 1971, and none of the difficulties which had been feared arose in practice. The very small amount of business from which they were excluded was handled by dividing meetings into two parts, the student members withdrawing at the conclusion of the first part.

Although student membership of the School Council had been accepted, when, in 1975, the question was raised of student membership of the Academic Board, the suggestion immediately encountered strong opposition – although several members of the Board equally strongly supported it. After a lengthy discussion it was decided to defer consideration of the matter for a year. But, as might have been expected, the idea did not go away. When it came up again in 1976 the Board grudgingly consented to the attendance at their meetings of student representatives provided they were selected by an agitator-proof process similar to that for the election of student members of the School Council, that they had no vote at meetings of the Board, and were excluded from discussions of the personal affairs of individual members of staff and students.

The extreme reluctance of the academic staff to accept the participation of students in their deliberations may seem surprising – student membership of committees at all levels was commonly accepted by the 1970s throughout the university world. The decision that although students could vote at meetings of the School Council on questions concerning the policy (including academic policy) and future of the School they must not be allowed to vote at meetings of the Academic Board on academic matters seemed to have no logic except that of dogged opposition. It was noticeable that the junior members of the Board were the most determined opponents, suggesting that opposition was based in the hierarchical structure of the academic, medical and dental professions; the right to exercise power was one to be earned by service and seniority, to be prized when gained and not to be given lightly. The Junior Staff Committee quickly raised the cry 'What about us?' and were permitted to send representatives to Board meetings on similar terms.

With hindsight, the logic becomes apparent. A case can be made for the right of students to help decide policy at the level of the School Council, but at the Academic Board different considerations apply. The Board was composed of teachers deciding how their subjects should be taught. They dealt with questions about which students, by definition, were incapable of judgement. Nevertheless, students might from time to time make useful comments and this the decision of the Board recognised.

In fact no noticeable harm resulted from the presence of students at meetings of the Academic Board and the School Council, and some good. It was a student member, Mr R Seymour, who drew the attention of the Council to the difficulties encountered by students in finding affordable accommodation in London and persuaded the Council to try to provide such facilities for them. As a result, the School acquired Nos. 24 and 26 Ferndale Road, in Clapham, and later No. 28. These provided single rooms for about 20 students at reasonable cost to them; but their provision involved a considerable expenditure of administrative time and effort.

The decision to embark upon this project, in January 1974, could not have been taken at a less propitious time, from a financial point of view. The welfare state inaugurated in 1945 was increasingly in trouble; inflation in the United Kingdom was running at just under 10 per cent per annum during the early 1970s and leaped to over 26 per cent in 1974/75. The efforts of successive Governments to curb it had been hampered by the commitment to full employment and their attempts to impose wage restraint led to extensive industrial unrest – nearly 24 million working days were lost in 1972 as a result of industrial action by workers. Basic interest rates were around 10 per cent. The worsening economic situation was aggravated in October 1973 when the Gulf oil-producing states announced a 70 per cent increase in the price of crude oil, an example which other oil producers rapidly followed. The Secretary of State for Trade and Industry asked motorists not to exceed 50 mph. and not to drive at all on Sundays.

The Heath Government which took office in 1970 had set the economy upon a rapid boom, after a period of stagnation, with a growth rate rising to 5 per cent per annum. But the resources generated were devoted to consumer spending rather than to investment in the economic infrastructure and public expenditure continued to rise. The Ministries of Health and Local Government spent freely and even Margaret Thatcher, soon to be the stern advocate of strict monetarist restrictions, as Minister of Education presided over the raising of the school leaving age and a huge investment in school building.

At the end of 1973 the bubble burst. In November, on top of the oil crisis, came a dispute with the coal miners which led to the declaration of a state of emergency and, to conserve energy, a three-day working week.

In these circumstances Government expenditure was cut, with serious results up and down the country. For the School's Student Residences Project the result was that the UGC grant towards the site cost which could have been expected failed to materialise. As if that was not sufficient of a disaster, the offer of a mortgage loan by the Bristol and West Building Society was withdrawn at the eleventh hour because the Society had run out of money to lend. Inflation combined with inadequate professional advice resulted in tenders for the conversion work which exceeded budget by nearly £20,000. However, with a generous grant of £20,000 from the Wolfson Foundation and another of £12,000 from the University of London, bridging loans from the School's bankers and its own Reserve Funds, all crises were overcome, the properties were bought and the conversion work carried out. By the beginning of 1975 the Building Society had gathered funds once again and the advance it made repaid the various bridging loans by means of which the project had been kept alive. By the time it was completed the School Secretary and his Administrative Officer, Fred Atkins, had learned a great deal about raising money, walking financial tightropes and controlling building operations, suffering numberless head-aches and sleepless nights in the process.

At about the same time the first of a series of re-organisations of the National Health Service descended upon the institution. The Board of Governors disappeared and was replaced by Merton, Sutton and Wandsworth Area Health Authority (Teaching), and the day-to-day administration of the Hospital became the responsibility of the Wandsworth and East Merton District Management Team. It became clear that the new structure failed entirely to make provision for the special nature of a dental hospital, the primary function of which is teaching, and seemed to provide quite inadequately for its administration. For a while it was only because the Dean was statutorily a member of the Area Health Authority and by invitation of the District Management Team that the needs of the institution were effectively represented. The Medical Committee became the Dental Advisory Committee (advisory to the District Management Team, that is) and before long its chairman was made a member of the Team.

One of the results of the re-organisation was to a diminution of the status of the Dental Hospital as a self-sufficient, stand-alone institution. Administratively, it became a unit in the Wandsworth and East Merton NHS District, and striking evidence of this was the change in the status of the Hospital's chief administrator. The two Secretary-Superintendents before the re-organisation were Ickeringill and his successor, Miss LJM Brace (Lola). Between them they served the institution for forty-three years. From 1972, when Lola left, and the closure in 1985, there were successively six different administrators seconded to the Hospital by the District Management Team. Despite their short tenure and because of their youth, energy and ambition, and with the support of the Team and its resources, they served the Hospital well.

Since 1967, as has been recorded, agreement existed at all levels that the School and Hospital should be redeveloped on the Tooting site in association with St George's Hospital and Medical School and the two Schools were actively involved together in planning their futures. In 1970, following the recommendation of the Royal Commission on Medical Education that all medical schools should be associated with multi-faculty institutions, St George's Hospital Medical School, with the concurrence of the Dental School, approached Chelsea College, which was also looking to be rebuilt on a site in south-west London. The three institutions agreed that their mutual collaboration was the best way forward for all. Higher authority concurred and in 1971 the UGC provisionally allocated funds for the rebuilding of Chelsea College at Tooting, on the Springfield site, as well as the Medical and Dental Schools.

Early in 1971 Dr MIA Hunter, the Dean of the Medical School, who had been a member of the Dental School's Council since 1952, was replaced by Dr RD Lowe. The change was one of style and method, as well as one of personality. Dr Hunter was a medical academic of the old school, mild-mannered and mindful of the views and interests of others. Dr Lowe, on the other hand, was a keenly ambitious academic politician with boundless energy, skilful in debate, single-minded in the furtherance of his aims and those of St George's Hospital Medical School and quick to adapt his tactics to changes in circumstances The advent of such a forceful personality added to the fears of those at Leicester Square who believed that the only way the Medical School was likely to associate with the Dental School was by swallowing it whole. He certainly failed to endear himself to Geoffrey Howe, the Dean of the Dental School. To such people the presence of Chelsea College in the down-to-earth practical person of Dr ME Gavin was a comfort; they felt that the Dental School had a better future in a three-sided partnership which included Chelsea College than they could expect if left alone at the mercy of the combative Medical School which Robert Lowe personified. It had to be acknowledged, however, that Dr Lowe was a redoubtable fighter in the cause of the Tooting development, including the rebuilding of the Royal there.

The 1970s were for the Royal a decade of intense planning and negotiation for a future in which it seemed the institution's whole way of life was to be changed out of recognition, and one of mounting frustration. For the staff of the Hospital the frustration was intense. Their fate, since the primary function of the Hospital was to provide clinical facilities for the School, was in the hands of others; all they could do was, through the cumbersome machinery of the Health Service authorities, try to ensure that what was planned was practicable from the clinical point of view, adequate for present use and containing provision for future development. In the event, when the soul of the School moved to London Bridge, the Hospital died instantly.

The School, on the other hand, was in the forefront of the battle for the future of the institution, and was closely engaged in it throughout the '70s. The problem was multi-faceted. At the beginning of the decade it was clear that the accommodation at Tooting for the pre-clinical departments of the School would, as the jargon had it, 'come on stream' before very long. But no date had yet been set for the start of the new clinical building there, so that the prospect was one of a School split in two for a long and indefinite period. Having at last achieved the aim of dentally orientated pre-clinical departments, the staff of which worked closely with their clinical colleagues, their separation in this way was seen as retrograde and potentially dangerously divisive. How to deal with this situation was one aspect of the problem.

Related to this was the question of student numbers. The pre-clinical accommodation at Tooting provided for an annual intake of 64; the clinical accommodation at Leicester Square could take not many more than 40. Were 24 places at Tooting to be wasted indefinitely? (Actually, the situation was much worse than this; what was being built at Tooting provided for a 2 year dental pre-clinical course, 128 places. Why this should be, no one seemed to know, because no one at any time had yet seriously considered a 2-year pre-clinical course for dental students. Somewhere in the heaps of paper which the Tooting Project had generated in the offices of the University, the UGC and the Department of Health, perhaps, there was a mistaken assumption, a slip of the pen even, which was in 1972 rapidly being perpetuated in bricks and mortar.)

The solution suggested to both these difficulties was the Interim Teaching Clinic at Tooting. Originally seen as a means of building up patient throughput at Tooting to a level necessary to provide adequate teaching facilities for the enlarged School and Hospital when they moved there, it came to be seen that it could also serve as an extension of the clinical facilities at Leicester Square to make possible an increase in clinical student numbers to match the higher numbers of pre-clinical students. Plans for the Clinic were discussed, and how it might best be used. The Dean, Professor Howe, set up a working party under the chairmanship of the Assistant Dean, Ivan Curson, to deal with the latter question.

The working party recommended the adoption of a proposal by Professor Houston that the Departments of Orthodontics and Children's Dentistry be moved to Tooting *en bloc* as soon as possible; there space could be provided for larger numbers of clinical students and the space at Leicester Square vacated would enable the remaining Departments to expand similarly. A number of teachers, as well as the working party, supported this scheme but Professor Howe spoke strongly against it. His opinion was that moving entire Departments away for some ten years or so would impose an unacceptable rigidity upon planning and thinking; in his view the Interim Clinic should contain elements of all the clinical teaching Departments, providing what at that time was called a 'polyclinic'; and his was the view which prevailed with the Academic Board and the School Council.

By December 1974 it was known that the new Dental Preclinical School at Tooting would open in October 1976, and plans for the necessary increase in clinical student numbers were being clarified. The Interim Teaching Clinic, it was thought, would provide space for 10 more, and the space at Leicester Square vacated by the Pre-clinical Departments could also be used. If the premises for the Interim Teaching Clinic failed to materialise, it was suggested to the School Council, the accommodation in multi-disciplinary laboratories provided for the non-existent second-year pre-clinical students should be adapted for the purpose. By this means the School thought it possible to increase the clinical student intake from 45 to 55 in 1976 and 64 in 1977.

That the Interim Teaching Clinic should fail to materialise was a distinct possibility. Negotiations for approval of the proposal were subject to delay and tergivisation on the part of the Department of Health, to whom detailed plans for a clinic providing some 189,000 square feet of accommodation were submitted in March 1973. Too big, said the Department, 10 months later, suggesting a 30 per cent reduction in area. Furthermore, they said, they were not going to pay for it – if it was to be built, the money must come from South West Thames Regional Health Authority. Aghast, the Chairman of the Authority said that they had no money for the project and, anyhow, they saw it as an integral part of the redevelopment of the Dental Hospital at Tooting and as such ranking for central funding.

Seven months elapsed while the discussion rumbled on until, in August 1975, an official of the Department helpfully summed up the situation in a letter to the Regional Development Officer, Bob Fairweather. The Interim Dental Clinic could not be centrally funded, she confirmed, and furthermore the Department could not justify expenditure in excess of half a million pounds for 'a development which was not necessary for service reasons, but only for manpower reasons' (she meant for training dentists, and only incidentally for treating patients). Since the new Dental Hospital was not likely to be completed before 1988, she went on to say, even the equipment put into the Interim Clinic would be too worn out to be transferrable. Wearily, because he had made the point so many times to so many officials, Fairweather explained that dental teaching hospitals existed primarily to enable dentists to be trained, and their provision could not be and was not related to service needs. Since it seemed to him that the Department's views were based upon a failure to understand this, he thought a meeting of all interested parties to discuss the matter would be helpful.

The refusal of the interim development coupled with the incidental introduction of a new and later date for the final move to Tooting produced dismay at Leicester Square. The Academic Board agreed that a space of thirteen years between the move of the Pre-clinical Departments and the establishment of any clinical dental facilities at Tooting should not be accepted and that if the Interim Clinic was denied 'alternative plans for the future of the School should be considered'. What alternative plans was not specified; indeed, it would have been difficult to do so. Robert Lowe, whose intelligence service and political acumen were at least as good as those of any at Leicester Square, wrote to Geoffrey Howe that any suggestion that the Royal might withdraw from the Tooting Project was potentially disastrous, advocating patience and restraint.

Miraculously, within a fortnight of the statement by the Academic Board, (although the event was almost certainly without reference to it), on 15th October 1975, Fairweather was able to tell the School Secretary that the Department of Health had withdrawn the August letter and now accepted that some interim teaching arrangements at Tooting were an essential part of the rebuilding project and that proposals for them should be accessible to central funds on the same basis as the main scheme. The repudiation of the lady who wrote the letter from which the fuss arose gave particular satisfaction.

But there was little other satisfaction to be gained. The economy of the country had not improved; in fact, in 1976 the (by then Labour) Government had no alternative to recourse to the International Monetary Fund. In return for a huge loan from the Fund the Government was obliged to make a cut of £1 billion in public spending in 1977/8 and a further cut of £1½ billion in the following year; and to sell its holding of British Petroluem shares for £500 million (so that Denis Healey became the first to privatise public assets to avoid taxation increases).

Enquiry revealed that the date of 1988 for the completion of the new clinical building was indeed the latest DHSS estimate; the government spending restrictions had forced the deferment – although the Pre-clinical School would open as planned, in 1976. The UGC took the view that it would be a mistake to detach portions of clinical departments for twelve or thirteen years and withdrew their support for the Interim Teaching Clinic. They acquiesced, however, in the School's suggestion that the first entry of dental students at Tooting be deferred until 1977 and agreed to press for funds to extend clinical facilities at Leicester Square so as to make it possible to take up the 64 places available at Tooting.

The move of Pre-clinical Departments was carried out smoothly and completed on 19th September 1976. The decision to defer the entry of students for a year turned out to be a wise one – the teething troubles experienced by the Medical School, whose intake had not been deferred, were such that to have had another 64 students on site would have converted confusion into chaos.

Not only hindsight supports Dr Lowe's warning that the Dental School would be in danger if it withdrew from the Tooting project. As early as June 1974 there came a warning for those who had ears to hear that the dental academic world was to be shaken up before very long. A meeting took place of representatives of the UGC, Chelsea College, St George's Medical School and the Dental School to discuss the financial implications of planning for an intake of medical and dental pre-clinical students at Tooting in 1976 and the possibilities of close association between the three institutions in the future. In the course of the discussion the UGC representative referred to current consideration of the national policy for dental student numbers, which had not been reviewed since 1956; he thought that there might be a reduction in the number, although he hastened to add that the Royal's intake of 55 when the Interim Clinic opened and 64 when the School was fully established at Tooting had been agreed.

The coming together of the three institutions in 1970 in response to pressure from above has been mentioned. In that year they set up a Joint Policy Committee and once the UGC had agreed in principle to the rebuilding of Chelsea College and Dr Lowe had replaced Dr Hunter as Dean of St George's Medical School they became more and more closely concerned in each other's affairs. This was in accordance with the policy of the UGC, to whom such arrangements offered two potential benefits; the supposed academic value of the association of medical and dental students with those studying other disciplines and the financial savings believed to be possible if several institutions merged. It behoved the Medical and Dental Schools and the College to be seen to be going along with this policy.

But the two Schools were very wary. The Dental School was especially suspicious of the intentions of the Medical School; the then Dean, Raleigh Lucas, had earlier reacted vigorously when the University referred in correspondence on an entirely different subject to the possibilities of amalgamation with St George's. 'No question' he wrote 'of amalgamation has ever been considered, nor is it on any agenda so far as we are concerned'. When Robert Lowe spoke airily at a meeting of the School Council of a University of South London, the Council quickly placed on record their view that something better than a conglomeration of St George's Hospital Medical School and Chelsea College would be necessary to constitute an institution 'of a real University character'; and that in any such evolution 'there should be adequate safeguards for the conduct of the Dental School'.

The three institutions felt it necessary to hammer out a common statement of policy for the benefit of higher authority and after several attempts it emerged in the following form:

1. We will plan our development at Tooting to make the most effective use of our common resources and in such a way as not to prejudice integration of the three institutions at a later date.

2. The rebuilding programme is of paramount importance. Until this is largely complete the three institutions should retain separate governing bodies but will arrange adequate machinery for joint consultation on all matters of common interest.

3. Our aim is to move towards functional integration of our various academic activities. In particular we will promote as soon as possible the co-ordination of teaching and research in the Basic Medical Sciences. Constitutionally, we are prepared either to continue as separate organis-ations or at a later date to consider amalgamation into a multi-faculty university, if this becomes the policy for London University. Amalgama-tion within the present constitution of the University appears to have serious disadvantages for the Medical and Dental Schools and is therefore not a satisfactory solution.'

This statement, the product of much earnest discussion, seemed to embody all that was required. It made satisfying noises about co-operation but shelved the question of amalgamation until some nebulous date in the distant future. It respected the desire of the Medical and Dental Schools for independence but nevertheless promulgated the ambition of the Basic Medical Sciences Departments of Chelsea College to take over their pre-clinical teaching.

Before long, in February 1973, the contract for Phase One of the rebuilding of the Medical and Dental Schools was let and work started. Phase One consisted of the accommodation for the Pre-clinical Schools together with the main central facilities block of the Medical School. It was agreed that 60,000 square feet of the accommodation being provided should be handed over to the Basic Medical Sciences Group of Chelsea College, in exchange for equivalent accommodation in the College's new building on the Springfield site in due course, and a Basic Medical Sciences Co-ordinating Committee was set up to make joint arrangements for teaching pre-clinical subjects. In this connection the Dental School insisted on retaining their own senior teachers to design and supervise the pre-clinical courses for dental students.

From this time regular meetings of the Heads and Secretaries took place to discuss informally the policies, problems and aspirations of the three institutions in the context of their developing association and future integration. In these discussions the objectives of the Royal's representatives were to ensure that the School maintained control over its curriculum and resources during the run-up to a single multi-faculty institution, and to ensure that dentistry was an autonomous faculty within that institution with control over the contributions made to its teaching by other faculties; and to ensure that dentistry received its appropriate share of the resources of the institution.

As the decade wore on and ministers made more strenuous efforts to reduce the Government's spending commitments this elaborate edifice in the clouds began to evaporate. The deferment of the rebuilding of the Dental Hospital and School has been referred to. In October 1978 the Chairman of the UGC said during a visit to Chelsea College that proposals to move the College south of the river 'if they were to materialise, would do so only slowly, and the College would be well advised to consolidate in the Chelsea area for the coming years'. The scheme to upgrade clinical facilities at Leicester Square was found to be likely to cost between £2.75 and £3 million and because of access difficulties and the need for the Hospital and School to continue to function while it was being carried out the work might extend over eight years. At this news the UGC and DHSS veered back to an acceleration of the move to Tooting, to which both re-affirmed their commitment.

Two new ways in which this might be possible were suggested; one was to use the accommodation already built which was to have housed Chelsea College's Basic Medical Sciences departments, but this was considered too small. The other suggestion was to use the Maybury Street site which was adjacent to but outside the main St George's site at Tooting. Here, it was thought, work to provide the clinical Dental Hospital and School would be able to proceed without the access, phasing and decantation constraints which working on the main site imposed.

So from the beginning of 1979 the Maybury Street site became the focus of efforts to get the Royal rebuilt at Tooting. The difficulty, as always, was that although the UGC could put up their share of the cost of the project, the Department of Health could not. Much ingenuity and persuasive effort was devoted to the task of finding ways of supplying this deficiency.

During these fateful negotiations three Deans held office. Raleigh Lucas relinquished the Deanship in 1973, having presided over the School's emergence from the criticisms of the UGC in 1956 and its blossoming during the 1960s. It seemed that he would be succeeded by Bryan Wade who became Dean-Elect; but upon examination Mr Wade found the terms of the appointment not to be what he had hoped and that in order to accommodate himself to them he needed to resign his academic post of Senior Lecturer in Periodontology. This he did, retaining his Hospital Consultantcy. The Academic Board, by whom he had been elected, did not take well to this change; the strictures of the UGC upon domination of the School by Hospital consultants had not been forgotten and, anyhow, the idea of a Dean with no academic role did not appeal.

In the ensuing election Geoffrey Howe was appointed Dean, taking up office on 1st October 1973. He strove to preserve the morale and the academic and clinical standing of the instititution during the dark days of rebuilding deferred and hopes dashed, of making do in the by then cramped and deteriorating Hospital building. He resigned in 1978, having been invited to the Chair of Oral Surgery and Oral Medicine and the office of Dean at the new Dental School then building in Hong Kong; an offer which, in all the circumstances, he understandably found it impossible to refuse.

It was early in Professor Howe's deanship that a solution was at last found to the perennial problem of the teaching of general medicine and surgery to the students of the School (see page 35). By 1939 the Middlesex and Kings College Hospitals had dropped out of the arrangement and the dental students went to Charing Cross Hospital for this part of their course. In 1948, when the School elected to join the St George's Hospital Group on the formation of the National Health Service, St George's Hospital Medical School took over the teaching. When they moved from Hyde Park Corner to Tooting difficulties soon arose because the Medical School had difficulty in meeting the needs of the dental students. Frustrated by the repeated failure of successive medical schools to provide an adequate course for the Dental School, Professor Howe decided to seek help from the staff of St Helier Hospital, which at that time had no commitment to medical students. The staff there responded to the suggestion with enthusiasm and a successful arrangement was made for third year dental students to spend a week in residence at St Helier Hospital and for members of the consultant staff of the Hospital to give lecture courses at Leicester Square.

Professor William Houston followed from 1st October 1978. All Deans of the Royal have had difficulties and dangers to contend with but from the outset Bill Houston was faced with potential disasters; financial restrictions and the need for retrenchment, the final fight for the move to Tooting, the battle for survival and the eventual closure. He faced these hectic and dangerous times with energy, courage and unremitting cheerfulness.

Early in his Deanship the Department of Conservative Dentistry became a centre of controversy again. When Professor Pickard retired the University was asked, in the normal way, to set up a Board of Advisors to select his successor. Ivan Curson, a long established and well respected Senior Lecturer in the Department was among those who applied for appointment to the Chair. In their wisdom the Board of Advisors decided upon Keith Mortimer, from Cardiff, to the intense disappointment of many members of the Department, who were convinced that Curson was the man for the job.

This view gained strength when Ivan Curson was appointed to a similar Chair at Kings College Hospital Dental School. Such was the strength of feeling that several members of the Department made clear to Professor Houston that the resulting situation of the Department was unacceptable. With the agreement of Professor Mortimer a meeting was held of all the academic staff of the Department at which a quite startling proposal was made.

It was that the Department should elect a Head of Department, Professor Mortimer agreeing to be a candidate and to accept the result of the election. Such a procedure, although by no means unknown elsewhere, was entirely unprecedented at the Royal and the procedure was most carefully thought through and agreed with all interested parties. What emerged was a recommendation, subsequently approved by the Academic Board, that the Head of the Department should be selected from the full-time members of the academic staff holding honorary consultant contracts by a ballot in which all members of the academic staff of the Department should participate.

The election was duly held and Ian Barnes, then Senior Lecturer, was appointed to direct the Department, which he did successfully until the School was closed.

9

From Hospital to Hotel

While these events were unfolding Sir Brian Flowers and the University of London's Working Party on Resources for Medical and Dental Teaching were addressing themselves to their task. Ever since the Report of the Royal Commission on Medical Education in 1968 – which, it will be remembered, was responsible for the inclusion of Chelsea College in the Tooting Project – discussion had continued in the University of London about the future of its Medical Schools. The problem was how to enable medical students to study the increasing range of subjects now considered essential to the education of a doctor within a restricted budget. The solutions advocated, as the academic politicians in the Basic Medical Sciences Departments of Chelsea College well knew, included encouraging co-operation between Medical Schools and multi-faculty institutions, and the concentration of some of the numerous small specialist departments which in many Medical Schools were competing for scarce funds.

During the 1970s the financial situation worsened; a Report by the University's Joint Planning Committee in October 1980 said:

Medical Schools began to fall into deficit. Posts had to be frozen, vacancies were left unfilled, students could not be given tutorials because staff were so stretched, and staff were unable to find adequate time for research.

Notwithstanding this, Medicine was taking an increasing share of the University's budget particularly because of the high cost of maintaining and operating the premises occupied by the Medical Schools associated with St George's, the Royal Free, and Charing Cross Hospitals, which had been rebuilt as part of large new modern hospitals. This was something which had affected the Royal, when its Pre-clinical Departments moved to Tooting in 1976; the contribution which the Dental School was required to make to the costs of heating, lighting, cleaning and maintaining the accommodation they shared with their Medical School colleagues made a huge hole in the School's budget and resulted in a situation similar to that depicted in the Joint Planning Committee's Report.

In this situation the University asked Sir Brian Flowers and his Working

Party to study the problem and to recommend how the resources available for medical and dental education and research in the University might best be redeployed to maintain them at their present standard. The terms of reference recognised that the recommendations might include the closure or amalgamation of some institutions, and asked the Working Party to suggest how any such re-arrangement might 'be achieved over a reasonable period in such a way as to minimise the consequential hardship to staff and the dislocation of students, teaching and research.'

Sir Brian reported early in 1980. He and his Working Party recommended in effect the closure of the equivalent of one clinical medical school and two pre-clinical schools and the attentuation of clinical teaching in one further medical school; coupled with the enlargement of two medical schools in the periphery of the capital. This would maintain student numbers and meet the situation which was developing on the National Health Service side in London.

It was known that in the Department of Health there had been for some time a conviction that London received more than its fair share of Health Service resources compared to the rest of the country, and their Resource Allocation Working Party (RAWP) had been working to find ways of redressing the balance. As a result, the Metropolitan Regional Health Authorities found themselves progressively deprived of funds. In 1980 the Department set up another working party, the London Health Planning Consortium, to report upon the situation of acute hospital services and clinical facilities generally. By chance or design, both Sir Brian and the Planning Consortium reported on the same day – the latter publishing a Green Paper with the encouraging title of 'Towards a Balance'.

The Green Paper said that the Consortium had found that population was draining from London and that the number of acute beds in the capital must decline accordingly – they suggested a reduction of some 20 to 25 per cent over the next ten years, a loss of roughly 2,300 beds in the Inner London Teaching Districts. Such a change was of considerable significance to the University, because the resources provided for medical education by the Department of Health, in the form of staff and facilities, far exceeded in value the contribution made by the UGC. The recommendations of the Consortium made it necessary to move London medical teaching from the centre to the periphery; and at the same time the activites of RAWP were reducing the Health Service input to the London area generally.

When the Flowers Working Party was set up a Labour Government was in power; the universities had been encouraged to take more students. The Flowers Working Party and the University assumed that funding would continue at the current levels, so the Working Party was not asked to save money – rather, to show how to use it more effectively. By the time its Report came out the first Thatcher Conservative Government was in power and the situation changed alarmingly.

At first the change of government did not appear to change the policy regarding university funding; universities were told that they could expect 'level funding' and the University of London continued to try to operate the Flowers policy of finding the best *academic* solution to the problems of London Medical Schools. However, in December 1980 the Government announced a $3\frac{1}{2}$ per cent cut in 1981/62 and in March 1981 said that further cuts would be made in successive years, rising to $8\frac{1}{2}$ per cent by 1983/84. It was clear that the rest of the University could not be expected to shield the Faculty of Medicine and Dentistry from their share of these cuts.

It was also clear that by 1983/84 the funds for the general medical schools of the University would be reduced by about 10 per cent – about £5 million in 1980/81 terms. The period of 10 years during which Flowers reckoned the necessary changes could be made, with staff reductions effected by natural wastage, was no longer available; the time to make them was now.

Flowers had suggested an examination of medical school costs and staffing levels, and this was duly carried out with the assistance of a firm of accountants and management consultants. It showed a wide disparity between individual Schools. A suggestion that the most cost-effective solution would be to close one Medical School down completely was not taken up – no school was going to volunteer and no one was prepared to nominate a victim for sacrifice – and the Joint Planning Committee decided that the required saving could be achieved if all Medical Schools brought their staff/student ratios to 1:7 in clinical departments and 1:10 in pre-clinical departments. To alleviate the difficulties which the reductions of staff would inevitably cause the Joint Planning Committee said 'the Schools must regroup so that the newly-built Schools, despite their higher running costs, can function more cost-effectively and so that each School supports the others in its own consortium'. The other Faculties were not going to support the expensive Medical Schools – they must look after themselves and each other. What emerged from the deliberations of the Flowers Working Party and the University's Joint Planning Committee was a decision that medical schools should be amalgamated ('twinned' was the word used) and the many isolated independent postgraduate medical institutions should be 'embedded' in one or other of the medical school consortia so formed.

As to the Royal Dental School, the Working Party had this to say:

> We believe it important that as far as possible medical and dental undergraduates are taught in the same environment, as we take the view that dentistry is in essence a branch of medicine.

The Working Party had been convinced, their Report said, 'that the pre-clinical courses for medical and dental students should be integrated'.

In their comments to the University's Joint Planning Committee the School Council were scathing, saying that these two statements disclosed a failure to understand what dental education at undergraduate level was, and pointing out that the suggestion of an integrated pre-clinical course was contrary to the General Dental Council's recommendation that dental students should have pre-clinical courses specifically designed for their needs taught by teachers with a special interest in dental and oral problems. Furthermore, the trend towards the integration of medical pre-clinical and clinical courses made the combined teaching of medical and dental pre-clinical students almost completely impossible.

The Working Party's view of the symbiotic relationship between dentistry and medicine and their zeal for larger organisations led them to the conclusion that the Royal should amalgamate with St George's Hospital Medical School. Why, the School Council asked the Joint Planning Committee, reiterating the advantages of independence for dental education, so long as those functions which can be economically and efficiently integrated are integrated? They drew attention to functions which the two Schools had already integrated; the shared pre-clinical school, which had existed since 1976, and the Joint Finance Office, set up in 1973 'without the necessity for either School to make any significant surrender of academic or financial independence'. The Schools expected in due course to extend this process into other areas, such as registration of students, maintenance of premises, management of residences and sports grounds and other appropriate functions as the move to Tooting progressed.

Apart from these matters and a proposal to turn the Institute of Dental Surgery into an undergraduate dental school associated with St Mary's Hospital Medical School (better to keep it as a postgraduate institution and merge it with an existing dental school, said the School Council, with an eye to its own ambitions) the Working Party did not really tackle the London Dental Schools. However, in April 1979 the Dean, Professor Houston, together with Professor Prophet, Dean of University College Hospital Dental School, had been invited to explain the situation of the dental schools to the Working Party. In the ensuing discussion the suggestion had been made that an effective way of making better use of resources would be to close one or more dental schools and re-allocate their student places to those remaining.

But consideration of dentistry in the University of London was hanging upon the recommendations of the Nuffield Foundation, which had been chewing over the questions of dental education and dental manpower for several years. The recommendations duly appeared soon after the Flowers Report. They were, in sum, that the number of dental students should be reduced by reducing the size of each and every dental school and that the resources saved be used to extend the present one-year pre-clinical course to two years. In March 1981 the Vice-Chancellor of the University, Lord Annan, set up another Working Party, under Dr David Ennis-Williams, to study the implications of the two Reports for dentistry in London University.

The situation was ominous because the suggestion of a two-year pre-clinical course was an obvious non-starter at a time of diminishing resources, as was the proposal that all dental schools should continue to operate with smaller numbers of students. In the circumstances the proposal to reduce student numbers threatened the existence of one or more dental schools.

Professor Houston had recognised from the outset that when consideration turned to the rationalisation of dentistry in the University, the dice would be loaded against the Royal. Hamish Stewart, the Clerk of the University Court, had recently pointed out that in 1976/77 the unit cost of academic departments at the Royal was higher than that at any of the other four London dental schools; the fact that the others were allied to medical schools (which were themselves hastily associating with one or other of the powerful multi-faculty colleges of the University) meant that not only were they able to share with their partners some of the expenses which the Royal had to bear on its own, but also that they had powerful allies to rely upon in a political battle.

Professor Houston opened a campaign to bring to the minds of those likely to influence decisions in the University the stature and status of the Royal, to suggest ways in which the Royal could help solve the University's problem, and to provide alternative targets. In a written submission he said that

> the plans to rebuild the School and its associated Hospital in association with St George's Hospital Medical School provide a unique opportunity for the University to rationalise its arrangements for dental education, to enhance their potential and to reduce their costs. This can be done by the provision at Tooting of a large institution with an intake of 100–120 students and a considerable postgraduate commitment, to which would be transferred the functions of other institutions within the University. The institution thus created would have its own pre-clinical school orientated to the needs of the dental curriculum and responsible to the authorities of the Dental School. It would be an institution with a long tradition of independence and responsibility for its own resources and activities, capable of close association with the Medical School while retaining the independence of action which we believe to be productive of the best in dental education.

Soon after the new Working Party was set up Dr Lowe and Professor Houston wrote jointly to its Chairman, reminding him of the Tooting plans for the Dental School, and telling him that there were beginning to emerge signs that the Health Service authorities might be able to fund their share of the development. They asked the Working Party to confirm the University's long-standing plans for the rebuilding of the Royal – 'this will enable the University to seize the opportunity which now exists (and is unlikely to recur) to provide itself with a large new dental school, integrated with an expanding Medical School, in an area which promises a plentiful supply of patients and where its associated Hospital can fulfill an important service need'.

The double provision for pre-clinical students already made at Tooting seemed to offer an immediate possibility for economy, they suggested; it could take the students from the London Hospital Dental School, for example. And if the opportunity were taken to make an even larger dental school at Tooting, closing one of the others, economies of scale would be obtained.

This robust defence was not calculated to arouse the enthusiasm of the other institutions whose functions, it suggested, should be transferred to the Royal at Tooting, nor did it do so.

But if this strategy was to work the Tooting plans had to become reality and Professor Houston soon became convinced that if the School waited too long in hope of rebuilding it would be overtaken by a decision by the University to close it. His concern was for members of the staff of the School and Hospital who, he feared, would be put out of work if this happened. His objective became a voluntary merger with another Dental School such that the combined student numbers would support the combined staffs at the approved staff:student ratios. At a social meeting, Donald Bompas, the Secretary of Guy's Hospital Medical School, suggested to the School Secretary that this condition might apply to a merger between the Royal and Guy's Hospital Dental School. When the two Deans and the two Secretaries sat down together with lists of staff it looked as if he was right.

There was another reason for urgency. Following the Nuffield Report the Department of Health's Dental Manpower Strategy Review Group had been considering the number of dentists likely to be needed in the future. If, as seemed likely, the Group recommended a reduction in their number, a reduction in the number of places for dental students would follow. The merger strategy, as has been explained, depended upon the maintenance of student numbers.

The Ennis-Williams Working Party decided that the number of Dental Schools in London should be reduced by one, and a Working Party of the five Dental Deans was instructed to decide how this should be done. Professor Houston, who was, of course, a member of this execution squad, explained his thoughts to the Academic Board when it met on 16th July 1981. He said that the need was urgent for the School to decide whether to maintain the commitment to the Tooting project or to merge with another School; in his view the two alternatives were mutually exclusive. He believed it unrealistic to hope that rebuilding could be achieved in the present circumstances and that if the School pursued that option any longer the opportunities for negotiation of a merger on acceptable terms would rapidly diminish. He proposed to ask the School Council in a week's time to make the decision.

Dr Lowe argued for optimism about the prospect of rebuilding, and put forward a plan for a reduced project at Tooting more compatible with the resources likely to be available. Professor Houston repeated his pessimism in this respect and reiterated his view that it was dangerous to wait too long. The Academic Board agreed to advise the School Council that 'the long-term interests of dental education in the University of London will best be served by the merger of this School with one of the other dental schools of the University', suggesting Guy's for preference, King's College otherwise.

The School Council, having heard the views of the Dean, and those of Dr Lowe, decided to postpone their decision until their next meeting, asking the Academic Board to consider in the meantime the academic practicality of the smaller Tooting project suggested by Dr Lowe. Thus commenced a struggle between two factions within the School which continued, not without asperity, until resolved by extraneous force, as will be seen.

A principal protagonist of fighting for Tooting to the bitter end was Professor HJJ Blackwood. He took the view that it was better to go down fighting than to surrender to being absorbed by another School. When the School Council's request came before the Academic Board in September he persuaded the Board, in a detailed paper, that the new Tooting plan would provide adequate accommodation for the School and the Board agreed, with some misgiving, that it was acceptable.

Harry Blackwood was joined by other members of the School Council; in particular, Mrs Alison Munro, Chairman of Merton, Sutton and Wandworth Area Health Authority, Mr SP Doughty, who lobbied local Members of Parliament, as well as Dr Lowe, were active in pressing South West Thames Regional Health Authority to find money from its own resources for the dental development at Tooting. So successful were their efforts that by the end of 1981 the Authority had agreed to use the prospective proceeds of the sale of the Atkinsons Morley, Leicester Square and Hyde Park Corner sites for the purpose.

This was reported to the School Council in December, at a meeting at which Professor Houston announced that the view of the majority of the Dental Deans in the Working Party was that the reduction in the number of Dental Schools should be effected by the merger of the Royal with Guy's, with some of the staff from the Royal transferring to King's College Hospital Dental School. He asked the Council whether in these circumstances they wanted to adhere to the policy of rebuilding at Tooting. He said that in his opinion the reduced Dental School and Hospital which it was now proposed to build at Tooting 'which would be planned to standards of maximum economy, would be unpleasing, unsuitable and difficult to work in', but nevertheless if the Council so decided he would continue vigorously and conscientiously to argue the case for the development; but he asked that if the rebuilding project was achieved someone else should be appointed to conduct the transfer to the new site.

The School Council decided that their view was unchanged, that the best policy for the School and for the University was to rebuild the School and Hospital at Tooting and asked the Dean to continue his efforts to obtain the support of the University for this. They agreed, however, that if the University did not support it, the School should accept the merger arrangements proposed by the Dental Dean's Working Party.

This decision caused murmurings at Guy's, where Professor Houston, and the School Secretary had for some weeks been engaged in informal discussions about how the staffs of the two Dental Schools could be dovetailed. It was seen there as something of a double-cross. At the other extreme, the negotiations with Guy's were seen by Harry Blackwood in particular as an act of treachery in view of the School Council's steadfast adherence to the Tooting project and independence.

The negotiations with Guy's were, as they were intended to be, a sort of life insurance policy, the wisdom of which soon became apparent. At about the time of the School Council's decision the Dean's fears were realised; the DHSS Dental Manpower Strategy Group recomended that the entry to dental schools be reduced by 10 per cent; and the UGC let it be known that if the recommendation was accepted (by DHSS) 'they would feel unable to proceed with the rebuilding of the RDH'.

While this was going on the School faced a financial crisis which had to be dealt with. Following the announcements of UGC grants after the Government-imposed cuts, the School's budget indicated deficits of £114,000 in 1981/82, £214,000 in 1982/3 and £247,000 in 1983/4; between 10 and 12 per cent of total expenditure. The School Council adopted proposals by the Dean involving economies in general expenditure, suspension of six posts due to become vacant in 1981/82 by resignation, retirement and expiry of tenure, and eight redundancies. As well, the District Management Team was told that the School was no longer able to meet expenditure identified as the responsibility of the NHS, such as the consultancy in Oral Surgery, the training of student technicians, and technical work for patients prescribed by members of the Hospital staff, together costing some £78,000 a year. While not disputing the School's logic, the DMT said that they could not meet the bill either, unless economies could be made elsewhere, and asked the Dental Advisory Committee to suggest how this might be done.

Thus to the existing stress which affected every member of the staff of the institution was added tension between School and Hospital over the apportionment of costs. To the question why this and the other measures of economy were necessary if the School was likely to disappear, Professor Houston's answer was that while the School existed it was necessary to balance the books; and that if amalgamation was to be the School's future, when all were in deep financial trouble, no other institution was likely to agree to amalgamate with a partner in deficit.

The beginning of 1982 found opinion in School and Hospital split. Some were deeply pessimistic, believing that the School was doomed and the

Hospital with it and that it was ignoble and dishonourable to suggest that it might be saved by amalgamation with another dental school. Some thought that salvation for both lay in whole-hearted amalgamation with St George's Hospital Medical School and, in fact, in April the School Council approved such a merger in principle, arguing that it would effect as much of a saving as one with Guy's Hospital Dental School; and in doing so abandoned the safeguards for the independence of dentistry so long insisted upon in this connection, asking only that the merger arrangements be such as to preserve as much independence for dentistry as possible in the new structure.

A more pragmatic view was that the struggle to save the Royal was lost and that every effort should be directed to minimising the hardship which its demise would inflict upon its staff. In June the University's Joint Medical Advisory and Joint Planning Committees endorsed the recommendations of the majority of the Dental Deans' Working Party, including the amalgamation of the Royal with Guy's. It remained for them to be approved by the Senate. Professor Houston told the School Council that he thought it unlikely that the decisions of the two Committees would be over-ruled and he asked them to face realities and authorise him to start formal discussions with Guy's about merger arrangements forthwith. His fear was that the staff of the School would be in great danger if the DHSS agreed to the recommended cut in dental student numbers; but he believed that the danger would be reduced if a firm plan for amalgamation with Guy's Hospital Dental School was in being.

The question was closely argued at the June meeting of the School Council, Mrs Munro, Professor Blackwood and Mr Orton speaking strongly against discussion of merger plans at that stage with anybody except St George's Hospital Medical School and advocating political action to get the authorities to accept the Tooting plan. Professor Houston maintained his view that the prudent course in the interests of the staff of the School was to discuss their redeployment quickly.

The School Council agreed in the end to ask the Dean to explore with the Deans of the other Dental Schools ways in which the recommendations of the Working Party might be implemented, if the Senate decided that they should be implemented; but they maintained their view that the Tooting Dental Project was the best option for the University, the School, and the staff of the School.

The political action, which included letters to the press and a demonstration at Senate House by students at the Royal, culminated in an adjournment debate in the House of Commons on 8th July 1982. Thomas Cox, Labour member for Tooting, raised the matter, saying that he was trying 'to find out from the Minister what is to be the future of the Royal Dental Hospital and whether it is to move to the facilities that exist for it at the St George's Hospital, Tooting'. His attack upon the Royal/Guy's merger proposal showed every sign of being based upon briefing by Harry

Blackwood, but his argument for pressing on with the move to Tooting was fatally flawed. He spoke of the detriment to dental services in Tooting if the move did not take place – 'the people affected would be children, the less well-off members of the community, the elderly and the phyisically handicapped', sentiments reminiscent of the Hospital's pre-NHS public appeals for funds. He said that it would be extremely short-sighted of the Minister not to allow the development at Tooting to take place and that he should examine every aspect of the issue before making a decision.

Geoffrey Ginsberg, Under-Secretary of State for Health and Social Security, had no difficulty in disposing of the argument and washing his hands of the matter. Dental Hospitals existed primarily to provide facilities for dental education, he said. His Department had not been convinced that there was a service need for a dental hospital in Tooting; nevertheless, they were ready to meet their share of the cost of transferring the Hospital provided that the University of London, which had a key role in the decision, agreed to transfer the School there. The University, he understood, was likely to reach a decision soon, and that was where the matter rested at the moment.

The University Senate endorsed the recommendations in the Majority Report of the Dental Dean's Working Party on 14th July 1892. As has been noted, Professor Houston had anticipated this decision and prepared for it. When the School Council met on 22nd July he was able to report the results of discussions with Guy's Hospital Medical School about ways of implementing it and the principles which had been agreed. These were:

> That the aim should be to achieve the formal merger of the two Schools by 1st August 1983 and that their Governing Bodies should subscribe to a statement of intent to that effect forthwith.
>
> Of the 45 clinical student places at the Royal, 23 would remain with the merged School, 17 would go to King's College Hospital Dental School and 5 to the Dental School at the London Hospital.
>
> Each of the merging Schools should adjust its establishment to the 1982/83 level of funding and the merger should take place on that basis.
>
> There should be no intake of students to the Royal after October 1982; the pre-clinical school at Tooting should close on 31st July 1983 and a phased transfer of clinical activity from Leicester Square to London Bridge should take place, to be completed by the end of 1985.
>
> All the clinical teachers together with six pre-clinical teachers, all the technical instructors, and all the non-academic staff employed by the School would be able to transfer to the merged School if they wished, with the exception of the staff of the Athletic Ground, some catering staff, and the Hospital-funded dental technicians..

The Dean was also able to report that these arrangements had been discussed with the Vice-Chancellor and Principal of the University, to whom they were acceptable. They were sympathetic to a proposal that the merged School should be granted a temporary financial cushion during the process of integration and agreed that no member of staff should be penalised as a result of the merger.

In a paper circulated with the agenda for the meeting Professor Houston repeated his words to the Academic Board earlier in the month:

I am confident that the opportunity exists for us to join with the staff of Guy's Dental School in full and equal partnership and for a new and exciting departure in dental education and research. There will be a multitude of difficulties but with effort, understanding and, above all, goodwill, they will be overcome. I have no doubt at all that the result will repay the effort. I believe that the outcome of my discussions is very satisfactory and I have no hesitation in recommending that the School proceeds with the merger on the basis of our agreed proposals.'

The School Council agreed, but by no means unanimously, Mrs Munro, Professor Blackwood, Mr Orton and Mr Dougherty voting to the contrary.

There remained a number of loose ends, not the least of which were the three categories of staff excluded from the offer of transfer to the merged School. The transfer of the staff at the Athletic Ground to St George's Hospital Medical School was made a condition of a lease by which the Medical School took over the Ground and Pavilion on 1st August 1983. In 1987 the Medical School exercised an option to buy the property; the Dental School's share of the purchase price, together with £41,000 from the surrender of the lease of 39 Orange Street, was used by UMDS to establish a fund of some £378,000 to be used for the benefit of students.

The catering staff had no difficulty in finding new jobs and, a vacancy occuring, the Manageress was transferred to Guy's Hospital Medical School.

The transfer of the Hospital-funded dental technicians was more troublesome to arrange. They worked for the Hospital, their job being the production of the appliances prescribed for patients by the staff and students but the Hospital was unable to recruit or retain them because the salaries it was allowed to pay were inadequate. In the early 1960s, with the agreement of the Board of Governors, the School, which was less restricted in such matters, agreed to employ them on behalf of the Hospital, offering much better salaries and conditions and recovering the cost from the Hospital.

The difficulty was to get agreement for the transfer of funds between Regional Hospital Authorities. In theory, it should have been straightforward. The 23 student places moved to London Bridge took with them a commitment for their clinical support – the financial burden on South-West Thames Regional Health Authority had been reduced and that of South-East Thames Regional Health Authority correspondingly increased. But this simple logic was obscured by the complicated logic of National Health Service finance under the Resource Allocation Working Party's rulings. A convoluted negotiation resulted which eventually resolved the matter satisfactorily.

In these ways it proved possible to redeploy the students and staff of the School with the minimum of distress. The position of the staff of the Hospital was less satisfactory. While clinical activities continued at Leicester Square it was essential to retain there a staff adequate to support them; but, unlike their School-employed colleagues, the individual members of staff had no guarantee of employment when the Hospital closed down. The natural reaction was for them to look for new jobs as soon as it became clear that the Hospital's life was limited, and to leave as soon as they found them.

In March 1983 there were about 150 people involved, excluding the clinical staff, comprising domestic workers and porters, engineers and clerks, radiographers, dental surgery assistants, nurses and hygienists, a significant number of whom had been with the Hospital for twenty years or more. Brian Goode, the Hospital Administrator, arranged to talk to each individual about their redeployment hopes, and asked the Personnel Departments of Guy's and King's College Hospitals to help. Most people, it turned out, wanted to move to Guy's. He sent the results of these talks to the Regional Treasurer in the hope that they might help him in considering the redeployment of funds when the Hospital closed.

Relevant to this was the consideration of what was to be the shape of the Dental Unit at Tooting, which was not to be closed. Wandsworth District Health Authority spent some time discussing this during 1982 and 1983. What they decided upon, and what exists now, was a Dental Unit consisting of clinics in Oral Surgery, with 4 chairs, 2 operating theatres and 6 day beds, Restorative Dentistry (5 chairs, including two for hygienists) and Orthodontics, with 10 chairs, including one paediadontist, with appropriate supporting staff. It was agreed that King's College Hospital Dental School should set up a general practice clinic within the Unit, and that their undergraduate students should attend it and the consultant clinics in the Unit; and that some postgraduate teaching, together with training for NHS clinical staff, should be carried out there. The present St George's Hospital Dental Unit can be said to constitute the Royal Dental Hospital in vestigial form.

So much so that, early in 1984, solicitors for the District Management Team were able to persuade themselves and the Team that because the Dental Unit was to survive the Royal Dental Hospital was not closing at all – it was being moved to Tooting. If the Royal was moving to Tooting so, of course, was the money due from the sale of its premises in Leicester Square. The District Management Team received this advice with enthusiasm, and suggested that the 'Royal' title should also move to Tooting. Other lawyers, acting for other authorities with their own interests in view, took a contrary view, and the proposal evaporated.

An attempt to use the merger of the two Dental Schools to get the 'Royal' title transferred to the United Medical and Dental Schools also failed. The formal application to the Home Secretary drew the enigmatic response that he 'was unable to recommend it to the favourable consideration of Her Majesty consistent with the accepted practice in these matters'.

Despite Brian Goode's efforts, which included making contact with the personnel departments of many hospital authorities in and around London for help in placing members of the non-clinical Hospital staff, nothing definite emerged. Those members of staff who could do so helped them-selves, with Brian's encouragement, by finding new jobs and were replaced where necessary by temporary staff on short-term contracts. In March 1984, worried for their futures, twelve members of the clerical staff wrote formally protesting at the delay and the apparent lack of planning.

Members of the clinical staff of the Hospital were better placed to make their own arrangements and to attract the attention of the District Personnel Department. Three elected to take early retirement; several transferred their sessions to University College Hospital where, ironically, they soon found themselves under threat again when the Dental School there was closed. Others went to Guy's, and to the Dental Unit at Tooting; all were re-established elsewhere more or less satisfactorily in the end. But it was very much at the end. It was not until October 1985, with closure three months away, that Brian Goode was able to announce that all remaining non-clinical staff who had permanent posts had been offered re-employment with St George's Hospital.

At the end of that month the RDH Dental Advisory Committee protested that 'the relocation of staff has been handled by the Wandsworth and Regoinal Administrators with culpable mismanagement and an absence of a proper level of care for the wellbeing of permanent staff', pointing out that most members of staff had still not received positive information about their futures. Their strictures, the DAC was careful to record, did not apply to Brian Goode and his staff who, in their opinion, had done their utmost to bring things to a satisfactory conclusion.

In retrospect it seems unlikely that the blame can fairly be laid upon individual managers. In fact, in October 1984 the District Management Team had ordered that all vacant posts anywhere in the District be offered first to people from the Royal. But in the climate of financial uncertainty which bedevilled the Health Service at that time, if it was a question of creating new posts no National Health Service authority could offer employment unless it was sure of funding for the new posts; and until the disposal of the funds released by the closure of the Royal was decided no one could be sure.

Some of the Hospital's activities were transferred *en bloc*; the schemes for training dental technicians and dental surgery assistants went to Guy's Dental Hospital and the School of Dental Hygiene to the Eastman Dental Hospital. This settled, the share-out of money could be agreed. Of the £2½ million allocated for the Royal Dental Hospital annually, £120,000 went with the School of Hygiene to the Eastman and £223,000 to Guy's, while £622,000 went to South East Thames Regional Health Authority to cover the additional cost of supporting the increased student numbers following the merger of the two dental schools. Setting aside £393,500 for the annual cost of the Dental Unit at Tooting, there was left a net saving to the National Health Service of just over one million pounds a year.

The prospect of their imminent vacation and sale focussed attention once more upon the ownership of the Leicester Square premises. The protracted and vexatious negotiations on this subject have been mentioned in Chapter 7. It was not until 1977 that the Department of Health formally accepted the School's contention that the ownership of the property should be apportioned on the basis of its occupation by the parties on the 'appointed day', 5th July 1948; that is to say, 24.06 per cent to the hospital authority, 39.10 per cent to the School and 36.84 per cent to the Endowment Fund. Since it had already been agreed that half of what belonged to the Endowment Fund belonged to the School the latter, with a total of 57.52 per cent, emerged as the majority shareholder.

This was not quite the end, however. By 1977, following the 1974 National Health Service re-organisation, the Board of Governors had been replaced as the relevant Hospital Authority by the Wandsworth and East Merton District Management Team. In 1980, when the Management Team were adding up their resources for funding the dental development at Tooting they turned up a reference to the apportionment of the Leicester Square premises. As had been the habit of Health Service authorities throughout the apportionment discussions, their reaction to the idea that they were entitled to a minority share only in the property, which they believed to be worth £2,235,000, was one of total disbelief. The District Administrator told the School Secretary that as the Team had not been involved in the discussions they did not propose to sign any agreement without further consideration. In fact, they were not required to sign anything, since the agreement had been settled; as no doubt they were in due course advised, because nothing further was heard on the matter.

In June 1983 the Senate of the University resolved that the Royal Dental Hospital of London cease to be a School of the University with effect from 1st August 1983. The merger of Guy's and St Thomas's Hospitals Medical Schools, to form the United Medical and Dental Schools of Guy's and St Thomas's Hospitals had already been approved and it was to this new conglomerate that the spirit of the School, if not all of its body, was joined.

The process was a prolonged one, spread over two years as had been agreed, and for those involved in it, a painful one. Staff and students of the School moved by instalments to the London Bridge site, as did many of the Hospital staff. As people left and equipment and furniture was moved out the Leicester Square buildings became more and more desolate; empty of people, holes in the floors of the clinical departments left when the chairs had been taken away, the entire place dirty, dusty and disconsolate.

Those who transferred to the London Bridge site were received like survivors from a sunken ship, metaphorically wrapped in warm blankets and given mugs of cocoa; accepted readily, they blended quickly into their new surroundings. But the ways of Guy's Hospital Dental School were not those of the Royal, the teaching and clinical staff of which were accustomed to be closely involved in all decisions of importance to the institution and its staff, patients and students. Other staff, too, through trades unions and other means had ready access to the decision making machinery. To the people from the Royal it seemed that Guy's had a more autocratic system of governance, decisions being handed down from on high, and they did not all readily adapt to the change.

Two tasks remained to complete the demise of the Royal. The first was the transfer of the many trust, prize and scholarship funds vested in the School Council to the United Medical and Dental Schools for the benefit of the Dental School, which was carried out with the assistance of the Charity Commission. As well, the Centenary Fund and the Peter Lunt Scholarship and Prize Fund, of £221,000 and £72,000 respectively, which were administered by independent trustees, had their terms of trust altered so that they could be used for the purposes of the merged school. With the prize and scholarship funds already possessed by Guy's Hospital Dental School these made it after the merger probably the best- endowed dental school in the country.

The second task was the disposal of the Leicester Square premises, 21 Irving Street and 6 Longs Court. Because of the many interests involved a large committee was set up to deal with the sale, on which were represented the Hospital and School, although the latter by then had legally ceased to exist, together with the Regional and Area Health Authorities and the District Management Team. A prestigious firm of estate agents having been appointed, the meetings of the committee took place in their palatial premises in Jermyn Street. It was decided that it would be folly to split so desirable a West-End site into separate packages, but to put the premises on the market as a whole. Marketing took a long time, during which rumours about possible buyers and the size of the sale price came and went – at one stage it was confidently stated that the People's Government of China was making a bid of eleven million pounds for the site, in order to establish a Chinese Cultural Centre in the heart of London.

In the event the whole package was bought in May 1987 for £7,510,000 for conversion into an expensive hotel; of this sum the agents took £141,500 and the School's share came to £3,651,431. At a singularly undramatic meeting of all concerned at the Headquarters of South-West Thames Regional Health Authority papers were signed and exchanged and the School Secretary (by then translated into an Assistant Secretary of UMDS) received the biggest cheque he had ever seen and, clutching it, trotted round to the Bank of England to pay it in to the account of Guy's Hospital Medical School.

The University Grants Committee, having contributed to the maintenance of the building during the greater part of its life, claimed 28 per cent of the School's share, leaving £2,629,030 in the possession of UMDS.

The building upon which Joseph Walker and his colleagues spent so much time, energy and money nearly a century ago and for which their successors struggled to pay during the first three decades of this century, still stands in Leicester Square, in the guise of the Hampshire Hotel. Although it remains by and large the familiar building it has been rebuilt inside and prettified externally in various unsubtle ways. The result, to say the least, seems to have been unfortunate.

So that guests of the Hotel should be aware of the building's former life the Royal Dental Hospital Students' and Staff Association commissioned a plaque which, with the permission of the hotel management, has been installed in the hotel lobby. It reads as follows:

The
HAMPSHIRE HOTEL
occupies the building which from
1901–1985 housed the
ROYAL DENTAL HOSPITAL and
SCHOOL OF DENTAL SURGERY
the oldest dental school in the United Kingdom.
These institutions opened in Soho in 1858 and
1859 and later moved to this site.

The Royal Dental Hospital of London and its School of Dental Surgery lasted one hundred and twenty-seven years, no more than the blink of an eyelid in the context of history. There were a great many similar institutions with much longer histories, many of which still exist, although most are being transformed beyond recognition as society itself changes. But the Royal's unique place in history is assured because, with the Odontological Society, it provided the basis for the establishment of dentistry as a regulated and registered profession. Incidentally, it was the first school of dental surgery in the United Kingdom and, importantly, after 1914, the only one that was independent, the others being adjuncts of medical schools.

These facts influenced the people who worked and studied at the Royal. They were proud of their School and Hospital, conscious of its contribution to the status and progress of dentistry and to the dental care of the people of London. They felt that they were part of something special and that they had standards to maintain. Because of this background the Royal inspired those who worked there; and because they were inspired the people made the Royal the place it was. They felt that their jobs were important and carried them out accordingly.

It has been very difficult to incorporate in this acount of the History of the Royal a proper recognition of the contribution they made. The deliberations of committees, the formulation of plans, the financial contrivances and the to-ings and fro-ings of public policy are what the archives record; but it was really the daily activity of all the people who worked at the Royal that made its History. It has been impossible to mention more than a few and might be invidious to try. Suffice it to say that as a group they were conscientious and dedicated; they considered themselves members of a family and acted like one. It was a privilege to be of their number and this book is intended to be a tribute to them all.

Appendix 1

The 'Memorialists' of 1843

*Samuel Cartwright, FRS

John H Parkinson
John H Parkinson, Jun.,MRCS

*Edwin Saunders, FRCS

William M Bigg

*Samuel Cartwright, Jnr.,MRCS

GA Ibbetson, MRCS
James Parkinson

*John Tomes, FRS

HJ Featherstone
Alfred Canton, MRCS
Robert Nasmyth, MD, MRCS
JL Craigie, FRCS
HJ Barrett, MRCS

*Arnold Rogers, FRCS

Thomas A Rogers, MRCS
Hubert Shelley, MB, London, MRCS
S James A Salter, MB, MRCS, FLS

*Those subsequently involved in the foundation of the Dental Hospital and School.

Appendix 2

Staff, Students and Former Students killed in the Great War 1914–18

The following names appeared on the Roll of Honour, near the main entrance to the hopital building, which consisted of a group of portraits with names and descriptions as below, framed in mahogany and sur-mounted by the RDH monogram:-

FJ ARBERY, Captain, lst Duke of Cornwall's Light Infantry. Died of wounds, October 9, 1917. (LDSEng)

VLS BECKETT, Major, Yorkshire Regiment. Died of wounds in France, July 14, 1916. (LDSEng)

CECIL W BOND, Captain, RAMC (MRCS, LRCP, DSEng)

JAB CARSON, Captain Dental Surgeon, attached RAMC. Died in Egypt. (LDSEng)

FRANK W COWLEY, Lieutenant, 11th Battalion, E. Yorkshire Regiment. MC with bar. Killed in France, August 9, 1918. (Student).

DEBENHAM STUART COOMBS, Lieutenant, 7th Essex Regiment. Died November 1, 1918. (Student).

NEVILLE GEORGE COMPTON, 2nd Lieutenant, Worcester Regiment. Killed April 19, 1916. (Student).

GORDON CRAIG, 2nd Lieutenant, Bedfordshire Regiment. Died of wounds, April 3, 1918. (LDSEng)

ALBERT COLLIS, Corporal Artists' Rifles. Died of wounds, November 23, 1917. (LDSEng)

LC CROCKETT, Captain Dental Surgeon, attached RAMC Died on Service, October 17, 1918.

E DINSMORE, Captain Dental Surgeon, attached RAMC Died on Service at Curragh, November 12, 1918. (LDSEng)

AW DOLAMORE, Captain, 10th Middlesex Regiment, attached lst Buffs. Mentioned in Dispatches. Killed in Mesopotamia, April 14, 1917. (Student)

LAR FENNELL, Private, Artists' Rifles. Died in training, April, 1917. (LDSEng)

ROBERT H HEATH, Private, London Regiment. 'Missing', October 1916. (LDSEng)

REM HOFMEYR, 2nd Lieutenant, 3/5th Yorks Regiment, attached MGC, 63rd Company. Killed in action in France, April 24, 1917. (Student).

FC HARRISON, Captain, RAMC Killed in Belgium, October 13, 1918. (MRCS, LRCP, LDSEng).

OWEN HAIRSINE, MC, Captain RAMC. Killed June 7, 1917 at the Battle of Messines. (MRCS, LRCP, LDSEng)

HB HOPE, 2nd Lieutenant, 2/ Northamptons, attached RAF 'Missing', May 7, 1917. (Student).

TC KIDNER, Captain, RAMC, attached Middlesex Regiment. Killed in action. (MRCS, LRCP) (Student).

HERBERT ALFRED POTTER, Surgeon Probationer, RNVR Killed in action, September 19, 1917. (Student).

FRED QUAYLE, Private, 10th Royal Fusiliers. Killed in action on the Somme, July 15, 1916. (LDSEng)

WF READ, Lieutenant, Hampshire Regiment. Died on active service. (Student)

RA RAIL, Lieutenant, Coldstream Guards. Killed in action, October 9, 1917. (LDSEng)

HR SEARS, Lieutenant Dental Surgeon, attached RAMC, and afterwards Royal Fusiliers. Killed February 17, 1917. (LDSEng)

C SHELTON, Captain, Norfolk Regiment. Killed in France, October 21, 1916. (Student).

STANLEY CLARENCE TOMKINSON, Lance-Corporal, 1/12th London Regiment (Rangers). Killed in action, April 9, 1917. (Student)

JE WHEELER, Captain, RGA. Killed November 10, 1916. (LDSEng)

KEITH ERIC WOOD, Lieutenant, 23rd London Regiment. Killed in action, May 26, 1915 at Givenchy. (LDSEng)

PAUL BERNARD WOOD, Lieutenant, 5th Royal Fusiliers, attached 7th Battalion Royal Fusiliers. Killed in action, April 23, 1917, near Gavrille. (LDSEng, MACantab., LLB)

Appendix 3

Annual General Meeting of Governors of the Royal Dental Hospital of London
March 11th, 1909
Chairman's Address

LADIES AND GENTLEMEN,

It is a matter for congratulation to the Governors of this Charity, that they are in possession of a freehold site, in the centre of London, readily reached from every part of the metropolis and its suburbs – to have erected upon that site a hospital, sanitary and hygienic, and in every way efficient for the work that has to be done it it – a building so well constructed that it will last for many years without serious dilapidations, and so situated that neither from the north or south can the light ever be interrupted by surrounding buildings.

The gentlemen whom you have elected to represent you as Members of the Committee of Management are anxious that their actions may be justified in the eyes of the Governors, and so your chairman to-day gives an account of their stewardship.

Our critics have said that the cost has been great, that there is no need to deny, not only has it been costly in money but also in time and anxiety. It is not possible to purchase a Stradivarius violin or a Velasquez's Venus, or an American Liner, unless a large sum be paid for it, and as a 'Strad' is to violins and the Liner to a penny steamboat so is our site to others that could be obtained; it is obvious, therefore, that there must be a large expenditure to obtain a freehold site and building such as we possess. The present value of them has much increased, and Mr Warner, of the firm of Messrs. Lofts and Warner, who generously act as our honorary surveyor, values them as follows:-

The site, for which £45,000 was paid, is at present valued at £75,000, and the building cost about £56,000. The site and buildings together would certainly now sell for £120,000 – a profit of £20,000 on the transaction.

The sanction of the Charity Commissioners to the expenditure is a guarantee there has been no extravagance. The King's Hospital Fund gives a large annual contribution towards the maintenance of the hospital, and, in this our Jubilee year, has given an additional £1,000 towards our debt, and those who know the methods of careful investigation made by the Executive of that Fund before a grant is given will understand what an assurance of our worthiness that is. The Hospital Sunday and Saturday Funds, both of which are very careful in their distribution, give yearly contributions, that from the Sunday Fund this year being larger than before. It may be said that is all very well, but are financial matters sound? This is vouched for by the fact that the Prudential Insurance Company accepted a mortgage on it. It is financially sound enough, but let us see what being so means. It means too few paid officials, one person doing two persons work, too little painting and decorating; it has had neither since it was built in 1900, and you all know what that means in smoky London. A second Anaesthetic Room only partially worked because we cannot afford a House Surgeon and Nurse. No lift for either patients or staff, although the building has five stories. All these economies and many others could be dispensed with if some of those worth too much wealth would pay our debt and set the charity free to develop its full possibilities.

We have done our best and we intend to struggle along with faith and hope strong in us, and some day realization must come, for the work is good and it must prosper.

Other critics say we should not have moved at all, but been content with our old building. We were not only 'cribbed, cabined, and confined,' but it was unclean, uncleanly and uncleanable, insanitary, unsavoury, undes-irable and unfitted for its purpose, unworthy of the profession of which it was the leading hospital in the Kingdom. Every impartial visitor admitted our needs.

Other critics say that special hospitals are not needed, and that all the branches of the healing art should be taught at general hospitals.

Dentistry is the only speciality of medicine that has a special curriculum, diploma and register, and it is impossible for dental surgery to be efficiently practised and taught in a special department of a general hospital – there is not space enough. What general hospital could spare the room necessary for such a hospital as this.

Your Executive would have rejoiced had it been possible to save our successors the responsibility of the debt it was necessary to incur, for they are not of those who say: 'Why should I do anything for posterity, it has done nothing for me!' However, by building shops under the hospital we have helped to provide some of the money to pay our annual debt, and the school generously gives 20 per cent of the students' fees and the balance we leave our excellent Secretary to find, to whose devotion to this hospital I should like here to bear public testimony; to him and to Mrs Pink we are deeply indebted, and I doubt very much had it not been for them if we should have been in this building today.

1908 was our Jubilee year, and a real effort has been made to pay off some of our debt, and in response to an appeal issued by Sir Frederick Treves and in virtue of the £1,000 from the King's Hospital Fund, we are in the proud position to state that our debt has been reduced to £43,000. In twenty-three years that debt must be paid, and what is that time in the history of a hospital. Those who succeed us will be in possession of a freehold site and building which will enable the Executive of that day to more fully and efficiently develop the enormous capabilities and possibilities of this great charity.

It is the duty of a Chairman on these occasions to say something to the public as well as to the Governors of the Hospital to justify the appeal we make for funds. On looking at the report the temptation is to enlarge on the figures found there, but I propose rather to refer to two interesting subjects, viz., the anaesthetic work and the school of the Hospital.

Nitrous oxide gas has been administered daily within the Hospital for nearly forty years, so that more than half-a-million patients have been anaesthetised during that time without the anaesthetic having caused one fatal case. Truly the Hospital has always been fortunate in having the most distinguished anaesthetists as members of its staff, and to-day in the person of Dr Dudley Buxton we are more than fortunate in the services of a gentleman whose scientific attainments are unusual, and who for more than twenty years has unsparingly given his time to promote the welfare of this Institution, and who is so prodigal of his time for the good of the patient and student that he attends far more frequently than he is required to do, in order that he may give a general superintendence to the department that is greatly valued and appreciated. The point, however, which I wish to make is that this Hospital has established the safety of nitrous oxide anaesthesia beyond any question, so that the public need have no fear of taking that anaesthetic, and need not run after the so-called local anaes-thetics that are not local only, for no drug inserted hypodermically can be restricted to the region where injected, and the deaths from which are far too numerous. Moreover, with the general anaesthetic the patient neither sees, hears nor feels the operation, while with the local one he in a sense does all three.

Such a contribution to the well-being of the community appears to me to deserve the recognition of the public, for it is through the work done here that largely the comfort and safety of this anaesthetic has been estab-lished.

The school attached to this Hospital is not like one at general hospitals, for they can be carried on without students, while here it is impossible, and they learn their art and science under very careful supervision in the actual treatment of patients; this ensures that, when they are qualified they have an accurate knowledge of their profession, and the public benefit by the teaching here given. There are many thousands of the rich to-day all over the Empire who have comfortable and happy mouths because of the dentists who have learned to make them so in this Hospital. There are other Dental Hospitals in Great and Greater Britain, but all of them have one or more old students of this place upon their staff, and we can say the Royal Dental Hospital is the mother of them all. Both rich and poor owe a deep debt of gratitude to the founders of this charity, who now alas! have passed to their rest without seeing the full development and evolution of their foundation. There is, I am glad to say, one still with us in the person of Mr Thomas Arnold Rogers, the first Dean of the school.

There are other reasons, however, why our appeals should be responded to. The reports which you hold in your hands, and which it is my privilege to propose for adoption, tells of much excellent work. To minister to the well-being of 70,000 suffering people is no mean record for the year. I once heard Canon Liddon say that Christ's work on earth was very like that of a hospital physician, and it is equally true about a hospital dentist; he is doing good and healing the sick, and in these days is doing what is even better, for his chief work is prevention rather than cure. The aspect of the whole of medicine to-day is remarkable, for by its scientific and preventive work it is endeavouring to prevent the very things upon which it can flourish financially.

If we look upon suffering as an entity and consider the accumulation of pain in humanity, what an awful thing it is, and how large a proportion of it is made up of tooth troubles and the attendant disorders which they produce. It is beyond denial that if the mouths of mankind could be made and kept sanitary, clean and efficient for the work for which they are intended, physical suffering would be materially decreased; it is to this work that this Charity is devoting its energies, and steps have been taken here not only to cure disease, but also by the circulation of printed instructions enforcing mouth cleanliness, to prevent it, and so perhaps the Hospital may say with the Prophet Amos, 'I have given you cleanliness of teeth in all your cities.'

The mouth may be considered the vestibule of the body, and if that vestibule be allowed to go to ruin without care and without repair, producing a mouth that is painful and insanitary, rendering mastication impossible and even poisoning the food itself – general disease must arise, due development and metabolism prevented, and a stunted, ill-developed unhealthy race be the result – a humanity with poor vitality to resist the attacks of disease – with no opsonic power to destroy the germs that find entrance with the air and food, and the consequent danger of that degeneracy of the race so much talked about to-day.

This hospital endeavours to meet these dangers by insisting that the patients who come here, be they adults or children, shall at once have their mouths made sanitary; it ensures that the operations shall be as painless as possible – extractions are performed under anaesthetics, thanks to the much valued work of the anaesthetic staff. It saves either by stopping or crowning all teeth that can be saved. It regulates the teeth of young children, giving them both efficient mastication and pleasing appearance, as as far as it is able, supplies the deficiency of teeth in the aged; this latter process, as present, it is only possible to do after some small payment has been made, because we have no fund upon which we may call to defray the expense of this department. It is hoped that some day such a fund may be established, and the nation's old aged pensioners, who have little to eat and nothing to eat it with, may be provided, without cost to themselves, with the necessary masticatory apparatus to make their few remaining years of life happier and more comfortable.

If it be the duty of a chairman on such an occasion as this to say that which will commend the charity to the generosity of the public, I trust there has been no failure to-day. It is all so obvious to us that fears must be entertained by the speaker that too little has been said. I know, after an experience of twenty years as Dean of this Hospital School, how excellent the work of the staff is, how for many years they have laboured, practically gratuitously, for the well-being of the patients and the proper education of young dentists. Yet this should not be so, for the dental labourer is as worthy of his hire as any other labourer, and this hospital should be in such a flourishing financial position as to be able to distribute to its officers such remuneration as would induce them to remain members of its staff. It cannot be expected that dentists of position, now that the enthusiasm that surrounded the first establishment of this hospital is passed, will surrender lucrative time at home to do voluntary hard work here. This can only be accomplished if our debt can be paid, then the 20 per cent of the students' fees now paid to the charity would be set free for distribution.

My last words are an appeal to that magnificently generous public to help us with donations, subscriptions and legacies. If members of that public would only come and see what is done and how well it is all done, the money would soon be forthcoming, for they could see for themselves how great a benefit this hospital is to the poor and through them to the wealthy also. May I appeal to the press to give us the benefit of their help, the publication of our appeal, and its advocacy would undoubtedly ensure the realization of our desires.

Let me summarize them.

1. That the debt may be discharged, which amounts to £43,000.
2. Failing that, that the sum be lent without interest to be repaid by twenty-one annual payments.
3. Failing either of these, that 4,000 donations of ten guineas be contributed, which constitutes every donor a life governor, and entitles him or her to four tickets of admission for special operations each year for life.

Before sitting down may I from this place, and with the authority of this great charity supporting me, issue one word of warning to the public about irregular dental practice.

The penal Clause of the Dentists' Act is as follows:-

3. From and after the first day of August, one thousand eight hundred and seventy-nine, a person shall not be entitled to take or use the name or title of 'dentist' (either alone or in combination with any other word or words), or of 'dental practitioner', or any name, title, addition, or description implying that he is registered under this Act or that he is a person specially qualified to practise dentistry, unless he is registered under this Act. *It is hereby declared that the words 'title, addition, or description', where used in the Dentists' Act, 1878, include any title, addition to a name, designation or description, whether expressed in words or by letters, or partly in one way and partly in the other.*

Any person who, after the first day of August, one thousand eight hundred and seventy-nine, not being registered under this Act, takes or uses any such name, title, addition, or description as aforesaid, shall be liable, on summary conviction to a fine not exceeding twenty pounds; provided that nothing in this section shall apply to legally qualified medical practitioners.

Today there are a large number of men whose only education has been received in a Dentists' Mechanical Laboratory, and who are not more entitled to practice as dentists than lawyers' clerks to practice as lawyers, but who do so practise, avoiding the wording of the clause I have just read by refraining from using any of the titles there mentioned, and by calling themselves makers and adapters of artificial teeth, dental institutes, tooth companies, and kindred titles. When it is remembered how difficult the photographer found it to take Mark Twain 'as a group', we cannot help admiring the ease with which these gentlemen have solved the perplexing problem of plural personality, and alone and unaided have become institutions and companies.

Let me advise both rich and poor to see to it that anybody whom they may consult about their teeth uses the titles of dentist, dental surgeon or surgeon dentist.

The question of irregular practice by unqualified and unregistered practitioners has assumed serious proportions, and menaces the health and well-being of the community, not only as regards dentistry, but equally so in relation to medicine and surgery. The public, particularly the poor and uneducated portion of it, can only be protected from the ravages of charlatans if the Legislature will pass an Act penalising practice instead of, as is the case now, penalising only the use of *titles*.

Bibliography

Best, G, *Mid-Victorian Britain, 1851–75* (London: Weidenfeld & Nicholson, 1971).

Bryce, J *The American Experience in the Relief of the Poor* (n. p., n. pub., 1871).

Cameron, HC *Mr Guy's Hospital*, 1726–1948 (London: Longmans Green & Co., 1954).

Dickens, C *Great Expectations* (London: Chapman & Hall, 1899).

Godwin, G *(Ed.) Town Swamps and Social Bridges* (Leicester: Leicester University Press, 1972).

Harte, N *The University of London 1836–1986*, (London: Athlone, 1989).

Hill. A *History of the Reform Movement in the Dental Profession* (London: Trubner & Co., 1877).

Luffkin, AW *A History of Dentistry* (London, Kimpton 1948)

Mayhew, H *London Labour and the London Poor* (London: Kimber 1861–62)

Minney, RJ *The Two Pillars of Charing Cross* (London, Cassell, 1967).

Tomes, J *A Course of Lectures on Dental Physiology and Surgery* (London: Wilson & Ogilvy, 1846).

Waite, G *An Appeal to Parliament, the Medical Profession and the Public* (London: (n. pub), 1841).

Index